밀당PT 영어

책은 일단 샀는데,
언제 다 외우지?

또 귀찮게 깜지 쓰면서 외울 거야?
눈으로만 대충 외울 거야?

그럼 시험기간 안에 절대 못 끝내!

밀당PT 영어가 외우는 속도를 절반으로
줄여주는 **문장 암기 프로그램**을 보내줄게!

짧은 시간 안에 가장 빠르게
내신 문장이 외워지도록
설계된 **학습 프로그램**이야.

다음 페이지로 넘겨봐!

잘 왔어! ***문장암기 정말 어렵지 않아!***

별도로 시간 쓰고 노력하지 않아도, 우리 프로그램만 따라오면 돼!

본문에 있는 QR을 찍으면 쌤이 말한 암기 프로그램이 뜰 거야

1과 본문 ①

The Final Touchdown

With only two minutes to play, both teams were fighting for the football. It was the last home game for the seniors of Winston High, and they were determined to win. Since it had been a close game the whole evening, the best players of each team hadn't left the field. Once Winston High's coach finally knew that victory was theirs, all the seniors on the sidelines were allowed to play for the last few seconds. One of the seniors, Ethan, was especially happy. He had never played in any of the games before. Now, Ethan was finally getting the chance to step onto the grass. …

김온택

여러 가지 프로그램이 있네요?

순서 맞추기

문장을 순서대로 선택해 내용을 완성해주세요.

문장을 선택하면 여기에 나타나요 7 COMBO

Why Do People Learn Foreign Languages?

Many others learn them for fun.

Learn a New Language, Find a New World

How can I improve my Spanish?

맞아! 프로그램만 순서대로 따라가면 그 지문은 완전 ***쉽게 암기*** 할 수 있어

앞으로도 이 프로그램만 잘 따라가면 정말 잘 외워질거야

1과 본문 ②

All eyes were on Ethan. With the ball in his hands, everything seemed to be moving in slow motion, like in a Hollywood movie. People kept their eyes on him as he made his way to the end zone. They saw him cross the goal line right before the clock ran out. …

1과 본문 ③

Well, Ethan is only five feet tall, and his legs unnaturally bend away from each other. It is difficult for him to walk, run, or move around. Because of his condition, he decided to leave his crowded high school in the big city. He moved to our school in the middle of his first year in high school. That following summer, he asked the coach if he could join the football team as a sophomore. The coach wasn't sure at first, but in the end he allowed Ethan to come to practice. …

+ #

김온택

게임하듯이 재밌게 하는데 정말 쉽게 암기가 되고 있어요!

1과 본문 ④

Over time, however, Ethan became valuable to the team in different ways. His passion for the game was an inspiration to all his teammates. Because Ethan motivated and encouraged them, they became his most passionate fans. Day in and day out, seeing Ethan's smile, positive attitude, and hard work lifted everyone's spirits. Right before every game, Ethan would always be in the middle of the group offering motivational words. He had a special talent for calming people down and bringing out the best in them. Ethan was also Winston High's loudest supporter. He always observed each play carefully from the sidelines. Although he wasn't the one making the actual plays on the field, Ethan's mind was always right there with his teammates. Everyone could sense his love for football, and the coaches admired his commitment.

1과 본문 ⑤

For the past three years, Ethan has been schooling us all in the game of life. He always reminds us that everyone is important to a team's success, though their role on the team may be small. Instead of putting all his efforts into trying to be the team's best player, he has done everything he can to make the team better. As Ethan has shown us, lifting up those around us is also of great worth. When we help others shine, their light will shine on us in return. Yes, sometimes there is something better than being the best.

전보다 더 빠르게 외울 수 있지?

After You Read

Winston High News

Winston High finished its season with an inspiring victory. It defeated Stark High by a score of 20-6. About 30 seconds before the final whistle, victory was already certain. However, the best moment of the game began shortly after. The coach sent all the seniors onto the field. Among them was Ethan. He joined the team in his sophomore year. Ethan doesn't look like a typical football player. He is only five feet tall and his legs are too weak to run fast. Nevertheless, Ethan is the team's most important player, as his great attitude motivates everyone around him. In the game's final seconds, Ethan scored the last touchdown. A teammate passed the ball to Ethan so that he could score. It was a touching moment and a fantastic way to finish the season!

김온택

이젠 진짜 단어만 봐도 쉽게 문장을 만들 수 있을 것 같아요.
시간도 오래 안 걸렸는데 문장이 외워졌어요!

그치? 학생들이 가장 쉽고 빠르게 외울 수 있도록 학습이 설계됐거든!

생각보다 더 쉽지? 앞으로 우리 책 공부하면서,
암기 걱정은 밀당PT 영어 로 해결해 봐!

페이지를 오려서 활용해 봐! :)

능률 PT

집　　　필 아이헤이트플라잉버그스㈜ 영어콘텐츠본부
편　　　집 설북
표지디자인 ㈜다츠
내지디자인 엘림
맥　편　집 엘림
영　　　업 한기영, 이경구, 박인규, 정철교, 하진수, 김남준, 이우현
마　케　팅 박혜선, 남경진, 이지원, 김여진
펴　낸　이 주민홍
펴　낸　곳 서울시 마포구 월드컵북로 396(상암동) 누리꿈스퀘어 비즈니스타워 10층
㈜NE능률 (우편번호 03925)
펴　낸　날 2023년 4월 14일 초판 제 1쇄
전　　　화 02-2014-7114
팩　　　스 02-3142-0357

능률 내신 PERSONAL TEACHING

능률 PT

NE능률 고등영어 (김성곤)

Lesson 1.
The Part You Play

/ 머리말 /

내신 만점을 위한 성공적인 준비

Personal Teaching for Your Precious Time

능률PT는 고등영어-NE능률(김성곤) 교과서 해당 시험 범위의 중간·기말고사를 대비하는 학생들을 위해 기획된 교재입니다. 본 교재는 실제 전국 내신 기출문제 100세트를 문장 단위로 철저하게 분석하여, 한 단원 기준 평균 300개 이상의 출제 포인트를 정리하였습니다.

실제 기출문제에 자주 등장한 출제 포인트 순서대로 내신 고득점을 위해 꼭 알아야 하는 내용을 먼저 학습할 수 있도록 구성하였고, 핵심 출제 포인트 내용 설명과 내용 이해를 확인할 수 있는 문제를 제시함으로써 필수 학습 내용을 완벽히 익힐 수 있도록 돕습니다. 핵심 포인트를 확실하게 학습할 수 있는 기출 변형 문제를 포함한 충분한 연습 문제를 제공하며, 최중요 출제 포인트를 모두 포함하는 시험 문제 미리보기를 통해 효율적이고 성공적인 내신 준비를 책임집니다.

본 교재로 학습하는 경험을 통해 출제 포인트에 접근하는 인사이트(insight)를 바탕으로 자기 주도적이고 효과적인 내신 대비 감각을 기를 수 있도록 설계되었습니다.

교재의 특징

- **실제 내신 기출문제 100세트 분석**
  해당 범위 내신 기출문제 100세트와 각 단원 내용과 관련된 시험 문제를 분석하여
  데이터화하였습니다.

- **문장 단위(sentence-by-sentence) 분석**
  본문을 문장 단위로 분석하여, 각 문장에서 시험 문제의 출제 포인트가 된 부분을 정리하고,
  각 출제 포인트의 출제 확률을 산출하였습니다.

- **우선순위 순으로 출제 포인트 제시**
  실제 기출문제에 많이 등장한 출제 포인트들에 대해 빈도순으로 학습 자료를 제공하여
  학습의 우선순위를 명확히 제시하였습니다.

- **풍부한 연습 문제 제공**
  기출 변형 문제, 출제 포인트 연습 문제, 시험 문제 미리보기 등 300문항 이상 수록하였습니다.

교재의 구성

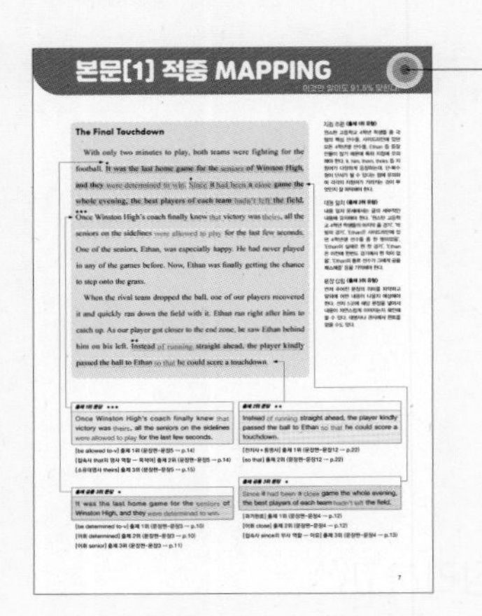

적중 MAPPING

출제율 최상위권 문장과 문제 유형을 한눈에 볼 수 있습니다.

시간이 없다면! (문장편 / 문단편)

- **최중요 출제 포인트** 각 문장/문단의 출제 확률과 실제 출제될 경우 포인트가 될 수 있는 부분에 대한 통계적 데이터를 참고하여 우선순위 순으로 핵심을 확인할 수 있습니다.
- **최중요 연습 문제** 핵심 출제 포인트 학습을 바탕으로 이해를 점검할 수 있는 문제를 통해, 실제 문제에 포인트가 적용되는 것을 확인하며 이해도를 체크할 수 있습니다.

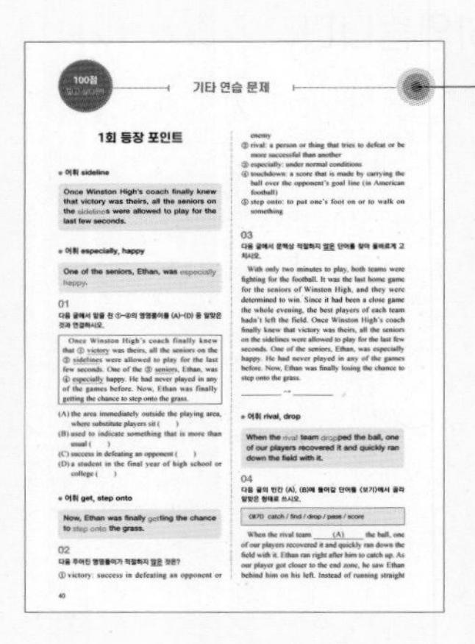

100점 맞고 싶다면!

- **기타 연습 문제**

  실제 시험에 한 번 이상 출제된 포인트들을 모두 모아 학습하여 빈틈없이 내용을 익힐 수 있습니다.

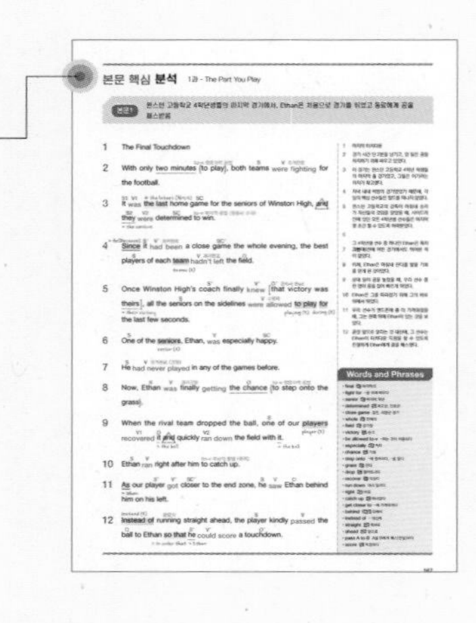

본문 핵심 분석

각 지문의 단어, 주제문, 주요 구문 등 출제 가능한 핵심 내용들을 심층 분석한 밀도 있는 자료를 통해 시험 직전 이해를 확인하는 용도로 사용할 수 있습니다.

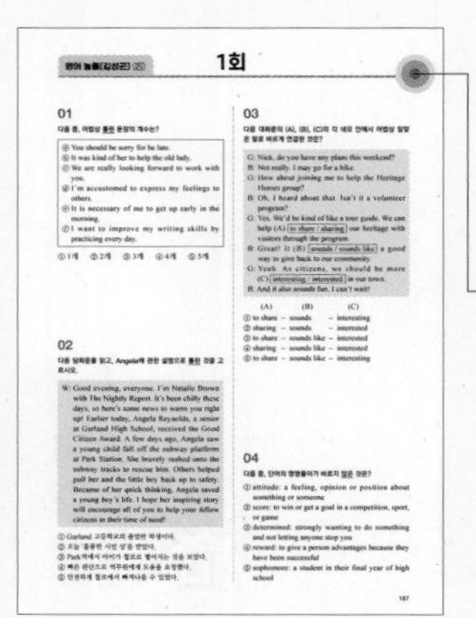

시험 문제 미리보기

최중요 출제 포인트를 활용한 시험 문제 2회분을 풀어 보며 자신의 실력을 점검하고 실전 감각을 끌어 올릴 수 있습니다.

목차

본문

Listen & Speak

Grammar & Vocabulary

시험 문제 미리보기

리딩 본문[1]

23.8% 확률로 본문[1]에서 출제

본문[1] 적중 MAPPING

이것만 알아도 91.5% 맞힌다!

The Final Touchdown

With only two minutes to play, both teams were fighting for the football. ★It was the last home game for the seniors of Winston High, and they were determined to win. ★Since it had been a close game the whole evening, the best players of each team hadn't left the field. ★★★Once Winston High's coach finally knew that victory was theirs, all the seniors on the sidelines were allowed to play for the last few seconds. One of the seniors, Ethan, was especially happy. He had never played in any of the games before. Now, Ethan was finally getting the chance to step onto the grass.

When the rival team dropped the ball, one of our players recovered it and quickly ran down the field with it. Ethan ran right after him to catch up. As our player got closer to the end zone, he saw Ethan behind him on his left. ★★Instead of running straight ahead, the player kindly passed the ball to Ethan so that he could score a touchdown.

지칭 추론 〈출제 1위 유형〉

윈스턴 고등학교 4학년 학생들 중 각 팀의 핵심 선수들, 사이드라인에 있던 모든 4학년생 선수들, Ethan 등 등장인물이 많기 때문에 특히 지칭에 유의해야 한다. it, him, them, theirs 등 지칭어가 다양하게 등장하는데, 단·복수형이 단서가 될 수 있다는 점에 유의하며 각각의 지칭어가 가리키는 것이 무엇인지 잘 파악해야 한다.

내용 일치 〈출제 2위 유형〉

내용 일치 문제에서는 글의 세부적인 내용에 유의해야 한다. '윈스턴 고등학교 4학년 학생들의 마지막 홈 경기', '박빙의 경기', 'Ethan은 사이드라인에 있던 4학년생 선수들 중 한 명이었음', 'Ethan이 실제로 뛴 첫 경기', 'Ethan은 이전에 한번도 경기에서 뛴 적이 없음', 'Ethan의 동료 선수가 그에게 공을 패스해줌' 등을 기억해야 한다.

문장 삽입 〈출제 3위 유형〉

먼저 주어진 문장의 의미를 파악하고 앞뒤에 어떤 내용이 나올지 예상해야 한다. 선지 5곳에 해당 문장을 넣어서 내용이 자연스럽게 이어지는지 확인해 볼 수 있다. 대명사나 관사에서 힌트를 얻을 수도 있다.

출제 1위 문장 ★★★

Once Winston High's coach finally knew that victory was theirs, all the seniors on the sidelines were allowed to play for the last few seconds.

[be allowed to-v] 출제 1위 (문장편-문장5 → p.14)
[접속사 that의 명사 역할 — 목적어] 출제 2위 (문장편-문장5 → p.14)
[소유대명사 theirs] 출제 3위 (문장편-문장5 → p.15)

출제 2위 문장 ★★

Instead of running straight ahead, the player kindly passed the ball to Ethan so that he could score a touchdown.

[전치사+동명사] 출제 1위 (문장편-문장12 → p.22)
[so that] 출제 2위 (문장편-문장12 → p.22)

출제 공동 3위 문장 ★

It was the last home game for the seniors of Winston High, and they were determined to win.

[be determined to-v] 출제 1위 (문장편-문장3 → p.10)
[어휘 determined] 출제 2위 (문장편-문장3 → p.10)
[어휘 senior] 출제 3위 (문장편-문장3 → p.11)

출제 공동 3위 문장 ★

Since it had been a close game the whole evening, the best players of each team hadn't left the field.

[과거완료] 출제 1위 (문장편-문장4 → p.12)
[어휘 close] 출제 2위 (문장편-문장4 → p.12)
[접속사 since의 부사 역할 — 이유] 출제 3위 (문장편-문장4 → p.13)

문장1

문장 출제 확률: 0.0%

The Final Touchdown

1과 본문의 제목이다. 제목에서 문제가 출제될 가능성은 거의 없다.

문장2

문장 출제 확률: 1.5%

With only two minutes to play, both teams were fighting for the football.

과거진행 (싸우고 있었다)

two minutes를 수식하는 to부정사의 형용사적 용법

출제 포인트

1위	2위	3위
to부정사의 형용사적 용법 – 명사 수식	**시제와 수 일치**	**전치사 with**
문장 내 출제 확률 38.5%	문장 내 출제 확률 30.8%	문장 내 출제 확률 23.1%
본문[1] 문장편 내 출제 확률 2.5%	본문[1] 문장편 내 출제 확률 2.0%	본문[1] 문장편 내 출제 확률 1.5%

● to부정사의 형용사적 용법 – 명사 수식

문장2에서 출제될 가능성은 1.5%이다. 이 문장에서 출제가 된다면, 38.5%의 확률로 to부정사의 형용사적 용법을 묻는다. 이 문장에서 to play는 to부정사의 형용사적 용법으로, 바로 앞에 있는 명사구 two minutes를 수식한다. With only two minutes to play는 '경기 시간 단 2분을 남기고'라는 뜻으로, With only two minutes left before closing 등과 같은 표현으로 바꿔 쓸 수 있다는 점에 유의하자.

Q. 다음 괄호 (A), (B) 안에 알맞은 말을 고르시오.

With only two minutes to (A) [play / playing], both teams were fighting for the football. It was the last home game for the seniors of Winston High, and they were determined to win. Since it had been a close game the whole evening, the best players of each team hadn't left the field. Once Winston High's coach finally knew that victory was theirs, all the seniors on the sidelines were allowed to play for the last few seconds. One of the seniors, Ethan, was especially happy. He had never played in any of the games before. Now, Ethan was finally getting the chance (B) [to step / stepping] onto the grass.

정답

(A) play (B) to step

(A)는 two minutes를 수식하는 형용사 역할의 to부정사, (B)에는 the chance를 수식하는 to부정사가 이어져야 알맞다.

● 시제와 수 일치

문장2에서 동사의 시제와 수 일치를 묻는 문제가 나올 확률은 30.8%이다. 본문은 전반적으로 과거의 이야기를 전달하는 방식으로 쓰여 있으므로, 이 문장에서도 '싸우고 있었다'는 의미를 나타내기 위해 과거진행 시제를 사용했다. 주어 both teams가 3인칭 복수이므로, be동사는 were를 사용한다. '양 팀은 공을 차지하기 위해 싸우고 있었다'는 내용을 '양 팀 모두 공에 대해 열정적이었다'는 뜻으로 변형하여 both teams were passionate for the football로 쓰거나, '양 팀 모두 공에 집중하고 있었다'는 뜻으로 both teams were focused on the football 등과 같이 나타낼 수도 있다는 점을 알아두자.

Q. 다음 글의 밑줄 친 부분 중 어법상 틀린 것은?

With only two minutes to play, both teams ① are fighting for the football. It was the last home game for the seniors of Winston High, and they were determined to win. Since it had been a close game the whole evening, the best players of each team ② hadn't left the field. Once Winston High's coach finally knew ③ that victory was theirs, all the seniors on the sidelines were allowed to play for the last few seconds. One of the seniors, Ethan, was especially happy. He had never played in any of the games ④ before. Now, Ethan was finally getting the chance ⑤ to step onto the grass.

정답 ①

글의 전체 시제는 과거 시제로, 맥락상 양 팀이 공을 차지하기 위해 싸우고 '있었다'라는 과거진행 시제가 들어가는 것이 자연스럽다. 따라서 are를 were로 바꿔야 한다.

② 부사절의 시제 had been과 같이 과거완료 시제 사용

③ knew의 목적어 역할을 하는 명사절을 이끄는 접속사 that

④ '이전에'라는 의미로, 완료시제와 함께 쓰이는 부사 before

⑤ 명사구 the chance를 수식하는 형용사적 용법의 to부정사

● 전치사 with

이 문장에서는 23.1%의 확률로, 전치사 with의 쓰임을 아는지 묻는 문제가 출제된다. 여기서 전치사 with는 문맥상 '~한 상태로'의 뜻을 나타낸다. 경기 시간이 2분 남은 상태에서 양 팀이 공을 차지하기 위해 싸우고 있었다는 뜻으로, 〈전치사 with+명사구〉가 쓰여 부사구를 이룬다는 점에 유의한다.

Q. 다음 우리말에 맞게 주어진 단어를 알맞게 배열하시오.

경기 시간을 단 2분 남기고, 양 팀은 공을 차지하기 위해 싸우고 있었다.

(only / to / with / minutes / play / two), both teams were fighting for the football.

____

정답

With only two minutes to play

With only two minutes(단 2분을 남기고)+to play(경기할)

문장3

문장 출제 확률: 2.5%

It was the last home game for the seniors of Winston High, and they were determined to win.

seniors: 4학년생

be determined to-v: ~하려는 결심이 확고하다

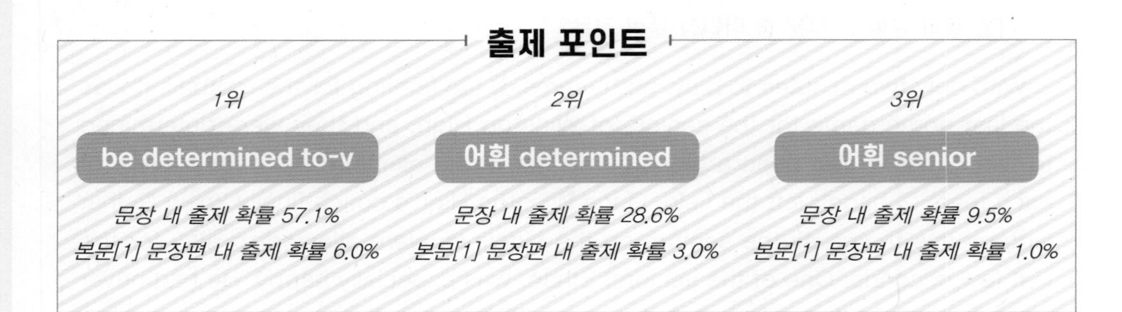

● be determined to-v

문장3에서 출제될 가능성은 2.5%이다. 이 문장에서 출제가 된다면, 57.1%의 확률로 〈be determined to-v〉의 쓰임에 대해 묻는다. determined는 '결심이 확고한'을 뜻하는 형용사이며, 〈be determined to-v〉 형태로 쓰여, '~하려는 결심이 확고하다'를 의미한다. 또한, 〈be determined to-v〉에서 to는 to부정사를 이루는 to이므로, 전치사 to와 구분하여 뒤에 동명사(v-ing)가 오지 않음에 유의하자.

Q. 다음 글의 빈칸에 들어갈 말을 괄호 안의 동사를 알맞게 변형하여 고쳐 쓰시오.

With only two minutes to play, both teams were fighting for the football. It was the last home game for the seniors of Winston High, and they were determined ______________(win). Since it had been a close game the whole evening, the best players of each team hadn't left the field.

정답 to win

형용사 determined는 '결심이 확고한'이라는 의미이고, 〈be determined to-v〉 형태로 쓰여 '~하려는 결심이 확고하다'를 뜻한다.

● 어휘 determined

이 문장에서 두 번째(28.6%)로 자주 출제되는 것은 어휘 determined가 문맥상 어울리는지 묻는 문제이다. 이번 경기는 윈스턴 고등학교의 4학년 학생들의 마지막 홈 경기였으므로, '결심이 확고한'이라는 의미를 지니는 어휘 determined를 사용해서, '이기려고 결심했다(이기려는 의지가 확고했다)'는 의미를 전달한다. 비슷한 의미를 지니는 유의어 resolved 또는 resolute와 바꿔 쓸 수 있다.

Q. 다음 빈칸에 들어갈 말로 가장 적절한 것은?

With only two minutes to play, both teams were fighting for the football. It was the last home game for the seniors of Winston High, and they were ______________ to win. Since it had been a close game the whole evening, the best players of each team hadn't left the field. Once Winston High's coach finally knew that victory was theirs, all the seniors on the sidelines were allowed to play

정답 ②

이번 경기는 윈스턴 고등학교 4학년 학생들의 마지막 홈 경기였으므로, 그들은 이기려는 '의지가 확고했다(resolute)'는 것을 유추할 수 있다.

① 마지못한, 꺼리는
③ 무관심한
④ 스트레스를 받는
⑤ 낙담한

for the last few seconds. One of the seniors, Ethan, was especially happy. He had never played in any of the games before. Now, Ethan was finally getting the chance to step onto the grass.

① reluctant ② resolute ③ uninterested
④ stressed ⑤ discouraged

● 어휘 senior

이 문장에서 어휘 senior를 물어볼 확률은 9.5%이며, 본문[1] 전체 내에서 이와 관련한 문제가 나올 확률은 1.0%이다. senior는 '(고교 · 대학의) 4학년생'을 의미하는데, 이 단어의 영영풀이를 묻는 문제가 나올 수 있다.

senior: a student in the final year of high school or college (고등학교나 대학의 마지막 학년의 학생)

Q. 다음 글의 밑줄 친 ⓐ~ⓔ의 영영풀이가 어색한 것은?

With only two minutes to play, both teams were fighting for the football. It was the last home game for the seniors of Winston High, and they were determined to win. Since it had been a ⓐ close game the whole evening, the best players of each team hadn't left the field. Once Winston High's coach finally knew that victory was theirs, all the ⓑ seniors on the sidelines were ⓒ allowed to play for the last few seconds. One of the seniors, Ethan, was especially happy. He had never played in any of the games before. Now, Ethan was finally getting the chance to step onto the grass.

When the rival team dropped the ball, one of our players ⓓ recovered it and quickly ran down the field with it. Ethan ran right after him to ⓔ catch up. As our player got closer to the end zone, he saw Ethan behind him on his left. Instead of running straight ahead, the player kindly passed the ball to Ethan so that he could score a touchdown.

① ⓐ: having only a small difference
② ⓑ: a student in the first year of high school or college
③ ⓒ: to let someone do or have something
④ ⓓ: to get back something lost
⑤ ⓔ: to move fast enough to reach somebody in front of you

정답 ②

a student in the first year of high school or college (고등학교나 대학의 1학년 학생)은 freshman(1학년, 신입생)에 대한 영영풀이다. senior(4학년생): a student in the final year of high school or college(고등학교나 대학의 마지막 학년의 학생)
① 막상막하의: 아주 작은 차이가 있는
③ 허락하다: 누군가가 무언가를 하거나 갖도록 허용하다
④ 되찾다: 잃어버린 것을 되찾다
⑤ 따라잡다: 앞에 있는 누군가에게 닿을 정도로 빠르게 움직이다

출제 포인트 2.9% 정복!

문장4

문장 출제 확률: 2.5%

접속사 since (~이기 때문에) / 과거완료 / close game 박빙의 경기

Since it had been a close game the whole evening, the best players of each team hadn't left the field.

과거완료

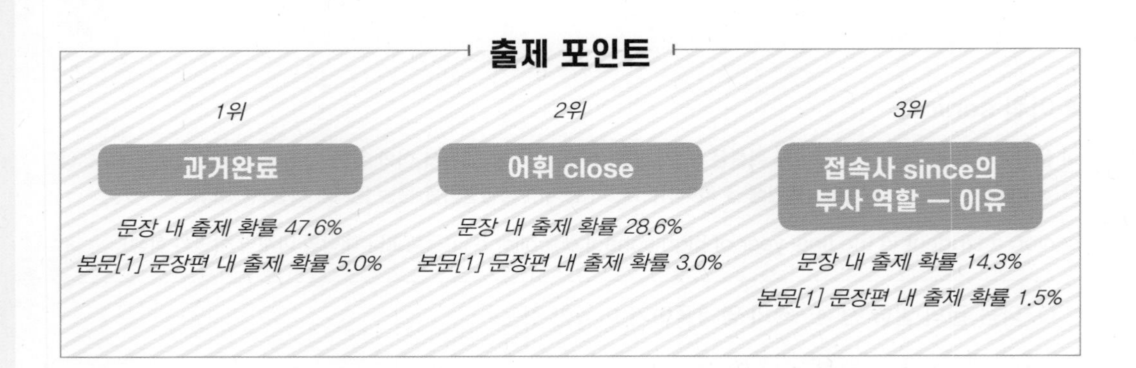

정답

(A) had (B) left

부사절에 the whole evening이 쓰여서 '저녁 내내 박빙의 경기가 계속되었다'는 의미를 나타내기 위해 과거완료의 계속 용법으로 쓴다. 이미 지나간 과거의 일을 기술하고 있으므로, 현재완료 시제는 알맞지 않다. 주절의 시제도 과거완료로 일치시켜 (A)에는 had, (B)에는 leave의 과거분사 left를 쓴다.

● 과거완료

문장4에서 출제될 가능성은 2.5%이다. 이 문장에서 출제가 된다면 47.6%의 확률로, 부사절과 주절의 동사의 형태를 묻는 문제가 출제된다. 특히, 부사절에 the whole evening이 쓰여서 '저녁 내내 박빙의 경기가 계속되었다'는 의미를 나타내기 위해 과거완료의 계속 용법으로 쓰인다는 점을 명심해야 한다.

Q. 다음 (A), (B)에 들어갈 알맞은 말을 고르시오.

It was the last home game for the seniors of Winston High, and they were determined to win. Since it (A) [has / had] been a close game the whole evening, the best players of each team hadn't (B) [leave / left] the field.

● 어휘 close

이 문장에서 출제가 된다면, close가 문맥상 어울리는 어휘인지 묻는 문제가 28.6%의 확률로 나온다. 본문에서 close는 '우열을 가리기 힘든, 막상막하의'라는 의미로 쓰였고, 영어로는 having only a small difference 또는 decided or won by a slight difference으로 설명할 수 있다.

Q. 밑줄 친 ⓐ~ⓔ를 제시된 표현으로 바꿔 쓸 수 없는 것은?

With only two minutes to play, both teams were fighting for the football. It was the last home game for the seniors of Winston High, and they were determined to win. ⓐ Since it had been ⓑ a close game the whole evening, the best players of each team hadn't left the field. Once Winston High's coach finally knew that victory was theirs, all the seniors on the sidelines were allowed to play for the last few seconds. One of the seniors, Ethan, was especially happy. He had never played in any of the games before. Now, Ethan was finally getting ⓒ the chance to step onto the grass.

When ⓓ the rival team dropped the ball, one of our players ⓔ recovered it and quickly ran down the field with it. Ethan ran right after him to catch up.

① ⓐ: Because
② ⓑ: a tight match
③ ⓒ: the opportunity
④ ⓓ: the opposing team
⑤ ⓔ: missed

정답 ⑤

밑줄 친 recovered는 떨어뜨린 공을 다시 잡았다는 의미이기 때문에 '놓쳤다'를 뜻하는 missed로 바꿔 쓸 수 없다. '잡다'라는 의미의 동사 catch의 과거형인 caught 등으로 바꿔 써야 한다.

● 접속사 since의 부사 역할 - 이유

이 문장에서 출제가 된다면 14.3%의 확률로, since가 본문에서 어떤 품사와 의미로 쓰였는지 확인하는 문제가 출제된다. 여기서 since는 '~ 때문에'라는 의미의 이유를 나타내는 접속사로 쓰였다. 시간을 나타내는 '~ 이후로 계속'이라는 의미와 혼동하지 않도록 주의하자.

Q. 다음 글의 (A)와 밑줄 친 부분의 의미가 같은 것을 모두 고르시오.

With only two minutes to play, both teams were fighting for the football. It was the last home game for the seniors of Winston High, and they were determined to win. (A) Since it had been a close game the whole evening, the best players of each team hadn't left the field.

① Two years have passed since I came here.
② We haven't seen each other since last summer.
③ We had a fight last week and haven't spoken since.
④ I can't raise a pet since my parents don't like animals.
⑤ Since the restaurant was full, we decided to eat at home.

정답 ④, ⑤

본문의 밑줄 친 (A) Since는 뒤에 주어+동사의 절이 오는 접속사로 쓰였으며, 이유를 나타낸다. Because 또는 As로 바꿔 쓸 수 있다. ①에서는 since가 접속사로 쓰였지만 '~이래로'라는 의미로 쓰였고, ②에서는 전치사, ③에서는 부사로 쓰였다.
① 내가 이곳에 온 지 2년이 지났다.
② 우리는 지난 여름 이후로 서로를 보지 못했다.
③ 우리는 지난주에 싸웠고 그 이후로 말을 하지 않았다.
④ 부모님께서 동물을 싫어하셔서 나는 동물을 키울 수 없다.
⑤ 식당이 꽉 찼기 때문에, 우리는 집에서 먹기로 결정했다.

● each + 단수명사

이 문장에서는 9.5%의 확률로 each가 단수명사를 수식한다는 사실을 아는지 확인하는 문제가 나오기도 한다. 따라서, 본문에서 each teams가 될 수 없다는 것을 명심하자.

Q. 다음 문장에서 어법상 틀린 부분을 찾아 바르게 고쳐 쓰시오.

Since it had been a close game the whole evening, the best players of each teams hadn't left the field.

________________ → ________________

정답

teams → team

each는 '각각의'라는 의미로 뒤에는 항상 단수명사를 쓴다.

출제 포인트 4.9% 정복!

문장5

문장 출제 확률: 5.2% (총 851개의 출제 포인트 중, 44회 출현, 45개 문장 중 1위)

Once Winston High's coach finally knew that victory was theirs, all the seniors on the sidelines were allowed to play for the last few seconds.

접속사 that의 명사 역할 – 목적어

소유대명사 '그들의 것'

A be allowed to-v: A가 ~하도록 허락받다

cf. allow A to-v: A가 ~하도록 허락하다

출제 포인트

1위	2위	3위
be allowed to-v	접속사 that의 명사 역할 – 목적어	소유대명사 theirs
문장 내 출제 확률 40.9% 본문[1] 문장편 내 출제 확률 9.0%	문장 내 출제 확률 15.9% 본문[1] 문장편 내 출제 확률 3.5%	문장 내 출제 확률 13.6% 본문[1] 문장편 내 출제 확률 3.0%

• be allowed to-v

문장5에서 출제될 가능성은 5.2%이며, 45개 문장 중 출제 확률 1위로 1과에서 가장 중요한 문장이다. 이 문장에서 출제가 된다면 40.9%의 확률로, 'A가 ~하도록 허락받다'라는 의미의 〈A be allowed to-v〉 형태를 묻는 문제나 이를 능동태 〈allow A to-v〉로 바꾸는 어법 문제로 나올 수 있다. 따라서 수동태 〈A be allowed to-v〉와 능동태 〈allow A to-v〉, 그리고 동사 allow는 목적격 보어로 to부정사를 취한다는 점을 꼭 명심하자.

Q. 다음 우리말에 맞게 괄호 안의 주어진 단어를 활용하여 빈칸에 채우시오.

Once Winston High's coach finally knew that victory was theirs, all the seniors on the sidelines ______________________(allow, play) for the last few seconds.

윈스턴 고등학교의 감독이 마침내 승리가 자신들의 것임을 알았을 때, 사이드라인에 있던 모든 4학년생 선수들은 마지막 몇 초간 뛸 수 있도록 허락받았다.

정답

were allowed to play

문맥상 주어 all the seniors가 경기를 뛸 수 있도록 '허락받은' 것이므로, 'A가 ~하도록 허락하다'라는 의미의 〈allow A to-v〉의 수동태인 〈A be allowed to-v(A가 ~하도록 허락받다)〉를 사용해야 한다. 이때, 주어가 복수명사이며 과거 시제이므로, be동사의 과거 시제 복수형 were을 활용한 were allowed to play가 알맞다.

• 접속사 that의 명사 역할 – 목적어

이 문장에서는 15.9%의 확률로, 접속사 that과 관계대명사 which, what을 비교하는 어법 문제가 나올 수 있다. 여기서 that은 동사 knew의 목적어절을 이끄는 명사절 접속사로, 뒤에 완전한 절이 온다. 반면, 관계대명사 which와 what은 뒤에 불완전한 절이 와야 하므로 해당 자리에 들어갈 수 없다는 점에 유의하자.

Q. 다음 문장에서 어법상 틀린 곳을 찾아 바르게 고쳐 쓰시오.

Once Winston High's coach finally knew what victory was theirs, all the seniors on the sidelines were allowed to play for the last few seconds.

______________ → ______________

정답

what → that

what은 뒤에 불완전한 절이 와야 하므로 해당 자리에 들어갈 수 없다. 동사 knew의 목적어 역할을 하는 명사절을 이끄는 접속사 that으로 바꿔야 어법상 적절하다.

● 소유대명사 theirs

이 문장에서는 13.6%의 확률로 소유대명사 theirs와 소유격 their을 비교하는 문제가 나올 수 있다. 소유대명사 theirs는 소유격과 명사가 합쳐진 개념으로, '그들의 것'을 의미한다. 이와 달리, 소유격 their은 '그들의'라는 의미로 뒤에 수식받는 명사가 필요하다.

Q. 다음 빈칸에 들어갈 말로 가장 적절한 것은?

With only two minutes to play, both teams were fighting for the football. It was the last home game for the seniors of Winston High, and they were determined to win. Since it had been a close game the whole evening, the best players of each team hadn't left the field. Once Winston High's coach finally knew that victory was ______________, all the seniors on the sidelines were allowed to play for the last few seconds. One of the seniors, Ethan, was especially happy. He had never played in any of the games before. Now, Ethan was finally getting the chance to step onto the grass.

① they ② them ③ their ④ theirs ⑤ themselves

정답 ④

주격보어 자리이고 뒤에 명사가 없으며, 문맥상 '그들의 것'이라는 내용이 되어야 하므로, 소유격과 명사가 합쳐진 '그들의 것'이라는 의미의 소유대명사 theirs가 들어가는 것이 적절하다. 소유격 뒤에는 명사가 와야 한다는 것에 유의한다.

● 어휘 allow

이 문장에서는 9.1%의 확률로 어휘 allow에 관한 문제가 나오기도 한다. 마지막 홈 경기로 핵심 선수들만 경기를 하다가 승리가 확실해지자 감독이 사이드라인에 있던 다른 선수들도 몇 초간 뛰게 '허락'했다는 내용이다. '허락하다'의 반대 의미인 '금지하다'라는 뜻의 영단어로 바꿔 문맥상 어울리는 낱말인지 물어볼 수 있다. 종종 영영풀이를 묻는 문제도 나오니 기억해 두자.

- 유의어 permit(허락하다) / 반의어 ban, forbid(금지하다)
- allow(허락하다): v. to give permission to have or do something(무언가를 가지거나 하도록 허락하다)

Q. 다음 글의 괄호 (A), (B) 안에서 문맥에 맞는 낱말로 가장 적절한 것을 고르시오.

With only two minutes to play, both teams were fighting for the football. It was the last home game for the seniors of Winston High, and they were (A) [resolute / reluctant] to win. Since it had been a close game the whole evening, the best players of each team hadn't left the field. Once Winston High's coach finally knew that victory was theirs, all the seniors on the sidelines were (B) [permitted / prohibited] to play for the last few seconds. One of the seniors, Ethan, was especially happy. He had never played in any of the games before. Now, Ethan was finally getting the chance to step onto the grass.

정답

(A) resolute

(B) permitted

(A) 마지막 홈 경기라, 학생들이 이기려는 의지가 확고했다(resolute)는 내용이어야 자연스럽다.

resolute: 확고한

reluctant: 꺼리는

(B) 경기의 승리가 확실해지자, 사이드라인에 있던 모든 학생들도 마지막 몇 초간 경기에서 뛸 수 있도록 허락받았다(permitted)라는 문맥이 자연스럽다.

permit: 허락하다

prohibit: 금지하다

● **few+복수명사**

이 문장에서 the last few seconds 부분을 묻는 문제도 6.8%의 확률로 나올 수 있다. few 뒤에는 항상 복수명사가 와야 한다.

Q. 다음 문장에서 어법상 틀린 곳을 찾아 바르게 고쳐 쓰시오.

Once Winston High's coach finally knew that victory was theirs, all the seniors on the sidelines were allowed to play for the last few second.

____________ → ____________

정답
second → seconds
few 다음에는 복수명사가 와야 하므로, second를 seconds로 고치는 것이 적절하다.

출제 포인트 8.4% 정복!

문장6

문장 출제 확률: 1.6%

One of the seniors, Ethan, was especially happy.
(One of the seniors: one of+복수명사 / was: 단수동사)

출제 포인트

1위

one of+복수명사+단수동사

문장 내 출제 확률 85.7%
본문[1] 문장편 내 출제 확률 6.0%

● **one of+복수명사+단수동사**

문장6에서 출제될 가능성은 1.6%이다. 그 중에서도 주어와 동사 부분인 〈one of+복수명사+단수동사〉에 대해 묻는 어법 문제가 나올 가능성이 85.7%로 가장 높다. 〈one of+복수명사〉는 '~들 중 하나'라는 의미로, 핵심이 되는 명사가 one이기 때문에 주어로 쓰인 경우에는 뒤에 동사가 단수로 일치되어야 한다.

Q. 다음 문장의 (A), (B) 안에서 어법상 맞는 것을 고르시오.

One of the (A) [senior / seniors], Ethan, (B) [was / were] especially happy.

정답
(A) seniors (B) was
'~들 중 하나'라는 의미의 〈one of+복수명사+단수동사〉 형태이므로, (A)에는 복수명사인 seniors, (B)에는 단수동사인 was가 들어가야 한다.

출제 포인트 9.5% 정복!

문장7

문장 출제 확률: 0.7%

He had never played in any of the games before.

과거완료 시제 (경험)

출제 포인트

1위

과거완료 시제

문장 내 출제 확률 100.0%
본문[1] 문장편 내 출제 확률 2.3%

● 과거완료 시제

문장7에서 출제될 가능성은 0.7%이다. 하지만, 이 문장이 나온다면 거의 100%의 확률로 시제에 대해 묻는 문제가 출제될 것이다. 내용상 Ethan이 경기를 뛰었던 시점(과거)보다 더 이전에(대과거) 경기를 한번도 뛴 적이 없었다고 서술하였기에 과거완료 시제가 사용되었다는 점을 명심하자.

Q. 주어진 단어를 사용하여 밑줄 친 (A)를 영작하시오. (단, 필요시 단어 변형 가능)

Ethan was especially happy. (A) 그는 이전에 어떤 경기에서도 뛰어본 적이 없었다.

he, in any of the games, never, play, before

____

정답

He had never played in any of the games before.

과거의 사건보다 더 이전의 과거(대과거)에 대한 서술은 과거완료 시제 had p.p.를 쓰는 것이 적절하다. 또한, 빈도부사의 위치는 had와 p.p. 사이이다.

출제 포인트 10.0% 정복!

문장8

문장 출제 확률: 1.2%

Now, Ethan was finally getting the chance to step onto the grass.

to부정사의 형용사적 용법 (the chance 수식)

출제 포인트

1위

to부정사의 형용사적 용법

문장 내 출제 확률 60.0%
본문[1] 문장편 내 출제 확률 3.0%

2위

표현 step onto the grass

문장 내 출제 확률 20.0%
본문[1] 문장편 내 출제 확률 1.0%

● to부정사의 형용사적 용법

문장8에서 출제될 가능성은 1.2%이다. 이 문장에 출제된다면, 60%의 확률로 to step에서 쓰인 to부정사에 대해 묻는 문법 문제가 나올 수 있다. 이 문장에서 쓰인 to부정사는 명사 the chance를 수식하는 형용사 역할을 하고 있으며, '~할, ~하려는'으로 해석된다. 본문[1]의 문장2에서 나온 to play 또한 앞에 오는 명사를 수식하는 형용사적 용법으로 쓰인 to부정사이므로, 같이 묶어서 기억해 두도록 하자.

Q. 다음 문장에서 어법상 틀린 부분을 찾아 올바르게 고쳐 쓰시오.

Now, Ethan was finally getting the chance step onto the grass.

__________ → __________

정답
step → to step
한 문장 내에서 본동사는 한 개만 있어야 하므로, step을 명사 the chance를 수식하는 형용사적 용법의 to부정사 to step으로 고쳐야 한다.

● 표현 step onto the grass

문장8에서 출제 가능성이 두 번째로 높은 포인트는 step onto the grass의 의미이다(20.0%). step onto the grass를 직역하면 '잔디를 밟다'이지만, Ethan이 이전에 어떤 경기에서도 뛰어본 적이 없었던 풋볼 선수라는 점으로 미루어 보아 해당 부분은 '경기 시합에 참가하게 되다[출전하다]'를 의미한다. 이와 같은 표현이 본문4에 making the actual plays[games] on the field로 언급이 되기 때문에 두 표현을 함께 알아두자.

Q. 다음 글의 밑줄 친 부분이 의미하는 바를 다음과 같이 정리할 때, 빈칸 (A), (B)에 들어갈 단어를 본문에서 찾아 각각 쓰시오.

With only two minutes to play, both teams were fighting for the football. It was the last home game for the seniors of Winston High, and they were determined to win. Since it had been a close game the whole evening, the best players of each team hadn't left the field. Once Winston High's coach finally knew that victory was theirs, all the seniors on the sidelines were allowed to play for the last few seconds. One of the seniors, Ethan, was especially happy. He had never played in any of the games before. Now, Ethan was finally getting the chance to step onto the grass.

→ to (A)__________ in the football (B)__________

정답
(A) play (B) game

출제 포인트 10.8% 정복!

문장9

문장 출제 확률: 2.2%

When the rival team dropped the ball, one of our players recovered it and quickly ran down the field with it.

recovered: 동사1(과거) 되찾다
ran: 동사2(과거)

출제 포인트

1위	2위
어휘 recover	시제 일치
문장 내 출제 확률 47.4%	문장 내 출제 확률 21.1%
본문[1] 문장편 내 출제 확률 4.5%	본문[1] 문장편 내 출제 확률 2.0%

● 어휘 recover

문장9에서 출제될 가능성은 2.2%이다. 이 문장이 출제된다면, 47.4%의 확률로 어휘 recover에 대해 묻는 문제가 나올 것이다. 보통 recover은 '(질병 등을) 회복하다'의 의미로 많이 알고 있으나, 여기서는 '(공을) 되찾다'의 의미로 쓰였다는 점을 반드시 알아야 한다. 특히, 영영풀이로 나오게 된다면 고난도 문제가 될 수 있으니, '되찾다'를 뜻하는 영영풀이 to get back something lost를 반드시 알아두자. recover의 유의어로는 catch, grasp(잡다) 등이 있으며, 반의어로는 drop, abandon(포기하다) 등이 있다. 헷갈리기 쉬운 낱말로는 recollect(기억해내다)가 있으니 문맥상 쓰인 뜻과 다양한 유의어들을 꼼꼼하게 대비해두자.

Q. 다음 빈칸에 들어갈 말로 적절하지 않은 것은? (단, 시제는 고려하지 않을 것)

Once Winston High's coach finally knew that victory was theirs, all the seniors on the sidelines were allowed to play for the last few seconds. One of the seniors, Ethan, was especially happy. He had never played in any of the games before. Now, Ethan was finally getting the chance to step onto the grass. When the rival team dropped the ball, one of our players ____________ it and quickly ran down the field with it. Ethan ran right after him to catch up. As our player got closer to the end zone, he saw Ethan behind him on his left. Instead of running straight ahead, the player kindly passed the ball to Ethan so that he could score a touchdown.

① grasp ② take ③ recover ④ recollect

정답 ④

상대 팀에서 공을 놓치고 이를 우리 팀의 선수 중 한 명이 되찾아 경기장을 뛰는 상황임을 고려했을 때 빈칸에는 '되찾다, 잡다' 등의 의미가 적절하다. ④ recollect는 '기억해내다'의 의미로 적절하지 않다.
① 꽉 잡다 ② 잡다
③ 되찾다

● 시제 일치

문장9에서 출제 가능성 2위(21.1%)를 차지한 포인트는 동사의 시제 일치에 대한 부분이다. 접속사 when으로 연결된 종속절의 동사 drop과 주절의 동사가 모두 과거 시제로 일치되어야 한다는 점과, 주절의 동사 recovered와 ran이 병렬 연결되어 있다는 점 모두 기억해두자.

Q. 다음 글에서 밑줄 친 (A), (B)에 들어갈 동사를 어법에 맞게 변형하여 쓰시오.

When the rival team ____(A)____(drop) the ball, one of our players ____(B)____ (recover) it and quickly ran down the field with it.

(A) ____________ (B) ____________

정답
(A) dropped
(B) recovered

(A) 주절의 동사가 과거 시제이므로, 접속사 when(~할 때)으로 이어진 부사절의 동사 drop도 문맥상 과거 시제 dropped로 고치는 것이 적절하다.
(B) 주절의 동사 recover와 ran이 등위접속사 and에 의해 연결되어 있으므로, recover 또한 과거 시제 recovered로 고치는 것이 적절하다.

• 동사 recover의 태

동사 recover의 태에 대해 묻는 문제가 출제될 가능성은 10.5%로, 문장9에서 출제 가능성 3위에 해당하는 문법 포인트다. 우리말로 '우리 선수 중 한 명이 공을 되찾고'라고 해석되는데, 수동의 의미로 혼동할 수 있는 부분이기 때문에 출제된 것으로 보인다. 주어 one of our players가 공을 능동적으로 되찾는 상황으로 능동태로 써야 한다는 사실을 잊지 말자.

정답 recovered

우리 팀의 선수 중 한 명이 공을 '되찾았다'는 문맥을 고려했을 때, 주어와 동사는 능동 관계이다. 따라서 recovered가 적절하다.

Q. 다음 괄호 안에 들어갈 말로 적절한 것은?

When the rival team dropped the ball, one of our players (recovered / was recovered) it and quickly ran down the field with it.

출제 포인트 12.2% 정복!

문장10

문장 출제 확률: 0.9%

Ethan ran right after him to catch up.

to catch up: to부정사의 부사적 용법 (~하기 위해) / 따라잡다[따라가다]

출제 포인트

1위	2위
to부정사의 부사적 용법	**어휘 catch up**
문장 내 출제 확률 50.0%	*문장 내 출제 확률 37.5%*
본문[1] 문장편 내 출제 확률 2.0%	*본문[1] 문장편 내 출제 확률 1.5%*

• to부정사의 부사적 용법

문장10에서 출제될 가능성은 0.9%이다. 이 문장에서 to catch up은 완전한 절에 이어지는 부사적 용법의 to부정사구이며, '~하기 위해'라는 의미로 목적을 나타낸다. 출제 가능성이 높은 편은 아니지만, 다른 문장에 나온 to부정사와 함께 밑줄 친 어법으로 출제될 수 있기 때문에 그 차이를 알아 두어야 한다.

정답 to catch up

완전한 절에 이어지는 부사적 용법의 to부정사구이며, 문맥상 목적의 의미(~하기 위해)를 나타낸다.

Q. 다음 괄호 안에 들어갈 말로 적절한 것은?

Ethan ran right after him (to catch up / to catching up). As our player got closer to the end zone, he saw Ethan behind him on his left.

• 어휘 catch up

문장10이 출제된다면, catch up의 to부정사 외에도 문맥상의 의미를 묻는 어휘 문제가 출제될 수 있다(37.5%). catch up은 본문에서는 '(먼저 간 사람을) 따라잡다[따라가다]'의 뜻으로 쓰였으며, 이에 대한 영영풀이는 to move fast enough to reach somebody in front of you이다. 영영풀이는 최대한 눈에 익혀 두는 것이 필요하다.

Q. 다음 글의 밑줄 친 부분 중, 주어진 영영풀이에 해당하는 낱말로 적절한 것은?

When the rival team ① dropped the ball, one of our players recovered it and quickly ② ran down the field with it. Ethan ran right after him to ③ catch up. As our player ④ got closer to the end zone, he saw Ethan behind him on his left.

to move fast enough to reach somebody in front of you

정답 ③

catch up은 '(먼저 간 사람을) 따라잡다[따라가다]'를 의미하므로, 주어진 영영풀이 '앞에 있는 누군가에 닿을 정도로 충분히 빠르게 움직이다'에 해당한다.

출제 포인트 12.8% 정복!

문장11

문장 출제 확률: 0.6%

접속사 as (~할 때)

As our player got closer to the end zone, he saw Ethan behind him on his left.

출제 포인트

1위

접속사 as

문장 내 출제 확률 80.0%

본문[1] 문장편 내 출제 확률 2.0%

● 접속사 as

문장11에서 출제될 가능성은 0.6%이다. 이 문장이 출제된다면, 접속사 as(~할 때)에 대한 문항으로 출제될 가능성이 가장 높다. 접속사 as는 시간, 이유, 방식 등의 다양한 의미를 가지고 있지만 이 문장에서는 시간을 나타내는 접속사로 쓰이고 있다. 시간의 접속사 as는 when, while 등으로 바꾸어 나올 수 있으니, 문맥상 쓰인 의미를 정확하게 알아두자.

Q. 다음 글의 밑줄 친 (a)~(d) 중, 다음과 같이 바꿔 쓸 때 의미가 달라지는 것은?

When the (a) rival team dropped the ball, one of our players recovered it and (b) quickly ran down the field with it. Ethan ran right after him to catch up. (c) As our player got closer to the end zone, he saw Ethan behind him on his left. Instead of running straight ahead, the player kindly passed the ball to Ethan (d) so that he could score a touchdown.

① (a): opponent ② (b): promptly
③ (c): Because ④ (d): in order that

정답 ③

우리 선수가 엔드존에 더 가까워졌을 때 Ethan을 발견했다는 해석이 자연스러우므로, 이유를 나타내는 접속사 Because가 아닌 시간을 나타내는 접속사 When 또는 While로 바꾸는 것이 적절하다.

출제 포인트 13.2% 정복!

문장12

문장 출제 확률: 4.6% (총 851개의 문제 중, 39회 출현, 45개 문장 중 4위)

Instead of running straight ahead, the player kindly passed the ball to Ethan so that he could score a touchdown.

(of running: 전치사+동명사 / so that: ~할 수 있도록)

출제 포인트

1위	2위
전치사+동명사	so that
문장 내 출제 확률 46.2%	*문장 내 출제 확률 35.9%*
본문[1] 문장편 내 출제 확률 9.0%	*본문[1] 문장편 내 출제 확률 7.0%*

● 전치사+동명사

문장12에서 출제될 가능성은 4.6%이며, 반드시 정복해야 할 문장에 해당한다. 이 문장에서도 특히 〈전치사+동명사〉의 형태에 대해 묻는 문제가 나올 가능성은 46.2%(1위)로, 반드시 암기해야 한다. instead of는 '~ 대신에'라는 의미의 전치사로, 뒤에 명사(구)가 와야 하고 to부정사나 동사원형은 올 수 없다. 특히, 이 부분은 서술형 문제로, 동사원형 run을 주고 "필요시 변형"이라는 조건을 주는 문제가 자주 나오므로, running으로 적절히 변형하여 답을 작성하는 연습이 필요하다.

Q. 밑줄 친 우리말에 맞게 〈보기〉의 단어를 활용하여 영작하시오. (단, 필요시 변형 가능)

〈보기〉 ahead, run, of, instead, straight

곧장 앞으로 달리는 것 대신에, the player kindly passed the ball to Ethan so that he could score a touchdown.

____

정답
Instead of running straight ahead
instead of는 '~대신에'의 의미를 가진 표현으로 뒤에는 반드시 명사 혹은 동명사(구)를 써야 한다. 때문에, 〈보기〉의 단어에서 run을 반드시 running으로 변형해야 한다.

● so that

문장12에서 두 번째로 출제 가능성(35.9%)이 높은 포인트는 so that 구문이다. 〈so that ... can ~〉은 '…가 ~할 수 있도록'의 의미를 가진 표현으로, so that은 in order that으로 바꾸어 쓸 수 있다. 〈so that ... can ~〉 구문의 that은 접속사이므로 생략 가능하며, 뒤에 완전한 절이 와야 한다. 또한, 해당 구문을 to부정사를 쓰는 구문(so as to-v, in order to-v, to-v)으로 변형하는 고난도 문제가 출제될 수 있으니 잘 대비해 두자.

Q. 다음 중, 빈칸에 들어갈 말로 적절하지 않은 것은?

Instead of running straight ahead, the player kindly passed the ball to Ethan ______________.

① so that he could score a touchdown
② in order for him to score a touchdown

정답 ⑤
〈so that ... can ~〉은 '…가 ~할 수 있도록'의 의미를 가진 표현으로, 같은 의미를 가진 표현으로는 〈in order that〉이나 to부정사를 활용한 〈in order for+의미상의 주어+to-v〉, 〈so as for+의미상의 주어+to-v〉 등이 있다. in that은 '~라는 점에서'의 의미를 가진 표현으로 적절하지 않다.

③ in order that he could score a touchdown
④ so as for him to score a touchdown
⑤ in that he could score a touchdown

● 어휘 instead of

instead of에 대한 문제는 어법 유형뿐만 아니라 어휘 유형으로도 출제될 수 있다(7.7%). instead of는 '~ 대신에'라는 의미의 전치사이다. 빈칸을 주고 because of(~ 때문에), in addition to(~에 더하여)와 같은 전치사로 오답 선지가 구성될 수 있으니, 혼동되는 전치사들을 알아두도록 하자.

Q. 다음 글의 빈칸에 들어갈 말을 〈보기〉에서 골라 쓰시오.

〈보기〉 Regardless of / Because of / Instead of / In addition to

As our player got closer to the end zone, he saw Ethan behind him on his left. ______________ running straight ahead, the player kindly passed the ball to Ethan so that he could score a touchdown.

____

정답 Instead of
공을 가진 선수가 곧장 달리지 않고 Ethan에게 공을 패스했다는 내용이므로, '달리는 것 대신에'의 의미가 담긴 Instead of가 빈칸에 적절하다.

출제 포인트 16.4% 정복!

01

다음 글의 주어진 단어를 활용하여 문맥에 맞게 빈칸에 들어갈 알맞은 말을 쓰시오.

With only two minutes to play, both teams were fighting for the football. It was the last home game for the seniors of Winston High, and they were determined to win. Since it had been a close game the whole evening, the best players of each team hadn't left the field. Once Winston High's coach finally knew that victory was theirs, all the seniors on the sidelines ____________________(allow, play) for the last few seconds. One of the seniors, Ethan, was especially happy. He had never played in any of the games before. Now, Ethan was finally getting the chance to step onto the grass.

____

02

다음 빈칸에 들어갈 말로 가장 적절한 것은?

With only two minutes to play, both teams were fighting for the football. It was the last home game for the seniors of Winston High, and they were determined to win. Since it had been a close game the whole evening, the best players of each team hadn't left the field. Once Winston High's coach finally knew __________ victory was theirs, all the seniors on the sidelines were allowed to play for the last few seconds. One of the seniors, Ethan, was especially happy. He had never played in any of the games before. Now, Ethan was finally getting the chance to step onto the grass.

① which ② what ③ that
④ how ⑤ when

03

다음 글의 빈칸 (A), (B)에 들어갈 말로 가장 적절한 것은?

When the rival team dropped the ball, one of our players recovered it and quickly ran down the field with it. Ethan ran right after him to catch up. ____(A)____ our player got closer to the end zone, he saw Ethan behind him on his left. ____(B)____ running straight ahead, the player kindly passed the ball to Ethan so that he could score a touchdown.

	(A)		(B)
①	When	–	Besides
②	Before	–	Despite
③	As	–	Instead of
④	Since	–	Due to
⑤	Once	–	Compared to

04

다음 글의 밑줄 친 부분 중, 문맥상 낱말의 쓰임이 적절하지 않은 것은?

With only two minutes to play, both teams were fighting for the football. It was the last home game for the seniors of Winston High, and they were ① <u>determined</u> to win. Since it had been a ② <u>close</u> game the whole evening, the best players of each team hadn't left the field. Once Winston High's coach finally knew that victory was theirs, all the seniors on the sidelines were ③ <u>forbidden</u> to play for the last few seconds. One of the seniors, Ethan, was especially happy. He had never played in any of the games before. Now, Ethan was finally getting the chance to step onto the grass.

When the rival team dropped the ball, one of our players ④ <u>recovered</u> it and quickly ran down the field with it. Ethan ran right after him to catch up. As our player got closer to the end zone, he saw Ethan ⑤ <u>behind</u> him on his left. Instead of running straight ahead, the player kindly passed the ball to Ethan so that he could score a touchdown.

05

다음 글의 밑줄 친 부분 중, 어법상 어색한 것은?

With only two minutes ① play, both teams were fighting for the football. It was the last home game for the seniors of Winston High, and they were determined ② to win. Since it had been a close game the whole evening, the best players of each team ③ hadn't left the field. Once Winston High's coach finally knew that victory was theirs, all the seniors on the sidelines were allowed to play for the last few seconds. One of the seniors, Ethan, was especially happy. He had never played in any of the games before. Now, Ethan was finally getting the chance to step onto the grass.

When the rival team dropped the ball, one of our ④ players recovered it and quickly ran down the field with it. Ethan ran right after him to catch up. As our player got closer to the end zone, he saw Ethan behind him on his left. Instead of ⑤ running straight ahead, the player kindly passed the ball to Ethan so that he could score a touchdown.

06

다음 글의 밑줄 친 부분 중, 문맥상 낱말의 쓰임이 적절하지 않은 것은?

With only two minutes to play, both teams were fighting for the football. It was the ① last home game for the seniors of Winston High, and they were determined to win. Since it had been a close game the whole evening, the best players of each team hadn't left the field. Once Winston High's coach finally knew that victory was theirs, all the seniors on the sidelines were ② allowed to play for the last few seconds. One of the seniors, Ethan, was especially happy. He had never played in any of the games before. Now, Ethan was finally getting the chance to ③ step onto the grass.

When the rival team dropped the ball, one of our players ④ recollected it and quickly ran down the field with it. Ethan ran right after him to catch up. As our player got ⑤ closer to the end zone, he saw Ethan behind him on his left. Instead of running straight ahead, the player kindly passed the ball to Ethan so that he could score a touchdown.

07

다음 빈칸에 들어갈 말로 적절한 것은?

With only two minutes to play, both teams were fighting for the football. It was the last home game for the seniors of Winston High, and they were determined to win. Since it had been a close game the whole evening, the best players of each team hadn't left the field. Once Winston High's coach finally knew that victory was __________, all the seniors on the sidelines were allowed to play for the last few seconds. One of the seniors, Ethan, was especially happy. He had never played in any of the games before. Now, Ethan was finally getting the chance to step onto the grass.

① they　② them　③ their
④ theirs　⑤ themselves

08

다음 밑줄 친 우리말 뜻과 일치하도록 〈보기〉의 단어를 알맞게 배열하시오.

〈보기〉 a touchdown / could / that / he / score / so

When the rival team dropped the ball, one of our players recovered it and quickly ran down the field with it. Ethan ran right after him to catch up. As our player got closer to the end zone, he saw Ethan behind him on his left. Instead of running straight ahead, the player kindly passed the ball to Ethan 그가 터치다운 득점을 할 수 있도록.

____

09

다음 글의 밑줄 친 부분 중, 어법상 틀린 것을 모두 고르시오.

With only two minutes to play, both teams were fighting for the football. It was the last home game for the seniors of Winston High, and they were determined to ① winning. Since it ② had been a close game the whole evening, the best players of each team hadn't left the field. Once Winston High's coach finally knew that victory was theirs, all the seniors on the sidelines were allowed ③ playing for the last few seconds. One of the seniors, Ethan, was especially happy. He had never played in any of the games before. Now, Ethan was finally ④ getting the chance to step onto the grass.

When the rival team dropped the ball, one of our players recovered it and quickly ran down the field with it. Ethan ran right after him to catch up. As our player got closer to the end zone, he saw Ethan behind him on his left. Instead of ⑤ run straight ahead, the player kindly passed the ball to Ethan so that he could score a touchdown.

10

다음 중, 문맥상 밑줄 친 ⓐ~ⓔ의 영영풀이가 어색한 것은?

With only two minutes to play, both teams were fighting for the football. It was the last home game for the seniors of Winston High, and they were ⓐ determined to win. Since it had been a close game the whole evening, the best players of each team hadn't left the field. Once Winston High's coach finally knew that ⓑ victory was theirs, all the seniors on the sidelines were allowed to play for the last few seconds. One of the seniors, Ethan, was especially happy. He had never played in any of the games before. Now, Ethan was finally getting the chance to step onto the grass.

When the rival team dropped the ball, one of our players ⓒ recovered it and quickly ran down the field with it. Ethan ran right after him to ⓓ catch up. As our player got closer to the end zone, he saw Ethan behind him on his left. Instead of running straight ahead, the player kindly passed the ball to Ethan so that he could ⓔ score a touchdown.

① ⓐ: having made a firm decision and not allowing anyone or anything to stop you
② ⓑ: success in defeating an opponent or enemy
③ ⓒ: to get back something lost
④ ⓓ: to cause someone or something not to move or walk
⑤ ⓔ: to get points or goals in a game or contest

11

다음 글의 밑줄 친 부분 중, 어법상 틀린 것은?

With only two minutes to play, both teams were fighting for the football. It was the last home game for the seniors of Winston High, and they were determined to win. Since it had been a close game the whole evening, the best players of each ① team hadn't left the field. Once Winston High's coach finally knew that victory was theirs, all the seniors on the sidelines ② were allowed to play for the last few seconds. One of the seniors, Ethan, ③ was especially happy. He had never played in any of the games before. Now, Ethan was finally getting the chance ④ to step onto the grass.

When the rival team dropped the ball, one of our players recovered it and quickly ran down the field with it. Ethan ran right after him to catch up. As our player got closer to the end zone, he saw Ethan behind him on his left. Instead of running straight ahead, the player kindly passed the ball to Ethan so ⑤ what he could score a touchdown.

12

다음 주어진 말을 바르게 배열하여 빈칸을 완성하시오.

When the rival team dropped the ball, one of our players recovered it and quickly ran down the field with it. Ethan ran right after him to catch up. As our player got closer to the end zone, he saw Ethan behind him on his left. Instead of running straight ahead, the player kindly passed the ball to Ethan ________________________ (score / to / for / a / touchdown / him).

____

13

다음 글의 (A), (B), (C)의 각 네모 안에서 어법에 맞는 표현으로 가장 적절한 것은?

With only two minutes to play, both teams were fighting for the football. It was the last home game for the seniors of Winston High, and they were determined to win. Since it (A) [has been / had been] a close game the whole evening, the best players of each team hadn't left the field. Once Winston High's coach finally knew that victory was theirs, all the seniors on the sidelines (B) [was / were] allowed to play for the last few seconds. One of (C) [the senior / the seniors], Ethan, was especially happy. He had never played in any of the games before. Now, Ethan was finally getting the chance to step onto the grass.

	(A)	(B)	(C)
①	has been	was	the senior
②	had been	were	the senior
③	had been	was	the seniors
④	has been	were	the seniors
⑤	had been	were	the seniors

14

다음 글의 밑줄 친 부분 중, 문맥상 낱말의 쓰임이 적절하지 않은 것은?

With only two minutes to play, both teams were fighting for the football. It was the last home game for the seniors of Winston High, and they were ① determined to win. Since it had been a ② close game the whole evening, the best players of each team hadn't left the field. Once Winston High's coach finally knew that victory was theirs, all the seniors on the sidelines were ③ allowed to play for the last few seconds. One of the seniors, Ethan, was especially ④ disappointed. He had never played in any of the games before. Now, Ethan was finally getting the chance to step onto the grass.

When the rival team dropped the ball, one of our players recovered it and quickly ran down the field with it. Ethan ran right after him to ⑤ catch up. As our player got closer to the end zone, he saw Ethan behind him on his left. Instead of running straight ahead, the player kindly passed the ball to Ethan so that he could score a touchdown.

15

다음 글의 (A), (B), (C)의 각 네모 안에서 어법에 맞는 표현으로 가장 적절한 것은?

With only two minutes to play, both teams were fighting for the football. It was the last home game for the seniors of Winston High, and they were (A) [determined / determining] to win. Since it had been a close game the whole evening, the best players of each (B) [team / teams] hadn't left the field. Once Winston High's coach finally knew that victory was theirs, all the seniors on the sidelines were allowed to play for the last few seconds. One of the seniors, Ethan, was especially happy. He had never played in any of the games before. Now, Ethan was finally getting the chance (C) [step / to step] onto the grass.

	(A)	(B)	(C)
①	determined	teams	step
②	determining	team	to step
③	determined	teams	to step
④	determined	team	to step
⑤	determining	teams	step

16

다음 글의 밑줄 친 부분의 동사원형을 어법에 맞게 고쳐 쓰지 않은 것은?

With only two minutes ① play, both teams were fighting for the football. It was the last home game for the seniors of Winston High, and they were determined to win. Since it ② be a close game the whole evening, the best players of each team hadn't left the field. Once Winston High's coach finally knew that victory was theirs, all the seniors on the sidelines ③ allow to play for the last few seconds. One of the seniors, Ethan, ④ be especially happy. He had never played in any of the games before. Now, Ethan was finally getting the chance ⑤ step onto the grass.

① play → to play
② be → been
③ allow → were allowed
④ be → was
⑤ step → to step

17

다음 글의 밑줄 친 문장 중, 어법상 틀린 것은?

① With only two minutes to play, both teams were fighting for the football. ② It was the last home game for the seniors of Winston High, and they were determined win. ③ Since it had been a close game the whole evening, the best players of each team hadn't left the field. ④ Once Winston High's coach finally knew that victory was theirs, all the seniors on the sidelines were allowed to play for the last few seconds. One of the seniors, Ethan, was especially happy. ⑤ He had never played in any of the games before. Now, Ethan was finally getting the chance to step onto the grass.

18

다음 글의 밑줄 친 부분에 들어갈 말을 주어진 말을 활용하여 쓰시오. (단, 필요시 단어를 추가 또는 변형할 것)

With only two minutes to play, both teams were fighting for the football. It was the last home game for the seniors of Winston High, and they were determined to win. Since it had been a close game the whole evening, the best players of each team hadn't left the field. Once Winston High's coach finally knew that victory was theirs, he ________________(all the seniors on the sidelines, play, allow) for the last few seconds. One of the seniors, Ethan, was especially happy. He had never played in any of the games before. Now, Ethan was finally getting the chance to step onto the grass.

____

19

다음 글의 밑줄 친 문장을 〈조건〉에 맞게 수동태 문장으로 바꿔 쓰시오.

With only two minutes to play, both teams were fighting for the football. It was the last home game for the seniors of Winston High, and they were determined to win. Since it had been a close game the whole evening, the best players of each team hadn't left the field. Once Winston High's coach finally knew that victory was theirs, the coach allowed all the seniors on the sidelines to play for the last few seconds. One of the seniors, Ethan, was especially happy. He had never played in any of the games before. Now, Ethan was finally getting the chance to step onto the grass.

〈조건〉 1. 행위자를 밝힐 것
2. 총 18단어로 영작할 것

____
________________.

20

다음 글의 밑줄 친 부분 중, 어법상 틀린 것은?

With only two minutes ① to play, both teams were fighting for the football. It was the last home game for the seniors of Winston High, and they were determined ② to win. Since it had been a close game the whole evening, the best players of each team ③ hadn't left the field. Once Winston High's coach finally knew that victory was theirs, all the seniors on the sidelines were allowed ④ to play for the last few seconds. One of the seniors, Ethan, was especially happy. He had never played in any of the games before. Now, Ethan was finally getting the chance ⑤ to stepping onto the grass.

21

다음 글의 밑줄 친 부분이 의미하는 바로 적절하지 않은 것은?

With only two minutes to play, both teams were fighting for the football. It was the last home game for the seniors of Winston High, and they were determined to win. Since it had been a close game the whole evening, the best players of each team hadn't left the field.

① The match was too close to call.
② Both teams were evenly matched in football.
③ It was easy to predict the winners of the game.
④ The gap between teams' scores hadn't been very big.
⑤ The seniors of Winston High were neck and neck with their rivals.

22

다음 중, 밑줄 친 that의 쓰임이 나머지 넷과 다른 것은?

① Winston High's coach finally knew that victory was theirs.
② He knew that he would never be a valuable player in any of the team's games.
③ He told the coach that he wanted to join the football team.
④ He always reminds us that everyone is important to a team's succes.
⑤ He wasn't the player that made the actual plays on the field.

23

다음 중, 밑줄 친 ⓐ~ⓔ의 문맥상 영영풀이가 적절하지 않은 것은?

With only two minutes to play, both teams were fighting for the football. It was the last home game for the seniors of Winston High, and they were determined to win. Since it had been a ⓐ close game the whole evening, the best players of each team hadn't left the field. Once Winston High's coach finally knew that victory was theirs, all the seniors on the sidelines were allowed to play for the ⓑ last few seconds. One of the seniors, Ethan, was especially happy. He had never played in any of the games before. Now, Ethan was finally getting the ⓒ chance to step onto the grass.

When the rival team dropped the ball, one of our players ⓓ recovered it and quickly ran down the field with it. Ethan ran right after him to catch up. As our player got closer to the end zone, he saw Ethan behind him on his left. Instead of running straight ahead, the player kindly passed the ball to Ethan so that he could ⓔ score a touchdown.

① ⓐ: decided or won by a slight difference
② ⓑ: final or coming after all others
③ ⓒ: an opportunity to do something
④ ⓓ: to get back something lost
⑤ ⓔ: to stay in the boundary line along the edge of the playing field

24

다음 글의 밑줄 친 ⓐ~ⓔ 중, 뜻풀이가 잘못된 것은?

ⓐ When the rival team dropped the ball, one of our players recovered it and quickly ran down the field with it. Ethan ran ⓑ right after him to catch up. ⓒ As our player got closer to the end zone, he saw Ethan behind him on his left. ⓓ Instead of running straight ahead, the player kindly passed the ball to Ethan ⓔ so that he could score a touchdown.

① ⓐ: ~할 때
② ⓑ: ~ 바로 뒤에서
③ ⓒ: ~하는 것처럼
④ ⓓ: ~하는 대신에
⑤ ⓔ: ~하도록

25

다음 글의 밑줄 친 부분 중, 어법상 옳은 것의 개수는?

With only two minutes ⓐ to play, both teams were fighting for the football. It was the last home game for the seniors of Winston High, and they were ⓑ determined winning. Since it had been a close game the whole evening, the best players of each team hadn't left the field. Once Winston High's coach finally knew that victory was ⓒ their, all the seniors on the sidelines were allowed to play for the last few seconds. One of the seniors, Ethan, was especially happy. He had never played in any of the games before. Now, Ethan was finally getting the chance ⓓ to step onto the grass.

When the rival team dropped the ball, one of our ⓔ player recovered it and quickly ran down the field with it. Ethan ran right after him ⓕ to catch up. As our player got closer to the end zone, he saw Ethan behind him on his left. Instead of ⓖ running straight ahead, the player kindly passed the ball to Ethan ⓗ in that he could score a touchdown.

① 3개 ② 4개 ③ 5개 ④ 7개 ⑤ 8개

26

다음 글의 밑줄 친 부분 중, 어법상 틀린 것은?

① With only two minutes to play, both teams were fighting for the football. It was the last home game for the seniors of Winston High, and ② they were determined to win. Since it had been a close game the whole evening, the best players of each team hadn't left the field. Once Winston High's coach finally knew that victory was theirs, ③ all the seniors on the sidelines were allowed to play for the last few seconds. One of the seniors, Ethan, was especially happy. He had never played in any of the games before. Now, Ethan was finally getting ④ the chance to step onto the grass.

When the rival team dropped the ball, one of our players recovered it and quickly ran down the field with it. ⑤ Ethan ran right after him caught up. As our player got closer to the end zone, he saw Ethan behind him on his left. Instead of running straight ahead, the player kindly passed the ball to Ethan so that he could score a touchdown.

27

다음 글의 밑줄 친 ①~⑤를 바르게 고치지 않은 것은?

With only two minutes to play, both teams ① fight for the football. It was the last home game for the seniors of Winston High, and they were determined ② win. Since it had been a close game the whole evening, the best players of each team hadn't ③ leave the field. Once Winston High's coach finally knew that victory was theirs, all the seniors on the sidelines ④ allowed to play for the last few seconds. One of the seniors, Ethan, was especially happy. He had never played in any of the games before. Now, Ethan was finally getting the chance ⑤ step onto the grass.

① fight → were fighting
② win → to win
③ leave → left
④ allowed → were allowing
⑤ step → to step

28

다음 글의 밑줄 친 우리말을 〈보기〉의 단어를 활용하여 영작하시오. (단, 필요시 단어를 어법에 맞게 변형하시오.)

When the rival team dropped the ball, one of our players recovered it and quickly ran down the field with it. Ethan ran right after him to catch up. As our player got closer to the end zone, he saw Ethan behind him on his left. 곧장 앞으로 달리는 대신에, 그 선수는 Ethan이 터치다운 할 수 있도록 Ethan에게 공을 패스했다.

〈보기〉 the ball / to Ethan / he / run / a touchdown / straight ahead / the player / could score / that / so / pass / instead of

____

____

____

29

다음 글의 (A), (B), (C)의 각 네모 안에서 어법상 옳은 것으로 짝지어진 것은?

With only two minutes to play, both (A) [teams / team] were fighting for the football. It was the last home game for the seniors of Winston High, and they were determined to win. Since it had been a close game the whole evening, the best players of each (B) [team / teams] hadn't left the field. Once Winston High's coach finally knew that victory was theirs, all the seniors on the sidelines were allowed to play for the last few seconds. One of the (C) [senior / seniors], Ethan, was especially happy. He had never played in any of the games before. Now, Ethan was finally getting the chance to step onto the grass.

	(A)	(B)	(C)
①	teams	team	senior
②	teams	teams	senior
③	teams	team	seniors
④	team	teams	seniors
⑤	team	team	seniors

30

다음 글의 (A), (B), (C)의 각 네모 안에서 문맥에 맞는 낱말로 가장 적절한 것은?

With only two minutes to play, both teams were fighting for the football. It was the last home game for the seniors of Winston High, and they were determined to win. (A) [Though / Since] it had been a close game the whole evening, the best players of each team hadn't left the field. Once Winston High's coach finally knew that victory was theirs, all the seniors on the sidelines were (B) [allowed / banned] to play for the last few seconds. One of the seniors, Ethan, was especially happy. He had never played in any of the games before. Now, Ethan was finally getting the chance to step onto the grass.

When the rival team dropped the ball, one of our players (C) [caught / abandoned] it and quickly ran down the field with it. Ethan ran right after him to catch up. As our player got closer to the end zone, he saw Ethan behind him on his left. Instead of running straight ahead, the player kindly passed the ball to Ethan so that he could score a touchdown.

	(A)	(B)	(C)
①	Though	allowed	caught
②	Since	banned	abandoned
③	Though	banned	abandoned
④	Since	allowed	caught
⑤	Since	allowed	abandoned

본문[1]

출제 포인트

1위	2위	3위
지칭 추론	내용 일치	문장 삽입
본문[1] 문단편 내 출제 확률 34.5%	본문[1] 문단편 내 출제 확률 32.8%	본문[1] 문단편 내 출제 확률 10.3%

● 지칭 추론

이 문단에서는 지칭 추론 유형이 34.5%의 확률로 가장 많이 출제될 수 있다. 많은 등장인물(윈스턴 고등학교 4학년 학생들 중 각 팀의 핵심 선수들, 사이드라인에 있던 모든 4학년생 선수들, Ethan 등)이 나오기 때문에, it, him, them, theirs 등의 대명사가 가리키는 것이 무엇인지 잘 파악해 두자.

Q. 다음 글의 밑줄 친 ⓐ~ⓔ 중, 가리키는 대상이 나머지 넷과 다른 것은?

With only two minutes to play, both teams were fighting for the football. It was the last home game for the seniors of Winston High, and they were determined to win. Since it had been a close game the whole evening, the best players of each team hadn't left the field. Once Winston High's coach finally knew that victory was theirs, all the seniors on the sidelines were allowed to play for the last few seconds. One of the seniors, Ethan, was especially happy. He had never played in any of the games before. Now, Ethan was finally getting the chance to step onto the grass.

When the rival team dropped the ball, ⓐ one of our players recovered it and quickly ran down the field with it. Ethan ran right after ⓑ him to catch up. As our player got closer to the end zone, ⓒ he saw Ethan behind ⓓ him on his left. Instead of running straight ahead, the player kindly passed the ball to Ethan so that ⓔ he could score a touchdown.

① ⓐ ② ⓑ ③ ⓒ ④ ⓓ ⑤ ⓔ

정답 ⑤

ⓔ는 Ethan, 나머지는 윈스턴 고등학교의 다른 선수들 중 한 명을 가리킨다.

● 내용 일치

이 문단에서 내용 일치 유형이 출제될 확률은 32.8%로, 두 번째로 높다. 글에서 알 수 있듯, Ethan은 이전에 어떤 경기에서도 뛰어본 적이 없었다. 하지만 내용과 일치하지 않는 선지로 '그는 이전에 경기에 출전한 경험이 있었다'와 같은 내용이 자주 등장한다. 이외에도 '윈스턴 고등학교 4학년 학생들의 마지막 홈 경기', '박빙의 경기', 'Ethan이 실제로 뛴 첫 경기', 'Ethan은 사이드라인에 있던 4학년생 선수들 중 한 명이었음', 'Ethan의 동료 선수가 그에게 공을 패스해 줌' 등과 같은 핵심 내용을 기억해두자.

1	The Final Touchdown	0%
2	With only two minutes to play, both teams were fighting for the football.	1.0%
3	It was the last home game for the seniors of Winston High, and they were determined to win.	16.2%
4	Since it had been a close game the whole evening, the best players of each team hadn't left the field.	10.1%
5	Once Winston High's coach finally knew that victory was theirs, all the seniors on the sidelines were allowed to play for the last few seconds.	20.2%
6	One of the seniors, Ethan, was especially happy.	6.1%
7	He had never played in any of the games before.	10.1%
8	Now, Ethan was finally getting the chance to step onto the grass.	10.1%
9	When the rival team dropped the ball, one of our players recovered it and quickly ran down the field with it.	5.0%
10	Ethan ran right after him to catch up.	2.0%
11	As our player got closer to the end zone, he saw Ethan behind him on his left.	3.0%
12	Instead of running straight ahead, the player kindly passed the ball to Ethan so that he could score a touchdown.	16.2%

Q. 글의 내용과 일치하면 T, 일치하지 않으면 F에 표시하시오.

(1) 윈스턴 고등학교의 감독은 승리를 확신하자 4학년 선수들을 경기에서 제외시켰다. (T / F)
(2) 이 게임은 윈스턴 고등학교 4학년들의 마지막 홈 경기였다. (T / F)
(3) Ethan의 동료 선수는 직접 터치다운을 하기 위해 계속 뛰었다. (T / F)
(4) 상대 팀은 핵심 선수들을 빼고 경기를 진행했다. (T / F)
(5) 경기는 접전이었다. (T / F)
(6) Ethan은 수많은 경기를 뛰어봤다. (T / F)
(7) Ethan은 단 하나의 경기도 뛰지 못하고 4학년을 마무리했다. (T / F)
(8) Ethan은 4학년이다. (T / F)
(9) 상대 팀 선수는 Ethan이 떨어뜨린 공을 들고 빠르게 경기장을 가로질렀다. (T / F)
(10) Ethan의 동료 선수는 엔드존에 다다랐을 때 Ethan이 자신의 뒤에 있는 것을 알지 못했다. (T / F)
(11) The game was the last away game for the seniors of Winston High. (T / F)
(12) Ethan's teammate passed the ball to Ethan. (T / F)
(13) Ethan was allowed to join the game for the second time. (T / F)
(14) For Ethan, it was the first game he took part in. (T / F)
(15) Ethan was pleased to take part in the game. (T / F)
(16) Ethan mistakenly dropped the ball during the game. (T / F)
(17) The player who held the ball saw Ethan behind him. (T / F)
(18) Since the game was close, Winston High's coach let the seniors play for the game. (T / F)

정답

1	F	2	T	3	F
4	F	5	T	6	F
7	F	8	T	9	F
10	F	11	F	12	T
13	F	14	T	15	T
16	F	17	T	18	F

(11) 이 경기는 윈스턴 고등학교 4학년들의 마지막 원정 경기였다.
(12) Ethan의 팀 동료가 Ethan에게 공을 패스했다.
(13) Ethan은 두 번째로 경기에 참여하도록 허락을 받았다.
(14) Ethan에게는, 그 경기가 그가 참여한 첫 번째 경기였다.
(15) Ethan은 경기에 참여하게 되어 기뻤다.
(16) Ethan은 경기 중 실수로 공을 떨어뜨렸다.
(17) 공을 잡은 선수는 그의 뒤에 Ethan이 있는 것을 보았다.
(18) 경기가 박빙이었기 때문에, 윈스턴 고등학교의 감독은 4학년들이 경기에 뛰도록 허락했다.

문장 삽입

이 문단에서 문장 삽입 유형은 10.3%의 확률로 출제될 수 있다. 우선 주어진 문장을 해석하여 앞뒤에 어떤 내용이 나올지 생각해보고, 선지 5개에 해당 문장을 넣어서 내용이 자연스럽게 이어지는지 확인해 볼 수 있다. 또한, 대명사나 관사에서 힌트를 얻을 수도 있다.

Q. 글의 흐름으로 보아, 주어진 문장이 들어가기에 가장 적절한 곳을 고르시오.

Once Winston High's coach finally knew that victory was theirs, all the seniors on the sidelines were allowed to play for the last few seconds.

With only two minutes to play, both teams were fighting for the football. It was the last home game for the seniors of Winston High, and they were determined to win. (①) Since it had been a close game the whole evening, the best players of each team hadn't left the field. (②) One of the seniors, Ethan, was especially happy. He had never played in any of the games before. (③) Now, Ethan was finally getting the chance to step onto the grass.

When the rival team dropped the ball, one of our players recovered it and quickly ran down the field with it. (④) Ethan ran right after him to catch up. As our player got closer to the end zone, he saw Ethan behind him on his left. (⑤) Instead of running straight ahead, the player kindly passed the ball to Ethan so that he could score a touchdown.

정답 ②

윈스턴 고등학교의 감독이 사이드라인에 있던 모든 4학년생 선수들이 경기에 출전하도록 허락했다는 내용의 주어진 문장은, 그 4학년생 선수 중 하나인 Ethan이 특히 기뻐했다는 내용 바로 앞인 ②에 오는 것이 글의 흐름상 자연스럽다.

등장인물의 심경

이 문단에서 등장인물의 심경을 물어보는 문제가 출제될 가능성은 8.6%이다. 등장인물의 심경/감정을 묻는 유형은 주어진 상황에서 등장인물이 어떻게 반응했는지를 살펴보며 추론할 수 있다. 이때, 감정을 나타내는 형용사나 분사가 힌트가 될 수 있다.

Q. 다음 글에서 Ethan의 심경으로 가장 적절한 것은?

With only two minutes to play, both teams were fighting for the football. It was the last home game for the seniors of Winston High, and they were determined to win. Since it had been a close game the whole evening, the best players of each team hadn't left the field. Once Winston High's coach finally knew that victory was theirs, all the seniors on the sidelines were allowed to play for the last few seconds. One of the seniors, Ethan, was especially happy. He had never played in any of the games before. Now, Ethan was finally getting the chance to step onto the grass.

When the rival team dropped the ball, one of our players recovered it and quickly ran down the field with it. Ethan ran right after him to catch up. As our player got closer to the end zone, he saw Ethan behind him on his left. Instead of running straight ahead, the player kindly passed the ball to Ethan so that he could score a touchdown.

① angry ② thrilled ③ cynical ④ disappointed ⑤ embarrassed

정답 ②

이전에 어떤 경기에서도 뛰어본 적이 없었지만 이제 마침내 잔디를 밟을 기회, 즉 경기에 출전할 기회를 얻게 된 상황이므로, Ethan의 심경으로 가장 적절한 것은 ② '아주 흥분한(thrilled)'이다.

① 화난
③ 냉소적인
④ 실망한
⑤ 당황스러운

● 글의 분위기

이 문단에서 글의 분위기와 관련된 문제가 출제될 가능성은 8.6%이다. 글의 분위기를 묻는 유형은 글의 전반적인 흐름을 이해하는 것이 중요한데, 윈스턴 고등학교 학생들이 마지막 홈 경기에서 승리하고자 하는 의지를 보여주며 박빙의 경기를 펼치고 있고, Ethan이 처음으로 경기에 뛸 수 있는 기회를 얻었다는 점을 이해해 보면 '극적인(dramatic), 신나는(exciting), 열정적인(enthusiastic)' 분위기인 것을 알 수 있다. 글에서 어떤 사건이 일어나고 있는지와 등장인물들이 어떻게 반응하고 있는지에 유의해야 한다.

Q. 다음 글의 분위기로 가장 적절한 것은?

With only two minutes to play, both teams were fighting for the football. It was the last home game for the seniors of Winston High, and they were determined to win. Since it had been a close game the whole evening, the best players of each team hadn't left the field. Once Winston High's coach finally knew that victory was theirs, all the seniors on the sidelines were allowed to play for the last few seconds. One of the seniors, Ethan, was especially happy. He had never played in any of the games before. Now, Ethan was finally getting the chance to step onto the grass.

When the rival team dropped the ball, one of our players recovered it and quickly ran down the field with it. Ethan ran right after him to catch up. As our player got closer to the end zone, he saw Ethan behind him on his left. Instead of running straight ahead, the player kindly passed the ball to Ethan so that he could score a touchdown.

① exciting and festive
② relaxing and peaceful
③ serious and urgent
④ lethargic and inactive
⑤ shameful and embarrassing

정답 ①

윈스턴 고등학교 4학년 학생들의 마지막 홈 경기에서 박빙의 경기 끝에 승리가 그들의 것임이 확실한 상황이므로, 이 글의 분위기로 가장 적절한 것은 ① '신나고 축제 기분의(exciting and festive)'이다.
② 편하고 평화로운
③ 심각하고 긴급한
④ 무기력하고 활발하지 않은
⑤ 창피하고 난처한

● 글의 순서

이 문단에서 글의 순서를 묻는 문제가 출제될 가능성은 5.2%이다. 순서 유형 문제를 풀 때는 가장 먼저 글의 흐름을 바꿀 수 있는 연결어가 있는지, 또는 관사나 대명사 등을 통해 힌트를 얻을 수 있는지 살펴봐야 한다.

Q. 주어진 글 다음에 이어질 글의 순서로 가장 적절한 것을 고르시오.

With only two minutes to play, both teams were fighting for the football.

(A) Once Winston High's coach finally knew that victory was theirs, all the seniors on the sidelines were allowed to play for the last few seconds. One of the seniors, Ethan, was especially happy.

(B) He had never played in any of the games before. Now, Ethan was finally getting the chance to step onto the grass.

(C) It was the last home game for the seniors of Winston High, and they were determined to win. Since it had been a close game the whole evening, the best players of each team hadn't left the field.

________ – ________ – ________

정답

(C) – (A) – (B)

경기 시간을 단 2분 남기고 양 팀이 공을 차지하기 위해 싸우고 있었다는 내용의 주어진 글 다음에 이 경기에 대해 부연 설명하는 (C)가 오고, 박빙의 경기 끝에 윈스턴 고등학교의 감독은 승리를 확신했고 사이드라인의 모든 4학년 학생들의 경기 출전을 허락했다는 내용의 (A)가 오며, 그 4학년생 선수 중 하나인 Ethan에 대해 설명하는 (B)가 마지막으로 온다.

출제 포인트 21.8% 정복!

최중요 연습 문제

01

다음 글의 내용과 일치하지 않는 것은?

With only two minutes to play, both teams were fighting for the football. It was the last home game for the seniors of Winston High, and they were determined to win. Since it had been a close game the whole evening, the best players of each team hadn't left the field. Once Winston High's coach finally knew that victory was theirs, all the seniors on the sidelines were allowed to play for the last few seconds. One of the seniors, Ethan, was especially happy. He had never played in any of the games before. Now, Ethan was finally getting the chance to step onto the grass.

When the rival team dropped the ball, one of our players recovered it and quickly ran down the field with it. Ethan ran right after him to catch up. As our player got closer to the end zone, he saw Ethan behind him on his left. Instead of running straight ahead, the player kindly passed the ball to Ethan so that he could score a touchdown.

① 이 경기는 윈스턴 고등학교 4학년 학생들의 마지막 홈 경기였다.
② 윈스턴 고등학교의 승리가 확실해지자 사이드 라인에 있던 모든 4학년 학생들이 경기에 뛸 수 있게 허용되었다.
③ Ethan은 마침내 경기를 할 수 있는 기회를 잡게 되어 기뻐했다.
④ Ethan은 같은 팀 선수를 따라잡기 위해 그의 바로 뒤에서 달렸다.
⑤ 팀 동료가 터치다운을 할 수 있도록 Ethan이 공을 패스해 주었다.

02

글의 흐름으로 보아, 주어진 문장이 들어가기에 가장 적절한 곳을 고르시오.

As our player got closer to the end zone, he saw Ethan behind him on his left.

With only two minutes to play, both teams were fighting for the football. It was the last home game for the seniors of Winston High, and they were determined to win. (①) Since it had been a close game the whole evening, the best players of each team hadn't left the field. (②) Once Winston High's coach finally knew that victory was theirs, all the seniors on the sidelines were allowed to play for the last few seconds. One of the seniors, Ethan, was especially happy. He had never played in any of the games before. (③) Now, Ethan was finally getting the chance to step onto the grass.

When the rival team dropped the ball, one of our players recovered it and quickly ran down the field with it. Ethan ran right after him to catch up. (④) Instead of running straight ahead, the player kindly passed the ball to Ethan so that he could score a touchdown. (⑤)

03

다음 글의 Winston High's coach의 심경으로 가장 적절한 것은?

With only two minutes to play, both teams were fighting for the football. It was the last home game for the seniors of Winston High, and they were determined to win. Since it had been a close game the whole evening, the best players of each team hadn't left the field. Once Winston High's coach finally knew that victory was theirs, all the seniors on the sidelines were allowed to play for the last few seconds. One of the seniors, Ethan, was especially happy. He had never played in any of the games before. Now, Ethan was finally getting the chance to step onto the grass.

① worried ② indifferent ③ upset
④ jealous ⑤ satisfied

04

다음 글의 밑줄 친 부분 중, 가리키는 대상이 나머지 넷과 다른 것은?

When the rival team dropped the ball, ① one of our players recovered it and quickly ran down the field with it. Ethan ran right after him to catch up. As ② our player got closer to the end zone, he saw Ethan behind ③ him on his left. Instead of running straight ahead, ④ the player kindly passed the ball to Ethan so that ⑤ he could score a touchdown.

05

다음 글의 분위기로 가장 적절한 것은?

With only two minutes to play, both teams were fighting for the football. It was the last home game for the seniors of Winston High, and they were determined to win. Since it had been a close game the whole evening, the best players of each team hadn't left the field. Once Winston High's coach finally knew that victory was theirs, all the seniors on the sidelines were allowed to play for the last few seconds. One of the seniors, Ethan, was especially happy. He had never played in any of the games before. Now, Ethan was finally getting the chance to step onto the grass.

When the rival team dropped the ball, one of our players recovered it and quickly ran down the field with it. Ethan ran right after him to catch up. As our player got closer to the end zone, he saw Ethan behind him on his left. Instead of running straight ahead, the player kindly passed the ball to Ethan so that he could score a touchdown.

① horrible ② calm
③ lively ④ boring
⑤ frightening

06

다음 글의 내용과 일치하지 않는 것은?

With only two minutes to play, both teams were fighting for the football. It was the last home game for the seniors of Winston High, and they were determined to win. Since it had been a close game the whole evening, the best players of each team hadn't left the field. Once Winston High's coach finally knew that victory was theirs, all the seniors on the sidelines were allowed to play for the last few seconds. One of the seniors, Ethan, was especially happy. He had never played in any of the games before. Now, Ethan was finally getting the chance to step onto the grass.

When the rival team dropped the ball, one of our players recovered it and quickly ran down the field with it. Ethan ran right after him to catch up. As our player got closer to the end zone, he saw Ethan behind him on his left. Instead of running straight ahead, the player kindly passed the ball to Ethan so that he could score a touchdown.

① Ethan's teammate picked up the ball that the opposing team's player dropped.
② It was not until Winston High's coach was convinced of victory that he put all the seniors into the game.
③ Ethan was delighted with the coach's permission to play in the final seconds of the game.
④ None of Ethan's teammates passed the ball to him.
⑤ Ethan ran right behind his teammate running fast to the end zone.

07

주어진 글 다음에 이어질 글의 순서로 가장 적절한 것을 고르시오.

With only two minutes to play, both teams were fighting for the football. It was the last home game for the seniors of Winston High, and they were determined to win.

(A) One of the seniors, Ethan, was especially happy. He had never played in any of the games before. Now, Ethan was finally getting the chance to step onto the grass. When the rival team dropped the ball, one of our players recovered it and quickly ran down the field with it.

(B) Since it had been a close game the whole evening, the best players of each team hadn't left the field. Once Winston High's coach finally knew that victory was theirs, all the seniors on the sidelines were allowed to play for the last few seconds.

(C) Ethan ran right after him to catch up. As our player got closer to the end zone, he saw Ethan behind him on his left. Instead of running straight ahead, the player kindly passed the ball to Ethan so that he could score a touchdown.

① (A) – (C) – (B)
② (B) – (A) – (C)
③ (B) – (C) – (A)
④ (C) – (A) – (B)
⑤ (C) – (B) – (A)

08

다음 글에 드러난 분위기로 가장 적절한 것은?

With only two minutes to play, both teams were fighting for the football. It was the last home game for the seniors of Winston High, and they were determined to win. Since it had been a close game the whole evening, the best players of each team hadn't left the field. Once Winston High's coach finally knew that victory was theirs, all the seniors on the sidelines were allowed to play for the last few seconds. One of the seniors, Ethan, was especially happy. He had never played in any of the games before. Now, Ethan was finally getting the chance to step onto the grass.

① shameful and embarrassing
② funny and humorous
③ calm and peaceful
④ boring and monotonous
⑤ lively and hopeful

09

다음 글에 드러난 Ethan의 심경으로 가장 적절한 것은?

With only two minutes to play, both teams were fighting for the football. It was the last home game for the seniors of Winston High, and they were determined to win. Since it had been a close game the whole evening, the best players of each team hadn't left the field. Once Winston High's coach finally knew that victory was theirs, all the seniors on the sidelines were allowed to play for the last few seconds. One of the seniors, Ethan, was especially happy. He had never played in any of the games before. Now, Ethan was finally getting the chance to step onto the grass.

When the rival team dropped the ball, one of our players recovered it and quickly ran down the field with it. Ethan ran right after him to catch up. As our player got closer to the end zone, he saw Ethan behind him on his left. Instead of running straight ahead, the player kindly passed the ball to Ethan so that he could score a touchdown.

① scared and terrified
② calm and indifferent
③ excited and anticipating
④ upset and irritated
⑤ regretful and determined

10

다음 글을 읽고 답할 수 있는 내용이 아닌 것은?

With only two minutes to play, both teams were fighting for the football. It was the last home game for the seniors of Winston High, and they were determined to win. Since it had been a close game the whole evening, the best players of each team hadn't left the field. Once Winston High's coach finally knew that victory was theirs, all the seniors on the sidelines were allowed to play for the last few seconds. One of the seniors, Ethan, was especially happy. He had never played in any of the games before. Now, Ethan was finally getting the chance to step onto the grass.

When the rival team dropped the ball, one of our players recovered it and quickly ran down the field with it. Ethan ran right after him to catch up. As our player got closer to the end zone, he saw Ethan behind him on his left. Instead of running straight ahead, the player kindly passed the ball to Ethan so that he could score a touchdown.

① Had Ethan ever played in the games before this one?
② Why did Ethan's teammate pass the ball to him?
③ Why did Winston High's coach let all the seniors play for the last few seconds of the game?
④ How did Ethan feel about his coach's decision to let him play?
⑤ What led Winston High to give up on their victory?

11

글의 흐름으로 보아, 주어진 문장이 들어가기에 가장 적절한 곳을 고르시오.

One of the seniors, Ethan, was especially happy.

With only two minutes to play, both teams were fighting for the football. (①) It was the last home game for the seniors of Winston High, and they were determined to win. Since it had been a close game the whole evening, the best players of each team hadn't left the field. (②) Once Winston High's coach finally knew that victory was theirs, all the seniors on the sidelines were allowed to play for the last few seconds. (③) He had never played in any of the games before. Now, Ethan was finally getting the chance to step onto the grass.

When the rival team dropped the ball, one of our players recovered it and quickly ran down the field with it. (④) Ethan ran right after him to catch up. As our player got closer to the end zone, he saw Ethan behind him on his left. (⑤) Instead of running straight ahead, the player kindly passed the ball to Ethan so that he could score a touchdown.

12

다음 글의 밑줄 친 부분 중, 가리키는 대상이 틀린 것은?

With only two minutes to play, both teams were fighting for the football. It was the last home game for the seniors of Winston High, and ⓐ they were determined to win. Since it had been a close game the whole evening, the best players of each team hadn't left the field. Once Winston High's coach finally knew that victory was theirs, all the seniors on the sidelines were allowed to play for the last few seconds. One of the seniors, Ethan, was especially happy. ⓑ He had never played in any of the games before. Now, Ethan was finally getting the chance to step onto the grass.

When the rival team dropped the ball, one of our players recovered ⓒ it and quickly ran down the field with it. Ethan ran right after him to catch up. As our player got closer to the end zone, ⓓ he saw Ethan behind ⓔ him on his left. Instead of running straight ahead, the player kindly passed the ball to Ethan so that he could score a touchdown.

① ⓐ: the seniors of Winston High
② ⓑ: Ethan
③ ⓒ: the ball
④ ⓓ: the rival team's player
⑤ ⓔ: our player

100점 맞고 싶다면!

기타 연습 문제

1회 등장 포인트

● 어휘 sideline

Once Winston High's coach finally knew that victory was theirs, all the seniors on the sidelines were allowed to play for the last few seconds.

● 어휘 especially, happy

One of the seniors, Ethan, was especially happy.

01

다음 글에서 밑줄 친 ①~④의 영영풀이를 (A)~(D) 중 알맞은 것과 연결하시오.

Once Winston High's coach finally knew that ① victory was theirs, all the seniors on the ② sidelines were allowed to play for the last few seconds. One of the ③ seniors, Ethan, was ④ especially happy. He had never played in any of the games before. Now, Ethan was finally getting the chance to step onto the grass.

(A) the area immediately outside the playing area, where substitute players sit (　　)
(B) used to indicate something that is more than usual (　　)
(C) success in defeating an opponent (　　)
(D) a student in the final year of high school or college (　　)

● 어휘 get, step onto

Now, Ethan was finally getting the chance to step onto the grass.

02

다음 주어진 영영풀이가 적절하지 않은 것은?

① victory: success in defeating an opponent or enemy
② rival: a person or thing that tries to defeat or be more successful than another
③ especially: under normal conditions
④ touchdown: a score that is made by carrying the ball over the opponent's goal line (in American football)
⑤ step onto: to put one's foot on or to walk on something

03

다음 글에서 문맥상 적절하지 않은 단어를 찾아 올바르게 고치시오.

With only two minutes to play, both teams were fighting for the football. It was the last home game for the seniors of Winston High, and they were determined to win. Since it had been a close game the whole evening, the best players of each team hadn't left the field. Once Winston High's coach finally knew that victory was theirs, all the seniors on the sidelines were allowed to play for the last few seconds. One of the seniors, Ethan, was especially happy. He had never played in any of the games before. Now, Ethan was finally losing the chance to step onto the grass.

__________ → __________

● 어휘 rival, drop

When the rival team dropped the ball, one of our players recovered it and quickly ran down the field with it.

04

다음 글의 빈칸 (A), (B)에 들어갈 단어를 〈보기〉에서 골라 알맞은 형태로 쓰시오.

〈보기〉 catch / find / drop / pass / score

When the rival team ____(A)____ the ball, one of our players recovered it and quickly ran down the field with it. Ethan ran right after him to catch up. As our player got closer to the end zone, he saw Ethan behind him on his left. Instead of running straight ahead, the player kindly passed the ball to Ethan so that he could ______(B)______ a touchdown.

(A) __________ (B) __________

● 어휘 closer

> As our player got closer to the end zone, he saw Ethan behind him on his left.

● 어휘 kindly, score a touchdown

> Instead of running straight ahead, the player kindly passed the ball to Ethan so that he could score a touchdown.

05

다음 글의 빈칸 (A), (B)에 들어갈 말로 알맞게 짝지어진 것은?

With only two minutes to play, both teams were fighting for the football. It was the last home game for the seniors of Winston High, and they were determined to win. Since it had been a close game the whole evening, the best players of each team hadn't left the field. Once Winston High's coach finally knew that victory was theirs, all the seniors on the sidelines were allowed to play for the last few seconds. One of the seniors, Ethan, was especially happy. He had never played in any of the games before. Now, Ethan was finally ______(A)______ the chance to step onto the grass.

When the rival team dropped the ball, one of our players recovered it and quickly ran down the field with it. Ethan ran right after him to catch up. As our player got closer to the end zone, he saw Ethan behind him on his left. Instead of running straight ahead, the player ______(B)______ passed the ball to Ethan so that he could score a touchdown.

	(A)		(B)
①	losing	–	kindly
②	getting	–	selfishly
③	losing	–	unselfishly
④	getting	–	kindly
⑤	getting	–	unkindly

06

다음 글을 읽고, 밑줄 친 (A)에서 the player가 Ethan에게 공을 패스한 목적으로 가장 적절한 것은?

One of the seniors, Ethan, was especially happy. He had never played in any of the games before. Now, Ethan was finally getting the chance to step onto the grass. When the rival team dropped the ball, one of our players recovered it and quickly ran down the field with it. Ethan ran right after him to catch up. As our player got closer to the end zone, he saw Ethan behind him on his left. Instead of running straight ahead, (A) the player kindly passed the ball to Ethan.

All eyes were on Ethan. With the ball in his hands, everything seemed to be moving in slow motion, like in a Hollywood movie. In this moment, all of Ethan's hard work and dedication was being rewarded with glory. Ethan's touchdown didn't win the game, but it will be worth remembering.

① to make Ethan stay off the sidelines
② to earn extra time before finishing the game
③ to show off his passing skills in front of the people
④ to give Ethan a chance to score a touchdown
⑤ to be a good friend of Ethan

● 어휘 pass, score

> Instead of running straight ahead, the player kindly passed the ball to Ethan so that he could score a touchdown.

07

다음 글의 밑줄 친 부분 중, 문맥상 낱말의 쓰임이 적절하지 않은 것은?

When the rival team ① dropped the ball, one of our players ② recovered it and quickly ran down the field with it. Ethan ran right after him to ③ catch up. As our player got closer to the end zone, he saw Ethan behind him on his left. Instead of running straight ahead, the player kindly ④ kept the ball to Ethan so that he could ⑤ score a touchdown.

기타 연습 문제

● **both의 쓰임**

> With only two minutes to play, both teams were fighting for the football.

● **시제와 수 일치**

> It was the last home game for the seniors of Winston High, and they were determined to win.

08

다음 글의 밑줄 친 부분 중, 어법상 틀린 것은?

With only two minutes to play, ⓐ each teams were focused on the football. It was the last home game for the seniors of Winston High, and they ⓑ were determined to win. Since it had been a close game the whole evening, the best players of each team hadn't left the field. Once Winston High's coach finally knew that victory was theirs, all the seniors on the sidelines ⓒ were allowed to play for the last few seconds. One of the seniors, Ethan, was especially happy. He ⓓ had never played in any of the games before. Now, Ethan was finally getting the chance to step onto the grass.

When the rival team dropped the ball, one of our players recovered it and quickly ⓔ ran down the field with it. Ethan ran right after him to catch up. As our player got closer to the end zone, he saw Ethan behind him on his left. Instead of running straight ahead, the player kindly passed the ball to Ethan so that he could score a touchdown.

① ⓐ ② ⓑ ③ ⓒ ④ ⓓ ⑤ ⓔ

09

다음 글의 밑줄 친 부분 중, 어법상 옳은 것을 모두 고르시오.

With only two minutes to play, both teams were fighting for the football. It was the last home game for the seniors of Winston High, and they were determined to win. Since it had been a close game the whole evening, the best players of each team hadn't left the field. Once Winston High's coach finally ① knew that victory was theirs, all the seniors on the sidelines were allowed to play for the last few seconds. One of the seniors, Ethan, ② was especially happy. He had never played in any of the games before. Now, Ethan was finally getting the chance to step onto the grass.

When the rival team dropped the ball, one of our ③ player recovered it and quickly ran down the field with it. Ethan ran right after ④ himself to catch up. As our player got closer to the end zone, he saw Ethan behind him on his left. Instead of ⑤ run straight ahead, the player kindly passed the ball to Ethan so that he could score a touchdown.

● **one of+복수명사**

> When the rival team dropped the ball, one of our players recovered it and quickly ran down the field with it.

● **목적격 대명사 him**

> Ethan ran right after him to catch up.

10

밑줄 친 우리말에 일치하도록 〈보기〉의 단어를 알맞게 배열하시오. (단, 필요시 단어 형태 변형 가능)

〈보기〉 it / of / our player / recover / one

When the rival team dropped the ball, 우리 선수들 중 한 명이 그것을 되찾았다 and quickly ran down the field with it. Ethan ran right after him to catch up. As our player got closer to the end zone, he saw Ethan behind him on his left. Instead of running straight ahead, the player kindly passed the ball to Ethan so that he could score a touchdown.

● **함축 의미**

> Once Winston High's coach finally knew that victory was theirs, all the seniors on the sidelines were allowed to play for the last few seconds.

11

다음 글의 밑줄 친 (A)에 대한 Winston High's coach의 의도로 가장 적절한 것은?

With only two minutes to play, both teams were fighting for the football. It was the last home game for the seniors of Winston High, and they were determined to win. Since it had been a close game the whole evening, the best players of each team hadn't left the field. Once Winston High's coach finally knew that victory was theirs, (A) all the seniors on the sidelines were allowed to play for the last few seconds. One of the seniors, Ethan, was especially happy. He had never played in any of the games before. Now, Ethan was finally getting the chance to step onto the grass.

① The coach tried to give the rival team the last chance to win.
② The coach intended to make all the seniors feel nervous.
③ The coach wanted to give all the seniors the chance to play in the last home game.
④ The coach didn't want to give the players a rest.
⑤ The coach tried to clean the sidelines.

• 문장 변형

본문에 나온 어휘와 혼동할 만한 어휘를 추가하면서 문장 구조를 변형하여, 어법상 틀린 곳을 찾으라는 문제가 출제될 수 있다.

12

다음 글의 밑줄 친 부분 중, 어법상 틀린 것은?

Two minutes ⓐ before the end of the game, both teams were fighting to take ⓑ possess of the ball. It was the last home game for the seniors of Winston High, and they ⓒ were determined to win. Since it had been a close game the whole evening, the best players of each team hadn't left the field. When the manager finally found out ⓓ that his team was the winner, all the senior players on the sideline were allowed to go on the field. One of the seniors, Ethan, was especially happy. He ⓔ had never played in any of the games before. Now, Ethan was finally getting the chance to step onto the grass.

① ⓐ ② ⓑ ③ ⓒ ④ ⓓ ⑤ ⓔ

출제 포인트 23.8% 정복!

리딩 본문[2]

18.8% 확률로 본문[2]에서 출제

본문[2] 적중 MAPPING

이것만 알아도 93.6% 맞힌다!

All eyes were on Ethan. With the ball in his hands, everything seemed to be moving in slow motion, like in a Hollywood movie. People kept their eyes on him as he made his way to the end zone. ★★★ They saw him cross the goal line right before the clock ran out.

Unexpectedly, everyone in the crowd leapt to their feet with their hands in the air. They were bursting with excited shouts and unending cheers for Ethan. ★★ In this moment, all of Ethan's hard work and dedication was being rewarded with glory. ★★ Ethan's touchdown didn't win the game, but it will be worth remembering. By now you're probably wondering why.

내용 일치 〈출제 1위 유형〉

해당 본문은 공을 패스받은 Ethan이 엔드존을 향해 달려가 터치다운에 성공하고 모두가 환호한다는 내용이다. Ethan의 움직임이 슬로우 모션과 같았다고 표현되는 부분이 Ethan이 실제로 천천히 움직였다는 내용으로 바뀌어 출제되거나, 관중들이 Ethan의 경기 수행에 실망했고 그동안의 Ethan의 노고가 수포로 돌아갔다는 내용이 틀린 내용 선지로 출제될 수 있다.

글의 순서 〈출제 2위 유형〉

Ethan이 터치다운을 하게 되는 과정을 파악하는 것이 중요하다. 공을 전달받은 Ethan은 엔드존을 향해 달려 경기 직전에 골라인을 넘으며, 'Unexpectedly ~' 이하 문장에서 관중들은 터치다운에 성공한 Ethan을 향해 환호를 보낸다. 'In this moment ~'의 'this moment'는 터치다운에 성공하여 환호를 받는 순간을 나타낸다.

글의 분위기 〈출제 3위 유형〉

처음으로 경기를 뛰게 된 Ethan이 터치다운에 성공하여 모두의 환호를 받는 상황으로, 해당 글의 분위기를 나타내는 말로는 festive(흥겨운, 축제와 같은), exciting(흥미진진한, 신나는), dramatic(감격적인, 인상적인), thrilling(황홀한, 아주 신나는), lively(활기찬, 발랄한), touching(감동적인), joyful(기쁜), enthusiastic(열광적인), impressive(인상 깊은) 등이 있다.

출제 1위 문장 ★★★

They saw him cross the goal line right before the clock ran out.

[지각동사+목적어+v/v-ing] 출제 1위 (문장편-문장4 → p.49)
[어휘 run out] 출제 2위 (문장편-문장4 → p.50)

출제 공동 2위 문장 ★★

Ethan's touchdown didn't win the game, but it will be worth remembering.

[be worth v-ing] 출제 1위 (문장편-문장8 → p.56)

출제 공동 2위 문장 ★★

In this moment, all of Ethan's hard work and dedication was being rewarded with glory.

[과거진행 수동태] 출제 1위 (문장편-문장7 → p.54)
[부분표현+of+명사] 출제 2위 (문장편-문장7 → p.54)

문장1

문장 출제 확률: 0.2%

수 일치 – 복수형

All eyes were on Ethan.

출제 포인트

1위

수 일치

문장 내 출제 확률 100.0%

본문[2] 문장편 내 출제 확률 1.4%

● 수 일치

문장1에서 출제될 가능성은 0.2%이다. 이 문장에서 출제가 된다면 100.0%의 확률로 수 일치를 묻는 어법 문제로 나올 수 있다. 주어가 All eyes라는 복수명사이므로 주어-동사 수 일치에 따라 복수형 동사 were이 쓰였다. 단수형 동사 was와 혼동하지 않도록 유의하자.

정답 were

주어가 All eyes라는 복수명사이므로 주어-동사 수 일치에 따라 복수형 동사 were이 어법상 적절하다.

Q. 다음 문장의 괄호 안에서 어법상 적절한 것을 고르시오.

All eyes (was / were) on Ethan.

출제 포인트 24% 정복!

문장2

문장 출제 확률: 2.0%

with+명사+전치사(구)

With the ball in his hands, everything seemed to be moving in slow motion, like in a Hollywood movie.

seem to be v-ing: ~하고 있는 듯하다

출제 포인트

1위	2위
seem to be v-ing	**with+명사+전치사(구)**
문장 내 출제 확률 76.5%	*문장 내 출제 확률 11.8%*
본문[2] 문장편 내 출제 확률 9.0%	*본문[2] 문장편 내 출제 확률 1.4%*

● seem to be v-ing

문장2에서 출제될 가능성은 2.0%이다. 이 문장에서 출제가 된다면 76.5%의 확률로 〈seem to-v〉 표현을 묻는 어법 문제로 나올 수 있다. '~하고 있는 듯하다'는 '~하는 듯하다'의 의미인 〈seem to-v〉와 '~하고 있다'의 의미인 진행형 〈be v-ing〉를 합쳐 〈seem to be v-ing〉의 형태로 나타낸다. 한편, 〈주어+seemed to-v〉는 〈It seemed that+주어+동사〉로 바꿔 쓸 수 있다.

Q. 다음 밑줄 친 우리말 뜻에 맞게 영작하시오. (7단어)

With the ball in his hands, everything 천천히 움직이고 있는 듯했다, like in a Hollywood movie.

____

정답

seemed to be moving in slow motion

'~하고 있는 듯하다'의 의미는 '~하는 듯하다'의 의미인 〈seem to-v〉와 진행형 〈be v-ing〉를 합쳐 〈seem to be v-ing〉가 된다. 한편, 과거에 관한 내용이므로 과거시제 seemed가 적절하며 '천천히'에 해당하는 표현은 부사구(전치사구) in slow motion이다.

● with+명사+전치사(구)

이 문장에서 두 번째로 출제 확률이 높은 것은 〈with+명사+전치사(구)〉로, 11.8%의 확률로 출제될 수 있다. 특히, with에 관해 묻는 어법 문제가 나올 수 있다. '~가 …한 채로'의 의미는 〈with+명사+현재분사〉로 나타낼 수 있는데, 현재분사가 being일 때는 종종 생략되어 그 뒤의 전치사(구)가 바로 올 수 있다.

Q. 다음 밑줄 친 우리말을 전치사 with를 활용하여 영작하시오. (6단어)

그의 손들에 공이 들린 채, everything seemed to be moving in slow motion, like in a Hollywood movie.

____

정답

With the ball in his hands

'~가 …한 채로'라는 의미는 〈with+명사+현재분사〉를 사용해서 With the ball being in his hands로 나타낼 수 있는데, 6단어로 써야 하므로 현재분사 being을 생략한 〈with+명사+전치사(구)〉 형태인 With the ball in his hands가 되어야 한다.

출제 포인트 25.4% 정복!

문장3

문장 출제 확률: 1.2%

People kept their eyes on him as he made his way to the end zone.

접속사 as 부사 역할 – 시간

keep one's eyes on: ~에서 눈을 떼지 않다

~로 나아가다

출제 포인트

1위	2위	3위
make one's way	접속사 as 부사 역할 – 시간	keep one's eyes on
문장 내 출제 확률 50.0%	문장 내 출제 확률 30.0%	문장 내 출제 확률 20.0%
본문[2] 문장편 내 출제 확률 3.5%	본문[2] 문장편 내 출제 확률 2.1%	본문[2] 문장편 내 출제 확률 1.4%

● make one's way

문장3에서 출제될 가능성은 1.2%이다. 이 문장에서 출제가 된다면 50.0%의 확률로 make one's way 표현을 묻는 문제로 나올 수 있다. 사람들은 Ethan이 엔드존으로 '나아갈(make one's way)' 때 그에게 시선을 고정했다는 내용이다. 또한, 주어가 he이며 문맥상 과거 시제로 쓰여 made his way로 쓰였음을 기억해두자.

Q. 다음 영영풀이를 참고하여, 빈칸 (A), (B)에 들어갈 말을 주어진 철자로 시작해 어법에 맞게 쓰시오.

to move forward by following a path

All eyes were on Ethan. With the ball in his hands, everything seemed to be moving in slow motion, like in a Hollywood movie. People kept their eyes on him as he ____(A)____ his ____(B)____ to the end zone. They saw him cross the goal line right before the clock ran out.

(A) m____________ (B) w____________

정답
(A) made (B) way
사람들은 Ethan이 엔드존으로 '나아갈(make one's way)' 때 그에게 시선을 고정했다는 내용이 흐름상 적절하다. 또한 글의 흐름상 과거 시제가 적절하므로 빈칸 (A)에는 made, (B)에는 way가 들어가야 한다.

● 접속사 as 부사 역할 – 시간

이 문장에서 두 번째로 높은 30.0%의 출제 확률을 보이는 것은 부사의 역할을 하며 시간의 의미를 표현하는 접속사 as이다. Ethan이 엔드존으로 나아갈 '때(as)' 사람들이 그에게 시선을 고정했다는 내용으로, 접속사 as(~할 때)의 의미를 파악하는 것이 중요하다. 또한, as와 마찬가지로 시간의 의미를 표현하는 접속사 when, while도 함께 알아두자.

Q. 다음 글의 밑줄 친 as와 바꿔 쓸 수 있는 것은?

All eyes were on Ethan. With the ball in his hands, everything seemed to be moving in slow motion, like in a Hollywood movie. People kept their eyes on him <u>as</u> he made his way to the end zone. They saw him cross the goal line right before the clock ran out.

① although ② when ③ since ④ because ⑤ whereas

정답 ② when
사람들은 Ethan이 엔드존으로 나아갈 '때(as)' 그에게 시선을 고정했다는 의미가 자연스럽다. 따라서, as와 바꿔 쓸 수 있는 것은 시간의 의미를 표현하는 접속사 ② 'when(~할 때)'이다.
① although: ~이긴 하지만
③ since: ~ 이후로, ~ 때문에
④ because: ~ 때문에
⑤ whereas: ~에 반하여

● keep one's eyes on

keep one's eyes on 표현에 관해 묻는 문제 또한 20.0%의 확률로 나올 수 있다. 〈keep one's eyes on A〉는 'A에서 눈을 떼지 않다'를 의미한다. 주어가 People이며 글의 흐름상 과거 시제가 적절하므로 kept their eyes on으로 쓰였다.

Q. 다음 영영풀이에 해당하는 표현으로 빈칸 (A), (B)를 채우시오. (단, 주어진 철자로 시작해 어법에 맞게 쓰시오.)

to pay close attention to someone or something

All eyes were on Ethan. With the ball in his hands, everything seemed to be

정답
(A) kept (B) on
주어진 영영풀이는 '누군가나 무언가에 세심한 주의를 기울이다'라는 의미이다. 이는 〈keep one's eyes on〉으로 표현할 수 있는데, 글의 흐름상 과거 시제가 적절하므로 빈칸 (A)에는 kept, (B)에는 on이 들어가야 한다.

moving in slow motion, like in a Hollywood movie. People ____(A)____ their eyes ____(B)____ him as he made his way to the end zone. They saw him cross the goal line right before the clock ran out.

(A) k______________ (B) o______________

출제 포인트 26.3% 정복!

문장4

문장 출제 확률: 3.4% (총 851개의 출제 포인트 중, 29회 출현, 45개 문장 중 9위)

They saw him cross the goal line right before the clock ran out.

saw him cross: 지각동사+목적어+v/v-ing

ran out: (시간 등이) 끝나다

출제 포인트

1위	2위
지각동사 + 목적어 + v/v-ing	어휘 run out
문장 내 출제 확률 82.8%	*문장 내 출제 확률 13.8%*
본문[2] 문장편 내 출제 확률 16.7%	*본문[2] 문장편 내 출제 확률 2.8%*

● 지각동사 + 목적어 + v/v-ing

문장4에서 출제될 가능성은 3.4%이다. 이 문장에서 출제가 된다면 82.8%의 확률로 〈지각동사+목적어+v/v-ing〉의 형식을 묻는 어법 문제로 나올 수 있다. '그들은 그가 (경기 종료 직전 골 라인을) 넘어선 것을 보았다'를 〈지각동사(see)+목적어+v/v-ing〉의 형식으로 나타냈다. 여기서는 목적격 보어로 동사원형이 쓰였다. 그 순간 일이 진행되고 있음을 강조할 때는 동사원형 대신 현재분사를 쓸 수 있다. to부정사는 쓸 수 없다는 것에 유의하자.

Q. 다음 문장에서 어법상 어색한 부분을 찾아 올바르게 고쳐 쓰시오.

They saw him crossed the goal line right before the clock ran out.

______________ → ______________

정답

crossed → cross/crossing

'그들은 그가 (경기 종료 직전 골 라인을) 넘어선 것을 보았다'를 표현할 때 〈지각동사(see)+목적어+v/v-ing〉의 형식이 적절하므로, 목적어 him에 대한 목적격 보어로 crossed가 아닌 cross/crossing이 와야 한다.

정답
(e) started running
→ ran out
이미 경기가 진행되고 있는 상황이므로 경기가 '시작되기' 전이 아니라 '종료되기' 직전에 Ethan이 골 라인을 넘어섰다는 내용이 흐름상 적절하다. 따라서 (e) started running을 ran out(끝나다, 다 되다)으로 고쳐야 한다.

● 어휘 run out

이 문장에서 13.8%의 확률로 두 번째로 높은 출제 확률을 보이는 것은 본문에서 '(경기가) 종료되다'를 의미하는 어휘 run out이다. 이미 경기가 진행되고 있는 상황이므로 경기가 '종료되기(ran out)' 직전에 Ethan이 골 라인을 넘어섰다는 내용이 흐름상 적절하다. 한편, 본문에서 run out은 자동사로 쓰였으며, '(남을) 내쫓다'를 의미하는 타동사 run ~ out / run out ~과 혼동하지 않도록 유의하자.

Q. 다음 글의 밑줄 친 (a)~(e) 중, 문맥상 적절하지 않은 것의 기호를 쓰고 바르게 고쳐 쓰시오.

(a) All eyes were on Ethan. With the ball in his hands, everything seemed to be moving (b) in slow motion, like in a Hollywood movie. People (c) kept their eyes on him as he made his way to the end zone. They saw him (d) cross the goal line right before the clock (e) started running.

(　　) ____________ → ____________

출제 포인트 28.9% 정복!

문장5

문장 출제 확률: 1.6%

Unexpectedly(뜻밖에), **everyone in the crowd leapt to their feet with their hands in the air.**

leap to one's feet: (기쁘거나 놀라서) 벌떡 일어서다
with + 명사 + 전치사(구)

출제 포인트

1위	2위	3위
leap to one's feet	with + 명사 + 전치사(구)	어휘 unexpectedly
문장 내 출제 확률 42.9%	문장 내 출제 확률 28.6%	문장 내 출제 확률 21.4%
본문[2] 문장편 내 출제 확률 4.2%	본문[2] 문장편 내 출제 확률 2.8%	본문[2] 문장편 내 출제 확률 2.1%

● leap to one's feet

문장5에서 출제될 가능성은 1.6%이다. 이 문장에서 출제가 된다면 42.9%의 확률로 leap to one's feet 표현을 묻는 문제로 나올 수 있다. leap to one's feet은 '(기쁘거나 놀라서) 벌떡 일어서다'를 의미한다. 본문에서 '그들은 Ethan을 향한 들뜬 외침과 끝없는 환호성을 터뜨렸다'는 내용이 바로 이어지므로 해당 부분은 '관중들이 Ethan의 터치다운에 매우 놀랐고 행복했다'는 것을 의미한다. 또한, 이 표현에서 전치사 to가 쓰인다는 점을 기억하자.

Q. 다음 글의 빈칸에 알맞은 말을 쓰시오.

All eyes were on Ethan. With the ball in his hands, everything seemed to be moving in slow motion, like in a Hollywood movie. People kept their eyes on him as he made his way to the end zone. They saw him cross the goal line right before the clock ran out.

Unexpectedly, everyone in the crowd leapt ____________ their feet with their hands in the air. They were bursting with excited shouts and unending cheers for Ethan. In this moment, all of Ethan's hard work and dedication was being rewarded with glory. Ethan's touchdown didn't win the game, but it will be worth remembering. By now you're probably wondering why.

____

정답 to

leap to one's feet은 '(기쁘거나 놀라서) 벌떡 일어서다'를 의미한다. 따라서 빈칸에 들어갈 말로 가장 적절한 것은 to이다.

● with + 명사 + 전치사(구)

이 문장에서 두 번째로 높은 출제 확률을 보이는 것은 〈with + 명사 + 전치사(구)〉이다. 28.6%의 확률로 〈with + 명사 + 전치사(구)〉 표현, 특히 with에 관해 묻는 어법 문제로 나올 수 있다. '그들의 손을 흔들며(공중에 두고)'를 의미하는 with their hands in the air 부분에 유의하자.

Q. 다음 글의 밑줄 친 우리말 뜻에 맞게 〈보기〉의 단어를 활용하여 영작하시오. (6단어)

〈보기〉 their hands / the air

Unexpectedly, everyone in the crowd leapt to their feet <u>그들의 손을 흔들며(공중에 두고)</u>. They were bursting with excited shouts and unending cheers for Ethan. In this moment, all of Ethan's hard work and dedication was being rewarded with glory. Ethan's touchdown didn't win the game, but it will be worth remembering. By now you're probably wondering why.

____

정답

with their hands in the air

〈with + 명사 + 전치사(구)〉는 '~가 …한 채로'를 의미한다. '공중에'라는 의미인 전치사구 in the air를 활용하여 with their hands in the air로 나타낸다.

● 어휘 unexpectedly

'뜻밖에'를 의미하는 부사 unexpectedly에 관해 묻는 문제 또한 21.4%의 확률로 나올 수 있다. 'everyone in the crowd leapt ~.'와 같은 문장을 수식하는 역할을 하는 것은 형용사가 아니라 부사이다. 한편, 사람들이 Ethan이 경기 종료 직전 골 라인을 넘어선 것을 보았다는 내용과 모든 관중들이 손을 흔들며 벌떡 일어섰다는 내용 사이에 '뜻밖에(Unexpectedly)'가 오는 것이 문맥상 자연스럽다.

Q. 다음 글에서 어법상 <u>틀린</u> 곳을 찾아 바르게 고쳐 쓰시오.

Unexpected, everyone in the crowd leapt to their feet with their hands in the air. They were bursting with excited shouts and unending cheers for Ethan. In this moment, all of Ethan's hard work and dedication was being rewarded with glory. Ethan's touchdown didn't win the game, but it will be worth remembering. By now you're probably wondering why.

____________ → ____________

정답

Unexpected
→ Unexpectedly

문장 'everyone in the crowd leapt ~.'을 수식하는 자리이므로 형용사가 아니라 부사를 써야 한다. 따라서, Unexpected(예기치 못한)를 부사 Unexpectedly(뜻밖에)로 고쳐야 한다.

출제 포인트 30.1% 정복!

문장6

문장 출제 확률: 1.9%

They were bursting with excited shouts and unending cheers for Ethan.

(bursting with — burst with: ~을 터뜨리다 / excited — 감정동사의 과거분사 / unending — 끝없는)

출제 포인트

1위	공동 2위	공동 2위
감정동사의 과거분사	어휘 burst with	어휘 unending
문장 내 출제 확률 50.0%	문장 내 출제 확률 18.8%	문장 내 출제 확률 18.8%
본문[2] 문장편 내 출제 확률 5.6%	본문[2] 문장편 내 출제 확률 2.1%	본문[2] 문장편 내 출제 확률 2.1%

● 감정동사의 과거분사

문장6에서 출제될 가능성은 1.9%이다. 이 문장에서 출제가 된다면 50.0%의 확률로 감정동사의 과거분사를 묻는 어법 문제로 나올 수 있다. '들뜨게 하다'를 의미하는 동사 excite와 명사 shouts가 수동 관계이므로 과거분사 excited가 쓰였다.

Q. 다음 글의 밑줄 친 (a)~(d) 중, 어법상 어색한 것을 골라 기호를 쓰고 바르게 고치시오.

Unexpectedly, everyone in the crowd (a) leapt to their feet with their hands in the air. They were bursting with (b) exciting shouts and unending cheers for Ethan. In this moment, all of Ethan's hard work and dedication (c) was being rewarded with glory. Ethan's touchdown didn't win the game, but it will be worth remembering. By now you're probably (d) wondering why.

(　　) ____________ → ____________

정답
(b) exciting → excited
'들뜨게 하다'를 의미하는 동사 excite와 명사 shouts가 수동 관계이므로 과거분사 excited가 적절하다.

● 어휘 burst with

이 문장에서 18.8%의 확률로 두 번째로 높은 출제 확률을 보이는 것은 '~을 터뜨리다', '~으로 터질 듯하다'를 의미하는 어휘 burst with이다. 본문에서는 경기 중인 상황이므로, 관중들이 Ethan을 향한 들뜬 외침과 끝없는 환호성을 '터뜨리고(bursting)' 있었다는 내용이 흐름상 적절하다. 또한, 주어 they(= everyone in the crowd)와 동사 burst가 능동 관계이므로 현재분사 bursting을 활용한 진행 시제가 쓰였다는 것도 기억하자.

Q. 다음 빈칸에 들어갈 말로 가장 적절한 것은?

Unexpectedly, everyone in the crowd leapt to their feet with their hands in the air. They were ____________ with excited shouts and unending cheers for Ethan. In this moment, all of Ethan's hard work and dedication was being rewarded with glory. Ethan's touchdown didn't win the game, but it will be worth remembering. By now you're probably wondering why.

① blinking ② bursting ③ boosting ④ breaking ⑤ breaching

정답 ② bursting
경기 중인 상황이므로, 관중들이 Ethan을 향한 들뜬 외침과 끝없는 환호성을 ② '터뜨리고(bursting)' 있었다는 내용이 흐름상 적절하다. burst with는 '~을 터뜨리다', '~으로 터질 듯하다'를 의미한다.
① 깜박이는
③ 북돋우는
④ 깨뜨리는
⑤ 위반하는

● 어휘 unending

마찬가지로 이 문장에서 18.8%의 확률로 두 번째로 높은 출제 확률을 보이는 것은 어휘 unending이다. '끝없는'을 의미하는 형용사 unending이 명사 cheers를 수식하고 있으며, 일반적으로 어법 문제에서 unending은 올바른 선지로 출제되는 경향이 있다.

Q. 다음 글의 밑줄 친 (a)와 (b)가 어법상 적절하다면 O, 적절하지 않다면 X를 고르고, 그 이유를 서술하시오.

Unexpectedly, everyone in the crowd leapt to their feet with their hands in the air. They were bursting with (a) excited shouts and (b) unending cheers for Ethan.

(a): (O / X) 이유: ______________________

(b): (O / X) 이유: ______________________

정답

(a): O / 이유: 그들(They)이 누군가를 '들뜨게 만드는' 외침이 아니고, 그들이 '들뜬' 외침을 한 것이므로 excited가 맞다.

(b): O / 이유: unending은 '끝없는'의 뜻을 가진 형용사로, 뒤에 있는 명사 cheers를 수식하는 자리로 알맞다.

● 동사의 태

동사 were bursting 부분의 시제와 태를 묻는 문제 또한 12.5%의 확률로 나올 수 있다. burst with는 '~을 터뜨리다', '~으로 터질 듯하다'라는 의미인데, 주어 they(= everyone in the crowd)와 동사 burst가 능동 관계이므로 현재분사 bursting을 썼다. 과거분사 bursted와 혼동하지 않도록 유의하자.

Q. 다음 글에서 어법상 틀린 곳을 찾아 바르게 고쳐 쓰시오.

Unexpectedly, everyone in the crowd leapt to their feet with their hands in the air. They were bursted with excited shouts and unending cheers for Ethan. In this moment, all of Ethan's hard work and dedication was being rewarded with glory. Ethan's touchdown didn't win the game, but it will be worth remembering. By now you're probably wondering why.

__________ → __________

정답

bursted → bursting

burst with는 '~을 터뜨리다', '~으로 터질 듯하다'를 의미하는데, 주어 they (= everyone in the crowd)와 동사 burst가 능동 관계이므로 현재분사 bursting으로 써야 한다.

출제 포인트 31.5% 정복!

문장7

문장 출제 확률: 2.9%

In this moment, all of Ethan's hard work and dedication was being rewarded with glory.

(all of: 부분표현+of+명사 / was being rewarded: 과거진행 수동태)

출제 포인트

1위	2위
과거진행 수동태	**부분표현+of+명사**
문장 내 출제 확률 56.0%	문장 내 출제 확률 20.0%
본문[2] 문장편 내 출제 확률 9.7%	본문[2] 문장편 내 출제 확률 3.5%

● 과거진행 수동태

문장7에서 출제될 가능성은 2.9%이다. 이 문장에서 출제가 된다면 56.0%의 확률로 과거진행 수동태를 묻는 어법 문제로 나올 수 있다. 주어인 'Ethan의 모든 노고와 헌신(all of Ethan's hard work and dedication)'이 동사 '보상하다(reward)'의 대상이므로 수동태를 쓰며, '보상받고 있었다'는 의미인 과거진행 시제를 써서, 과거진행 수동태 was being rewarded로 나타냈다는 것을 기억하자.

Q. 다음 밑줄 친 우리말 뜻에 맞게 주어진 단어를 활용하여 영작하시오. (단, 필요시 단어의 형태를 변형하여 12단어로 쓸 것)

In this moment, Ethan의 그 모든 노고와 헌신이 영광으로 보상받고 있었다.

____

(hard work and dedication, with, reward, glory, Ethan's, of, all)

정답

all of Ethan's hard work and dedication was being rewarded with glory

'Ethan의 그 모든 노고와 헌신'은 all of Ethan's hard work and dedication'으로 쓰고, '보상받고 있었다'는 '~받고[되고] 있었다'를 나타내는 과거진행 수동태 〈be동사의 과거형+being p.p.〉를 써서 was being rewarded로 쓴다.

● 부분표현+of+명사

이 문장에서 20.0%의 확률로 두 번째로 높은 출제 확률을 보이는 것은 〈부분표현+of+명사〉이다. 〈all of+명사〉와 같은 〈부분표현+of+명사〉는 동사를 명사의 수에 일치시킨다. 따라서, 단수 취급하는 불가산명사 Ethan's hard work and dedication에 수 일치시켜 단수형 동사 was를 썼다. 복수형 동사 were와 혼동하지 않도록 유의하자.

Q. 다음 글에서 어법상 어색한 곳을 찾아 바르게 고쳐 쓰시오.

Unexpectedly, everyone in the crowd leapt to their feet with their hands in the air. They were bursting with excited shouts and unending cheers for Ethan. In this moment, all of Ethan's hard work and dedication were being rewarded with glory. Ethan's touchdown didn't win the game, but it will be worth remembering. By now you're probably wondering why.

______________ → ______________

정답

were → was

〈부분표현+of+명사〉는 동사를 명사에 수 일치시키므로, 단수 취급하는 불가산명사 Ethan's hard work and dedication에 수 일치시켜 단수형 동사 was가 와야 하므로 복수형 동사 were를 was로 고쳐야 한다.

● 어휘 reward

reward를 묻는 문제 또한 12.0%의 확률로 나올 수 있다. 모든 관중들이 손을 흔들며 벌떡 일어선 채로 Ethan을 향한 끝없는 환호성을 터뜨리고 있는 상황이므로, 그의 모든 노고와 헌신이 영광으로 '보상받고(rewarded)' 있었다는 내용이 흐름상 적절하다. 're-'로 시작하는 생김새가 비슷한 단어와 혼동하지 않도록 유의하자.

Q. 다음 글의 (A), (B)의 각 네모 안에서 문맥에 맞는 낱말로 가장 적절한 것은?

(A) [All / No] eyes were on Ethan. With the ball in his hands, everything seemed to be moving in slow motion, like in a Hollywood movie. People kept their eyes on him as he made his way to the end zone. They saw him cross the goal line right before the clock ran out.

Unexpectedly, everyone in the crowd leapt to their feet with their hands in the air. They were bursting with excited shouts and unending cheers for Ethan. In this moment, all of Ethan's hard work and dedication was being (B) [recovered / rewarded] with glory. Ethan's touchdown didn't win the game, but it will be worth

정답 ①

(A) 사람들은 Ethan이 엔드존을 향해 갈 때 그에게 시선을 고정했다는 내용(People kept their eyes on him ~ the end zone.)으로 미루어 보아, '모든(All)' 시선이 Ethan을 향했다는 내용이 문맥상 적절하다.

(B) 모든 관중들이 Ethan을 향한 들뜬 외침과 끝없는 환호성을 터뜨리고 있는 상황이므로, 그의 모든 노고와 헌신이 영광으로 '보상받고(rewarded)' 있었다는 내용이 흐름상 적절하다.

recover: 회복하다, 되찾다

remembering. By now you're probably wondering why.

(A) (B)
① All – rewarded
② All – recovered
③ No – rewarded
④ No – recovered

● 어휘 dedication

dedication을 묻는 문제 또한 12.0%의 확률로 나올 수 있다. 모든 관중들이 손을 흔들며 벌떡 일어선 채 Ethan을 향한 들뜬 외침과 끝없는 환호성을 터뜨리고 있는 상황으로, 그의 모든 노고와 '헌신(dedication)'이 영광으로 보상받고 있었다는 내용이다. '-tion'으로 끝나는 철자가 비슷한 단어와 혼동하지 않도록 유의하자.

Q. 다음 글의 밑줄 친 부분 중, 문맥상 표현의 쓰임이 적절하지 않은 것은?

All eyes were on Ethan. ① With the ball in his hands, everything seemed to be moving in slow motion, like in a Hollywood movie. People kept their eyes on him as he ② made his way to the end zone. They saw him cross the goal line right before the clock ③ ran out.

Unexpectedly, everyone in the crowd ④ leapt to their feet with their hands in the air. They were bursting with excited shouts and unending cheers for Ethan. In this moment, all of Ethan's ⑤ hard work and donation was being rewarded with glory. Ethan's touchdown didn't win the game, but it will be worth remembering. By now you're probably wondering why.

정답 ⑤

모든 관중들이 손을 흔들며 벌떡 일어선 채 Ethan을 향한 들뜬 외침과 끝없는 환호성을 터뜨리고 있다고 했으므로, 그의 모든 노고와 '헌신(dedication)'이 영광으로 보상받고 있었다는 내용이 자연스럽다. donation은 '기부'라는 의미로, 문맥에 어울리지 않는다.

출제 포인트 33.8% 정복!

문장8

문장 출제 확률: 2.9%

Ethan's touchdown didn't win the game, but it will be worth remembering.

be worth v-ing: ~할 가치가 있다

출제 포인트

1위

be worth v-ing

문장 내 출제 확률 88.0%

본문[2] 문장편 내 출제 확률 15.3%

● **be worth v-ing**

문장8에서 출제될 가능성은 2.9%이다. 이 문장에서 출제가 된다면 88.0%의 확률로 〈be worth v-ing〉를 묻는 어법 문제로 나올 수 있다. 이는 '~할 가치가 있다'를 의미하는 표현으로, 〈be worthy of 명사/v-ing〉로 바꿔 쓸 수 있다. worth 뒤에 동사원형이나 to부정사는 올 수 없다는 점에 유의하자.

Q. 다음 문장의 괄호 안에 어법상 적절한 것을 고르시오.

Ethan's touchdown didn't win the game, but it will be worth (remembering / to remember).

정답 remembering

〈be worth v-ing〉는 '~할 가치가 있다'라는 의미로, worth 뒤에 동명사를 써야 한다.

출제 포인트 35.9% 정복!

문장9

문장 출제 확률: 0.7%

By now you're probably wondering why. (관계부사 why)

출제 포인트

1위

관계부사 why

문장 내 출제 확률 50.0%

본문[2] 문장편 내 출제 확률 2.1%

● **관계부사 why**

문장9에서 출제될 가능성은 0.7%이다. 이 문장에서 출제가 된다면 50.0%의 확률로 관계부사 why를 묻는 어법 문제로 나올 수 있다. 여기서는 선행사 the reason과 관계절의 '주어+동사'가 생략된 형태이다. 다음과 같이 바꿔 쓸 수 있는 표현도 함께 알아두자.

By now you're probably wondering (the reason) why[for which] it will be worth remembering.

Q. 다음 글의 밑줄 친 문장 중, 어법상 틀린 것은?

All eyes were on Ethan. ① With the ball in his hands, everything seemed to be moving in slow motion, like in a Hollywood movie. People kept their eyes on him as he made his way to the end zone. ② They saw him cross the goal line right before the clock ran out.

Unexpectedly, everyone in the crowd leapt to their feet with their hands in the air. They were bursting with excited shouts and unending cheers for Ethan. ③ In this moment, all of Ethan's hard work and dedication was being rewarded with glory. ④ Ethan's touchdown didn't win the game, but it will be worth remembering. ⑤ By now you're probably wondering the reason for why it should be remembered.

정답 ⑤

관계부사 why는 〈for(전치사)+which(목적격 관계대명사)〉의 역할을 하므로, 전치사 for가 중복되어 사용될 수 없다. why를 which로 고치거나 for을 없애야 한다.

출제 포인트 36.2% 정복!

최중요 연습 문제

01

다음 글의 문장 ①~⑤ 중, 어법상 어색한 것은?

① All eyes was on Ethan. ② With the ball in his hands, everything seemed to be moving in slow motion, like in a Hollywood movie. ③ People kept their eyes on him as he made his way to the end zone. ④ They saw him cross the goal line right before the clock ran out. ⑤ Unexpectedly, everyone in the crowd leapt to their feet with their hands in the air.

02

다음 글의 밑줄 친 부분 중, 문맥상 낱말의 쓰임이 적절하지 않은 것은?

① All eyes were on Ethan. With the ball in his hands, everything seemed to be moving in ② slow motion, like in a Hollywood movie. People kept their eyes on him as he made his way to the end zone. They saw him cross the goal line right before the clock ran out. ③ Unexpectedly, everyone in the crowd leapt to their feet with their hands in the air. They were bursting with excited shouts and unending cheers for Ethan. In this moment, all of Ethan's hard work and ④ prescription was being rewarded with glory. Ethan's touchdown didn't win the game, but it will be worth ⑤ remembering. By now you're probably wondering why.

03

다음 글의 밑줄 친 우리말 뜻에 맞게 〈보기〉의 단어를 활용해 어법에 맞게 영작하시오. (8단어)

〈보기〉 excited shouts, with, burst, unending cheers

Unexpectedly, everyone in the crowd leapt to their feet with their hands in the air. They 들뜬 외침과 끝없는 환호성을 터뜨리고 있었다 for Ethan. In this moment, all of Ethan's hard work and dedication was being rewarded with glory. Ethan's touchdown didn't win the game, but it will be worth remembering. By now you're probably wondering why.

____

____

04

다음 빈칸에 들어갈 말로 적절한 것은?

All eyes were on Ethan. With the ball in his hands, everything seemed ____________ moving in slow motion, like in a Hollywood movie. People kept their eyes on him as he made his way to the end zone. They saw him cross the goal line right before the clock ran out.

① be ② to be ③ being
④ been ⑤ to be been

05

다음 빈칸에 들어갈 말로 가장 적절한 것은?

____________ the ball in his hands, everything seemed to be moving in slow motion, like in a Hollywood movie.

① By ② With ③ Through
④ Like ⑤ Despite

06

다음 빈칸에 들어갈 말로 가장 적절한 것은?

All eyes were on Ethan. With the ball in his hands, everything seemed to be moving in slow motion, like in a Hollywood movie. People kept their eyes on him as he made his ____________ to the end zone. They saw him cross the goal line right before the clock ran out.

① eyes ② hands ③ time
④ way ⑤ walking

07

다음 글의 밑줄 친 부분 중, 어법상 어색한 것을 골라 번호를 쓰고 바르게 고쳐 쓰시오.

All eyes were on Ethan. With the ball in his hands, everything ① seemed to be moving in slow motion, like in a Hollywood movie. People ② kept their eyes on him as he made his way to the end zone. They saw him cross the goal line right before the clock ran out. Unexpectedly, everyone in the crowd ③ leapt to their feet with their hands in the air. They were bursting with excited shouts and unending cheers for Ethan. In this moment, all of Ethan's hard work and dedication ④ were being rewarded with glory. Ethan's touchdown didn't win the game, but it will ⑤ be worth remembering. By now you're probably wondering why.

(　　) ______________ → ______________

08

다음 글의 밑줄 친 우리말 뜻에 맞게 〈보기〉의 단어를 활용해 어법에 맞게 영작하시오. (단, 필요시 단어의 형태를 바꿔 쓸 수 있으며, 5단어로 작성할 것)

〈보기〉 worth, it, remember

Unexpectedly, everyone in the crowd leapt to their feet with their hands in the air. They were bursting with excited shouts and unending cheers for Ethan. In this moment, all of Ethan's hard work and dedication was being rewarded with glory. Ethan's touchdown didn't win the game, but 그것은 기억할 만한 가치가 있을 것이다. By now you're probably wondering why.

____

09

다음 글의 (A), (B), (C)의 각 네모 안에서 어법에 맞는 표현으로 가장 적절한 것은?

All eyes were on Ethan. With the ball in his hands, everything seemed to be (A) [moved / moving] in slow motion, like in a Hollywood movie. People kept their eyes on him as he made his way to the end zone. They saw him cross the goal line right before the clock ran out. Unexpectedly, everyone in the crowd leapt to their feet with their hands in the air. They were bursting with (B) [excited / exciting] shouts and unending cheers for Ethan. In this moment, all of Ethan's hard work and dedication was being rewarded with glory. Ethan's touchdown didn't win the game, but it will be worth remembering. By now you're probably (C) [wondered / wondering] why.

	(A)	(B)	(C)
①	moved	exciting	wondering
②	moving	excited	wondering
③	moving	exciting	wondering
④	moving	excited	wondered
⑤	moved	excited	wondered

10

다음 글의 (A), (B), (C)의 각 네모 안에서 어법에 맞는 표현으로 가장 적절한 것은?

All eyes (A) [was / were] on Ethan. With the ball in his hands, everything seemed (B) [be / to be] moving in slow motion, like in a Hollywood movie. People kept their eyes on him as he made his way to the end zone. They saw him (C) [cross / to cross] the goal line right before the clock ran out.

	(A)		(B)		(C)
①	were	–	to be	–	cross
②	were	–	be	–	to cross
③	were	–	be	–	cross
④	was	–	to be	–	to cross
⑤	was	–	be	–	cross

11

다음 중, 밑줄 친 (A) as와 쓰임이 가장 비슷한 것은?

All eyes were on Ethan. With the ball in his hands, everything seemed to be moving in slow motion, like in a Hollywood movie. People kept their eyes on him (A) as he made his way to the end zone. They saw him cross the goal line right before the clock ran out.

① She should pay taxes as a citizen.
② Doris used to be as tall as Tom was.
③ As you can see, honesty is important.
④ I often listen to music as I go to school.
⑤ As long as you love me, I will love you too.

12

다음 글의 밑줄 친 부분 중, 문맥상 낱말의 쓰임이 적절하지 않은 것은?

All eyes were on Ethan. With the ball in his hands, everything seemed to be moving in ① slow motion, like in a Hollywood movie. People kept their eyes on him as he made his way to the end zone. They ② saw him cross the goal line right before the clock ran out. Unexpectedly, everyone in the crowd leapt to their feet with their hands in the air. They were bursting with ③ excited shouts and unending cheers for Ethan. In this moment, all of Ethan's hard work and dedication was being ④ recovered with glory. Ethan's touchdown didn't win the game, but it will be worth remembering. By now you're probably ⑤ wondering why.

13

다음 글의 밑줄 친 부분을 한 문장으로 바꿔 쓸 때, 어법상 어색한 것은?

Unexpectedly, everyone in the crowd leapt to their feet with their hands in the air. They were bursting with excited shouts and unending cheers for Ethan. In this moment, all of Ethan's hard work and dedication was being rewarded with glory. Ethan's touchdown didn't win the game, but it will be worth remembering. By now you're probably wondering the reason. For the reason, it will be worth remembering.

① By now you're probably wondering the reason it will be worth remembering.
② By now you're probably wondering why it will be worth remembering.
③ By now you're probably wondering the reason why it will be worth remembering.
④ By now you're probably wondering the reason for why it will be worth remembering.
⑤ By now you're probably wondering the reason for which it will be worth remembering.

14

다음 글의 밑줄 친 부분 중, 어법상 틀린 것은?

Unexpectedly, everyone in the crowd leapt to their feet ① with being their hands in the air. They were bursting ② with excited shouts and unending cheers for Ethan. In this moment, all of Ethan's hard work and dedication ③ was being rewarded with glory. Ethan's touchdown ④ didn't win the game, but it will be worth ⑤ remembering. By now you're probably wondering why.

15

다음 글의 밑줄 친 부분 중, 어법상 틀린 것은?

All eyes ① were on Ethan. With the ball in his hands, everything seemed to be ② moving in slow motion, like in a Hollywood movie. People kept their eyes on him as he made his way to the end zone. They saw him ③ cross the goal line right before the clock ran out.

Unexpectedly, everyone in the crowd leapt to their feet with their hands in the air. They were ④ bursted with excited shouts and unending cheers for Ethan. In this moment, all of Ethan's hard work and dedication was being ⑤ rewarded with glory. Ethan's touchdown didn't win the game, but it will be worth remembering. By now you're probably wondering why.

16

다음 글의 (A), (B), (C)의 각 네모 안에서 문맥에 맞는 낱말로 가장 적절한 것은?

All eyes were on Ethan. With the ball in his hands, everything seemed to be moving in (A) [fast / slow] motion, like in a Hollywood movie. People kept their eyes on him as he made his way to the (B) [start / end] zone. They saw him cross the goal line right before the clock (C) [ran out / ran off].

	(A)	(B)	(C)
①	fast	end	ran off
②	slow	end	ran off
③	slow	start	ran off
④	slow	end	ran out
⑤	fast	start	ran out

17

다음 글의 밑줄 친 부분 중, 어법상 틀린 것은?

① Unexpected, everyone in the crowd leapt to their feet with their hands in the air. They ② were bursting with excited shouts and unending cheers for Ethan. In this moment, all of Ethan's hard work and dedication was ③ being rewarded with glory. Ethan's touchdown didn't win the game, but it will be worth ④ remembering. By now you're probably wondering ⑤ why.

18

다음 글의 (A), (B), (C) 각 네모 안에서 문맥에 맞는 낱말로 가장 적절한 것은?

All eyes were on Ethan. With the ball in his hands, (A) [nothing / everything] seemed to be moving in slow motion, like in a Hollywood movie. People kept their eyes on him as he made his way to the end zone. They saw him cross the goal line right before the clock ran out. Unexpectedly, everyone in the crowd (B) [leapt / led] to their feet with their hands in the air. They were bursting with excited shouts and unending cheers for Ethan. In this moment, all of Ethan's hard work and dedication was being rewarded with (C) [complaint / glory]. Ethan's touchdown didn't win the game, but it will be worth remembering. By now you're probably wondering why.

	(A)	(B)	(C)
①	nothing	– leapt	– glory
②	nothing	– led	– glory
③	nothing	– leapt	– complaint
④	everything	– led	– complaint
⑤	everything	– leapt	– glory

19

다음 글의 밑줄 친 부분 중, 어법상 틀린 것은?

All eyes were on Ethan. With the ball in his hands, everything seemed ① to be moving in slow motion, like in a Hollywood movie. People kept their eyes on him as he made his way to the end zone. They saw him ② cross the goal line right before the clock ran out.

Unexpectedly, everyone in the crowd leapt to their feet with their hands in the air. They ③ were bursting with excited shouts and unending cheers for Ethan. In this moment, all of Ethan's hard work and dedication ④ was being rewarded with glory. Ethan's touchdown didn't win the game, but it will be worth ⑤ to remember. By now you're probably wondering why.

20

다음 글의 (A), (B), (C)의 각 네모 안에서 어법에 맞는 표현으로 가장 적절한 것은?

All eyes were on Ethan. With the ball in his hands, everything seemed (A) [being / to be] moving in slow motion, like in a Hollywood movie. People kept their eyes on him as he made his way to the end zone. They saw him (B) [to cross / cross] the goal line right before the clock ran out. Unexpectedly, everyone in the crowd leapt to their feet with their hands in the air. They were bursting with excited shouts and unending cheers for Ethan. In this moment, all of Ethan's hard work and dedication was (C) [rewarding / being rewarded] with glory. Ethan's touchdown didn't win the game, but it will be worth remembering. By now you're probably wondering why.

	(A)	(B)	(C)
①	being	– cross	– rewarding
②	to be	– cross	– being rewarded
③	being	– cross	– being rewarded
④	being	– to cross	– being rewarded
⑤	to be	– to cross	– rewarding

본문[2]

출제 포인트

1위	2위	3위
내용 일치	글의 순서	글의 분위기
본문[2] 문단편 내 출제 확률 *31.7%*	*본문[2] 문단편 내 출제 확률* *20.0%*	*본문[2] 문단편 내 출제 확률* *18.3%*

● 내용 일치

이 문단에서는 내용 일치 유형이 31.7%로 가장 많이 출제되었다. 문단 내 각 문장들의 내용 일치 빈출도는 아래와 같다. Ethan이 경기 종료 전에 터치다운에 성공했는지 여부와, Ethan의 터치다운이 우승에 결정적인 영향을 끼치지는 않았지만 의미가 있다는 부분이 가장 많이 출제되었다.

1	All eyes were on Ethan.	3.2%
2	With the ball in his hands, everything seemed to be moving in slow motion, like in a Hollywood movie.	11.1%
3	People kept their eyes on him as he made his way to the end zone.	15.9%
4	They saw him cross the goal line right before the clock ran out.	22.2%
5	Unexpectedly, everyone in the crowd leapt to their feet with their hands in the air.	6.4%
6	They were bursting with excited shouts and unending cheers for Ethan.	12.7%
7	In this moment, all of Ethan's hard work and dedication was being rewarded with glory.	7.9%
8	Ethan's touchdown didn't win the game, but it will be worth remembering.	20.6%
9	By now you're probably wondering why.	0.0%

Q. 글의 내용과 일치하면 T, 일치하지 않으면 F에 표시하시오.

(1) Ethan은 경기 종료 전에 골을 성공시켰다. (T / F)
(2) Ethan의 득점은 팀의 승리에 지대한 영향을 끼쳤다. (T / F)
(3) Ethan이 공을 들고 사이드라인을 향해 달려갈 때 모두의 이목이 집중되었다. (T / F)
(4) 사람들은 터치다운에 성공한 Ethan에게 끊임없는 환호를 보냈다. (T / F)
(5) 막상 공을 잡은 Ethan은 평소처럼 달릴 수 없었지만, 관객들은 그를 응원했다. (T / F)
(6) 단 한 번의 터치다운은 그동안의 Ethan의 노고와 헌신을 보상하기에는 역부족이었다. (T / F)
(7) 관중 모두가 Ethan의 터치다운에 진심으로 기뻐했다. (T / F)
(8) 관중들은 공을 잡은 Ethan에게 일제히 집중했다. (T / F)
(9) People cheered up Ethan as he couldn't make it to the end zone. (T / F)
(10) Most people considered Ethan's touchdown no more than ordinary. (T / F)
(11) People couldn't keep their eyes off Ethan while he was running to the end zone. (T / F)
(12) Ethan bursted into tears as he successfully made his way to the end zone. (T / F)
(13) Ethan moved very slowly toward the end zone carrying the ball in his hands. (T / F)
(14) All of Ethan's hard work went down the drain in the end. (T / F)

정답

1	T	2	F	3	F
4	T	5	F	6	F
7	T	8	T	9	F
10	F	11	T	12	F
13	F	14	F	15	T
16	T				

(9) 사람들은 Ethan이 엔드존에 도달하지 못하자 그를 응원했다.
(10) 대부분의 사람들은 Ethan의 터치다운을 특별할 것 없다고 생각했다.
(11) Ethan이 엔드존으로 달려갈 때 사람들은 그에게서 눈을 뗄 수 없었다.
(12) Ethan이 성공적으로 엔드존에 갔을 때 그는 눈물을 터뜨렸다.
(13) Ethan은 손에 공을 들고 엔드존을 향해 아주 느리게 움직였다.
(14) 모든 Ethan의 노고가 결국에는 수포로 돌아갔다.
(15) 관중은 Ethan의 터치다운에 대해 엄청난 환호와 함께 갑자기 일어섰다.
(16) Ethan이 공을 가졌을 때, 그는 관중들로부터 모든 관심을 받았다.

(15) The crowd suddenly stood up with a great cheer for Ethan's touchdown. (T / F)
(16) When Ethan got the ball, he got all the attention from the crowd. (T / F)

● 글의 순서

이 문단에서는 글의 순서 유형이 20.0%로 두 번째로 많이 출제되었다. 이 문단의 순서 문제에 대비하기 위해서는, Ethan이 터치다운을 하게 되는 과정, 즉 공을 전달받은 Ethan이 엔드존을 향해 달려가 경기 직전에 골 라인을 넘고, 터치다운에 성공한 Ethan을 향해 관중이 환호를 보내는 과정을 이해할 필요가 있다.

Q. 주어진 글 다음에 이어질 (A)~(C)의 순서를 바르게 배열하시오.

All eyes were on Ethan. With the ball in his hands, everything seemed to be moving in slow motion, like in a Hollywood movie.

(A) Unexpectedly, everyone in the crowd leapt to their feet with their hands in the air. They were bursting with excited shouts and unending cheers for Ethan.
(B) People kept their eyes on him as he made his way to the end zone. They saw him cross the goal line right before the clock ran out.
(C) In this moment, all of Ethan's hard work and dedication was being rewarded with glory. Ethan's touchdown didn't win the game, but it will be worth remembering. By now you're probably wondering why.

__________ – __________ – __________

정답 (B) – (A) – (C)
Ethan의 손에 공이 들려 있는 주어진 글 뒤에는 가장 먼저 Ethan이 공을 들고 골 라인을 넘어서는 (B)가 오고, 그 다음으로는 Ethan의 터치다운에 대한 관중들의 반응을 보여주는 (A)가 와야 한다. 마지막으로, (C)의 'this moment'는 Ethan이 터치다운에 성공하여 모두의 환호를 받는 순간을 나타내므로, (A) 다음에는 (C)가 온다.

● 글의 분위기

이 문단에서는 글의 분위기를 묻는 문제가 18.3%의 비율로 출제되었다. 처음으로 실제 경기를 뛰게 된 Ethan이 터치다운에 성공하여 모두의 환호를 받았다는 내용으로, 해당 글의 분위기를 나타내는 말로는 festive(흥겨운), exciting(신나는), dramatic(감격적인), thrilling(흥분되는, 신나는), lively(활기찬), touching(감동적인), joyful(기쁜), impressive(인상 깊은), enthusiastic(열광적인) 등이 있다.

Q. 다음 글의 분위기를 나타내기에 적합한 말을 〈보기〉에서 모두 찾아 쓰시오.

〈보기〉 solitary / boring / frustrating / festive / calm / furious / lonely / mysterious / monotonous / gloomy / touching

When the rival team dropped the ball, one of our players recovered it and quickly ran down the field with it. Ethan ran right after him to catch up. As our player got closer to the end zone, he saw Ethan behind him on his left. Instead of running straight ahead, the player kindly passed the ball to Ethan so that he could score a touchdown. All eyes were on Ethan. With the ball in his hands, everything seemed to be moving in slow motion, like in a Hollywood movie. People kept their eyes on him as he made his way to the end zone. They saw him cross the goal line right before the clock ran out. Unexpectedly, everyone in the crowd leapt to their feet with their hands in the air. They were bursting with excited shouts and

정답
festive, touching
같은 팀 선수가 Ethan을 배려하여 자신이 가지고 있던 공을 넘겨주고, 공을 건네받은 Ethan이 터치다운에 성공하여 모두가 환호하는 상황이다. 따라서 글의 분위기로 알맞은 말은 festive(흥겨운), touching(감동적인)이다.

unending cheers for Ethan. In this moment, all of Ethan's hard work and dedication was being rewarded with glory. Ethan's touchdown didn't win the game, but it will be worth remembering.

____

● 지칭 추론

이 문단에서 출제된 문제들 중 13.3%가 지칭 추론 유형에 해당한다. 특히, 인칭대명사 he, him, his가 본문[1]에 나오는 '우리 선수들 중 한 명(one of our players)'과 Ethan 중 각각 누구를 가리키는지 파악하는 것이 중요하다.

Q. 다음 글의 밑줄 친 부분이 가리키는 대상과 같은 표현을 모두 찾아 쓰시오. (단, 대명사는 포함하지 말 것)

When the rival team dropped the ball, one of our players recovered it and quickly ran down the field with it. Ethan ran right after him to catch up. As our player got closer to the end zone, he saw Ethan behind him on his left. Instead of running straight ahead, the player kindly passed the ball to Ethan so that he could score a touchdown. All eyes were on Ethan. With the ball in his hands, everything seemed to be moving in slow motion, like in a Hollywood movie. People kept their eyes on him as he made his way to the end zone. They saw him cross the goal line right before the clock ran out.

____

정답
our player, the player
'우리 선수들 중 한 명(one of our players)'과 '우리 선수(our player)', '그 선수(the player)'는 모두 동일 인물을 지칭한다.

● 등장인물의 심경

이 문단에서는 등장인물의 심경을 묻는 문제가 5.0%의 비율로 출제되었으며, 중심 인물인 Ethan의 심경을 묻는 문제가 주로 출제되었다. Ethan의 심경을 나타내는 말로는 thrilled(황홀해하는, 신이 난), excited(신이 난, 들뜬), proud(자랑스러워하는) 등이 있다. Ethan의 심경 외에도, 각 구체적인 상황 별로 등장인물의 심경을 묻는 문제 또한 출제될 수 있으니 잘 파악해 두자.

Q. 다음 글의 Ethan의 심경으로 가장 적절한 것은?

All eyes were on Ethan. With the ball in his hands, everything seemed to be moving in slow motion, like in a Hollywood movie. People kept their eyes on him as he made his way to the end zone. They saw him cross the goal line right before the clock ran out. Unexpectedly, everyone in the crowd leapt to their feet with their hands in the air. They were bursting with excited shouts and unending cheers for Ethan. In this moment, all of Ethan's hard work and dedication was being rewarded with glory. Ethan's touchdown didn't win the game, but it will be worth remembering. By now you're probably wondering why.

① confused ② disappointed ③ thrilled
④ curious ⑤ indifferent

정답 ③
Ethan이 경기 종료 직전에 터치다운에 성공하여 모두가 환호를 보내는 상황이므로, Ethan의 심경으로 가장 적절한 것은 ③ 'thrilled(신이 난)'이다.
① 혼란스러운
② 실망한
④ 궁금한
⑤ 무관심한

문장 삽입

이 문단에서는 문장 삽입 유형이 3.3%의 비율로 출제되었다. 해당 문단에서는 '모든 것이 슬로우 모션으로 움직이는 듯했다(everything seemed to be moving in slow motion)'는 부분 뒤에 Ethan이 모든 시선을 한 번에 받으며 터치다운에 성공하는 장면이 Ethan의 움직임과 관객들의 반응에 따라 차근차근 묘사되고 있다. 아래 문제를 통해, Ethan이 터치다운에 성공하기까지의 과정을 사건 순서에 따라 촘촘하게 학습해 보자.

Q. 글의 흐름으로 보아, 주어진 문장이 들어가기에 가장 적절한 곳은?

People kept their eyes on him as he made his way to the end zone.

All eyes were on Ethan. With the ball in his hands, everything seemed to be moving in slow motion, like in a Hollywood movie. (①) They saw him cross the goal line right before the clock ran out. (②) Unexpectedly, everyone in the crowd leapt to their feet with their hands in the air. (③) They were bursting with excited shouts and unending cheers for Ethan. (④) In this moment, all of Ethan's hard work and dedication was being rewarded with glory. (⑤) Ethan's touchdown didn't win the game, but it will be worth remembering. By now you're probably wondering why.

정답 ①

주어진 문장은 Ethan이 엔드존을 향해 나아가는 장면이다. 따라서 주어진 문장은 Ethan이 공을 잡은 문장 2와, 골 라인을 넘는 문장3 사이인 ①에 들어가야 옳다.

이어질 내용

이 문단에서는 이어질 내용을 묻는 문제가 3.3%의 비율로 출제되었다. 글의 후반부에서, Ethan의 터치다운이 팀의 승리를 얻어낸 것이 아니었지만 기억할 만한 가치가 있을 것이라고 언급한 점을 유념하자.

Q. 다음 글에 이어질 내용으로 가장 적절한 것은?

All eyes were on Ethan. With the ball in his hands, everything seemed to be moving in slow motion, like in a Hollywood movie. People kept their eyes on him as he made his way to the end zone. They saw him cross the goal line right before the clock ran out. Unexpectedly, everyone in the crowd leapt to their feet with their hands in the air. They were bursting with excited shouts and unending cheers for Ethan. In this moment, all of Ethan's hard work and dedication was being rewarded with glory. Ethan's touchdown didn't win the game, but it will be worth remembering. By now you're probably wondering why.

① 관중의 응원이 경기력에 미치는 영향에 대한 통계 자료
② 모든 학생에게 동일한 기회가 주어지는 것의 중요성
③ 감독이 Ethan의 팀 선수들을 체계적으로 훈련시켜 온 과정
④ Ethan이 경기에서 얼마나 큰 활약을 했는지에 대한 분석
⑤ Ethan의 터치다운이 왜 의미 있는지에 대한 설명

정답 ⑤

글의 후반부에서, Ethan의 터치다운이 경기에서 이기는 데 결정적인 요소가 아니었음에도 불구하고 Ethan의 터치다운이 기억할 만한 가치가 있다고 한 후, '지금쯤 당신은 왜 그런지 궁금할 것이다(By now you're probably wondering why.)'라고 했으므로, 주어진 글 다음에는 왜 Ethan의 터치다운이 그렇게나 의미가 있는지에 관한 설명이 이어져야 한다.

01

다음 글의 내용과 일치하지 않는 것은?

All eyes were on Ethan. With the ball in his hands, everything seemed to be moving in slow motion, like in a Hollywood movie. People kept their eyes on him as he made his way to the end zone. They saw him cross the goal line right before the clock ran out.

Unexpectedly, everyone in the crowd leapt to their feet with their hands in the air. They were bursting with excited shouts and unending cheers for Ethan. In this moment, all of Ethan's hard work and dedication was being rewarded with glory. Ethan's touchdown didn't win the game, but it will be worth remembering. By now you're probably wondering why.

① Ethan이 공을 잡았을 때, 모든 관중이 그에게 시선을 집중했다.
② Ethan은 할리우드 영화 배우처럼 천천히 공을 잡고 움직였다.
③ Ethan은 경기가 끝나기 직전에 득점에 성공했다.
④ 모든 관중이 Ethan을 향해 끝없는 환호성을 터뜨렸다.
⑤ Ethan의 터치다운이 경기의 승패에 영향을 미친 것은 아니었다.

02

다음 글의 분위기로 가장 적절한 것은?

All eyes were on Ethan. With the ball in his hands, everything seemed to be moving in slow motion, like in a Hollywood movie. People kept their eyes on him as he made his way to the end zone. They saw him cross the goal line right before the clock ran out.

Unexpectedly, everyone in the crowd leapt to their feet with their hands in the air. They were bursting with excited shouts and unending cheers for Ethan. In this moment, all of Ethan's hard work and dedication was being rewarded with glory. Ethan's touchdown didn't win the game, but it will be worth remembering. By now you're probably wondering why.

① dull and boring
② noisy and irritating
③ lonely and gloomy
④ calm and encouraging
⑤ exciting and joyful

03

주어진 글 다음에 이어질 글의 순서로 가장 적절한 것은?

As our player got closer to the end zone, he saw Ethan behind him on his left. Instead of running straight ahead, the player kindly passed the ball to Ethan so that he could score a touchdown. All eyes were on Ethan.

(A) In this moment, all of Ethan's hard work and dedication was being rewarded with glory. Ethan's touchdown didn't win the game, but it will be worth remembering. By now you're probably wondering why.

(B) With the ball in his hands, everything seemed to be moving in slow motion, like in a Hollywood movie. People kept their eyes on him as he made his way to the end zone. They saw him cross the goal line right before the clock ran out.

(C) Unexpectedly, everyone in the crowd leapt to their feet with their hands in the air. They were bursting with excited shouts and unending cheers for Ethan.

① (A) – (C) – (B)
② (B) – (A) – (C)
③ (B) – (C) – (A)
④ (C) – (A) – (B)
⑤ (C) – (B) – (A)

04

다음 글의 밑줄 친 (a)~(e) 중에서 Ethan을 지칭하는 것의 개수는?

When the rival team dropped the ball, one of our players recovered it and quickly ran down the field with it. Ethan ran right after (a) <u>him</u> to catch up. As our player got closer to the end zone, he saw Ethan behind him on (b) <u>his</u> left. Instead of running straight ahead, the player kindly passed the ball to Ethan so that (c) <u>he</u> could score a touchdown.

All eyes were on Ethan. With the ball in his hands, everything seemed to be moving in slow motion, like in a Hollywood movie. People kept their eyes on (d) <u>him</u> as he made his way to the end zone. They saw (e) <u>him</u> cross the goal line right before the clock ran out.

① 1개 ② 2개 ③ 3개 ④ 4개 ⑤ 5개

05

주어진 글 다음에 이어질 글의 순서로 가장 적절한 것은?

> Once Winston High's coach finally knew that victory was theirs, all the seniors on the sidelines were allowed to play for the last few seconds. One of the seniors, Ethan, was especially happy. He had never played in any of the games before. Now, Ethan was finally getting the chance to step onto the grass.

(A) All eyes were on Ethan. With the ball in his hands, everything seemed to be moving in slow motion, like in a Hollywood movie. People kept their eyes on him as he made his way to the end zone. They saw him cross the goal line right before the clock ran out.

(B) When the rival team dropped the ball, one of our players recovered it and quickly ran down the field with it. Ethan ran right after him to catch up. As our player got closer to the end zone, he saw Ethan behind him on his left. Instead of running straight ahead, the player kindly passed the ball to Ethan so that he could score a touchdown.

(C) Unexpectedly, everyone in the crowd leapt to their feet with their hands in the air. They were bursting with excited shouts and unending cheers for Ethan. In this moment, all of Ethan's hard work and dedication was being rewarded with glory. Ethan's touchdown didn't win the game, but it will be worth remembering. By now you're probably wondering why.

① (A) – (C) – (B) ② (B) – (A) – (C)
③ (B) – (C) – (A) ④ (C) – (A) – (B)
⑤ (C) – (B) – (A)

06

다음 글에서 관중들의 심경으로 가장 적절한 것은?

All eyes were on Ethan. With the ball in his hands, everything seemed to be moving in slow motion, like in a Hollywood movie. People kept their eyes on him as he made his way to the end zone. They saw him cross the goal line right before the clock ran out.

Unexpectedly, everyone in the crowd leapt to their feet with their hands in the air. They were bursting with excited shouts and unending cheers for Ethan. In this moment, all of Ethan's hard work and dedication was being rewarded with glory. Ethan's touchdown didn't win the game, but it will be worth remembering. By now you're probably wondering why.

① disappointed ② jealous
③ tired ④ delighted
⑤ unconcerned

07

다음 글의 내용과 일치하는 것은?

All eyes were on Ethan. With the ball in his hands, everything seemed to be moving in slow motion, like in a Hollywood movie. People kept their eyes on him as he made his way to the end zone. They saw him cross the goal line right before the clock ran out.

Unexpectedly, everyone in the crowd leapt to their feet with their hands in the air. They were bursting with excited shouts and unending cheers for Ethan. In this moment, all of Ethan's hard work and dedication was being rewarded with glory. Ethan's touchdown didn't win the game, but it will be worth remembering. By now you're probably wondering why.

① Ethan got attention of everyone in the crowd while moving to the end zone.
② Ethan was moving in slow motion due to the ball in his hands.
③ As soon as the game ended, Ethan crossed the goal line.
④ Although the crowd was excited enough, they were seated all the time.
⑤ Ethan's touchdown didn't influence the game result, so it is not that worthwhile.

08

다음 글의 상황에 나타난 분위기로 가장 적절한 것은?

As our player got closer to the end zone, he saw Ethan behind him on his left. Instead of running straight ahead, the player kindly passed the ball to Ethan so that he could score a touchdown. All eyes were on Ethan. With the ball in his hands, everything seemed to be moving in slow motion, like in a Hollywood movie. People kept their eyes on him as he made his way to the end zone. They saw him cross the goal line right before the clock ran out.

Unexpectedly, everyone in the crowd leapt to their feet with their hands in the air. They were bursting with excited shouts and unending cheers for Ethan. In this moment, all of Ethan's hard work and dedication was being rewarded with glory. Ethan's touchdown didn't win the game, but it will be worth remembering. By now you're probably wondering why.

① humorous and funny
② touching and exciting
③ aggressive and competitive
④ dark and gloomy
⑤ serious and mysterious

09

글의 흐름으로 보아, 주어진 문장이 들어가기에 가장 적절한 곳은?

They saw him cross the goal line right before the clock ran out.

All eyes were on Ethan. With the ball in his hands, everything seemed to be moving in slow motion, like in a Hollywood movie. (①) People kept their eyes on him as he made his way to the end zone.

(②) Unexpectedly, everyone in the crowd leapt to their feet with their hands in the air. (③) They were bursting with excited shouts and unending cheers for Ethan. (④) In this moment, all of Ethan's hard work and dedication was being rewarded with glory. (⑤) Ethan's touchdown didn't win the game, but it will be worth remembering. By now you're probably wondering why.

10

주어진 글 다음에 이어질 (A)~(D)의 순서를 바르게 배열하시오.

> Once Winston High's coach finally knew that victory was theirs, all the seniors on the sidelines were allowed to play for the last few seconds. One of the seniors, Ethan, was especially happy.

(A) Ethan ran right after him to catch up. As our player got closer to the end zone, he saw Ethan behind him on his left. Instead of running straight ahead, the player kindly passed the ball to Ethan so that he could score a touchdown. All eyes were on Ethan.

(B) With the ball in his hands, everything seemed to be moving in slow motion, like in a Hollywood movie. People kept their eyes on him as he made his way to the end zone. They saw him cross the goal line right before the clock ran out.

(C) He had never played in any of the games before. Now, Ethan was finally getting the chance to step onto the grass. When the rival team dropped the ball, one of our players recovered it and quickly ran down the field with it.

(D) Unexpectedly, everyone in the crowd leapt to their feet with their hands in the air. They were bursting with excited shouts and unending cheers for Ethan. In this moment, all of Ethan's hard work and dedication was being rewarded with glory. Ethan's touchdown didn't win the game, but it will be worth remembering.

________ – ________ – ________ – ________

11

다음 중, (a)~(e)의 내용을 잘못 이해한 것은?

All eyes were on Ethan. (a) With the ball in his hands, everything seemed to be moving in slow motion, like in a Hollywood movie. (b) People kept their eyes on him as he made his way to the end zone. (c) They saw him cross the goal line right before the clock ran out.

(d) Unexpectedly, everyone in the crowd leapt to their feet with their hands in the air. They were bursting with excited shouts and unending cheers for Ethan. In this moment, all of Ethan's hard work and dedication was being rewarded with glory. (e) Ethan's touchdown didn't win the game, but it will be worth remembering. By now you're probably wondering why.

① (a): Ethan의 손에 들린 공과 함께, 모든 것이 할리우드 영화의 한 장면처럼 천천히 움직이는 듯했다.
② (b): 사람들은 Ethan이 엔드존을 향해 갈 때 그에게 시선을 고정했다.
③ (c): 사람들은 Ethan이 경기 종료 직전에 골 라인을 넘어선 것을 보았다.
④ (d): 뜻밖에 모든 관중이 손을 흔들며 벌떡 일어섰다.
⑤ (e): Ethan의 터치다운으로 경기에서 이겼기 때문에 그것은 기억할 만한 가치가 있을 것이다.

12

다음 글의 상황에 나타난 분위기로 가장 적절한 것은?

All eyes were on Ethan. With the ball in his hands, everything seemed to be moving in slow motion, like in a Hollywood movie. People kept their eyes on him as he made his way to the end zone. They saw him cross the goal line right before the clock ran out.

Unexpectedly, everyone in the crowd leapt to their feet with their hands in the air. They were bursting with excited shouts and unending cheers for Ethan. In this moment, all of Ethan's hard work and dedication was being rewarded with glory. Ethan's touchdown didn't win the game, but it will be worth remembering.

① urgent and chaotic
② enthusiastic and thrilling
③ serious and frightening
④ calm and solemn
⑤ funny and humorous

13

다음 글 뒤에 이어질 내용으로 가장 적절한 것은?

All eyes were on Ethan. With the ball in his hands, everything seemed to be moving in slow motion, like in a Hollywood movie. People kept their eyes on him as he made his way to the end zone. They saw him cross the goal line right before the clock ran out.

Unexpectedly, everyone in the crowd leapt to their feet with their hands in the air. They were bursting with excited shouts and unending cheers for Ethan. In this moment, all of Ethan's hard work and dedication was being rewarded with glory. Ethan's touchdown didn't win the game, but it will be worth remembering. By now you're probably wondering why.

① how playing football prevented the players from getting disease
② how to win a close game with a touchdown at the last moment
③ how Ethan committed himself to the team and earned admiration
④ how disappointing and neglectful Ethan was as a football player
⑤ how little the crowd expected about Winston High winning the game

14

다음 글을 통해 Ethan에 관해 알 수 있는 것은?

All eyes were on Ethan. With the ball in his hands, everything seemed to be moving in slow motion, like in a Hollywood movie. People kept their eyes on him as he made his way to the end zone. They saw him cross the goal line right before the clock ran out.

Unexpectedly, everyone in the crowd leapt to their feet with their hands in the air. They were bursting with excited shouts and unending cheers for Ethan. In this moment, all of Ethan's hard work and dedication was being rewarded with glory. Ethan's touchdown didn't win the game, but it will be worth remembering. By now you're probably wondering why.

① He was ignored by his teammates.
② He was famous for his outstanding talent.
③ He failed to make a touchdown.
④ He was a committed member of the team.
⑤ He was born with physical difficulties.

15

다음 글의 밑줄 친 ⓐ~ⓔ의 심경으로 알맞지 않은 것을 고르시오.

When the rival team dropped the ball, one of our players recovered it and quickly ran down the field with it. Ethan ran right after him to catch up. As our player got closer to the end zone, ⓐ he saw Ethan behind him on his left. Instead of running straight ahead, the player kindly passed the ball to ⓑ Ethan so that he could score a touchdown.

All eyes were on Ethan. With the ball in his hands, everything seemed to be moving in slow motion, like in a Hollywood movie. ⓒ People kept their eyes on him as he made his way to the end zone. They saw him cross the goal line right before the clock ran out.

Unexpectedly, everyone in the crowd leapt to their feet with their hands in the air. ⓓ They were bursting with excited shouts and unending cheers for ⓔ Ethan. In this moment, all of Ethan's hard work and dedication was being rewarded with glory. Ethan's touchdown didn't win the game, but it will be worth remembering. By now you're probably wondering why.

① ⓐ: envious　② ⓑ: thankful
③ ⓒ: anticipating　④ ⓓ: delighted
⑤ ⓔ: proud

16

다음 글의 밑줄 친 (a)~(e) 중, 가리키는 대상이 같은 것끼리 짝지은 것은?

When the rival team dropped the ball, one of our players recovered it and quickly ran down the field with it. Ethan ran right after (a) him to catch up. As our player got closer to the end zone, he saw Ethan behind (b) him on his left. Instead of running straight ahead, the player kindly passed the ball to Ethan so that (c) he could score a touchdown.

All eyes were on Ethan. With the ball in (d) his hands, everything seemed to be moving in slow motion, like in a Hollywood movie. People kept their eyes on him as he made (e) his way to the end zone. They saw him cross the goal line right before the clock ran out.

① (a), (b), (c)
② (a), (d), (e)
③ (b), (c), (d)
④ (b), (c), (e)
⑤ (c), (d), (e)

100점 맞고 싶다면!

기타 연습 문제

1회 등장 포인트

● 함축 의미

Ethan's touchdown didn't win the game, but it will be worth remembering.

01

다음 글의 밑줄 친 (A)가 의미하는 바로 가장 적절한 것은?

Unexpectedly, everyone in the crowd leapt to their feet with their hands in the air. They were bursting with excited shouts and unending cheers for Ethan. In this moment, all of Ethan's hard work and dedication was being rewarded with glory. (A) Ethan's touchdown didn't win the game, but it will be worth remembering. By now you're probably wondering why. Well, Ethan is only five feet tall, and his legs unnaturally bend away from each other. It is difficult for him to walk, run, or move around. (중략) Although he knew he would never be a valuable player in any of the team's games, he poured his heart and soul into practice every day. Over time, however, Ethan became valuable to the team in different ways. His passion for the game was an inspiration to all his teammates. Because Ethan motivated and encouraged them, they became his most passionate fans.

① To be a valuable player worth remembering, winning many points is considered most important.
② Because the spectators at the game pitied Ethan, they were not mad at him for not getting an extra score.
③ At the last moment, Winston High achieved a victory thanks to Ethan's touchdown, making everyone happy.
④ People were kind and encouraging enough to support Ethan even when he brought disgrace on the team.
⑤ No matter how small Ethan's role was on the team's success, people acknowledged Ethan's hard work and felt happy for his touchdown.

● 시제 일치

They saw him cross the goal line right before the clock ran out.

● 문장 변형

Unexpectedly, everyone in the crowd leapt to their feet with their hands in the air.

● 현재진행

By now you're probably wondering why.

02

다음 글의 밑줄 친 부분 중, 어법상 틀린 것은?

All eyes were on Ethan. With the ball in his hands, everything seemed ① to be moving in slow motion, like in a Hollywood movie. People kept their eyes on him as he made his way to the end zone. They saw him cross the goal line right before the clock ② ran out. It was unexpected ③ that everyone in the crowd leapt to their feet with their hands in the air. They were bursting with excited shouts and unending cheers for Ethan. In this moment, all of Ethan's hard work and dedication was being rewarded with glory. Ethan's touchdown didn't win the game, but it will be ④ worthy remembering. By now you're probably ⑤ wondering why.

● 무관한 문장

03

다음 글에서 전체 흐름과 관계 없는 문장은?

When the rival team dropped the ball, one of our players recovered it and quickly ran down the field with it. Ethan ran right after him to catch up. ① As our player got closer to the end zone, he saw Ethan behind him on his left. ② His anxiety grew that Ethan might take away his chance to score a touchdown. ③ Instead of running straight ahead, the player kindly passed the ball to Ethan so that he could score a touchdown. ④ All eyes were on Ethan. ⑤ With the ball in his hands, everything seemed to be moving in slow motion, like in a Hollywood movie. People kept their eyes on him as he made his way to the end zone. They saw him cross the goal line right before the clock ran out.

● 어휘 slow, seem

With the ball in his hands, everything seemed to be moving in slow motion, like in a Hollywood movie.

● 어휘 worth

Ethan's touchdown didn't win the game, but it will be worth remembering.

● 어휘 wonder

By now you're probably wondering why.

04

다음 글의 밑줄 친 부분 중, 문맥상 낱말의 쓰임이 적절하지 않은 것은?

All eyes were on Ethan. With the ball in his hands, everything ① seemed to be moving in ② slow motion, like in a Hollywood movie. People kept their eyes on him as he made his way to the end zone. They saw him cross the goal line right before the clock ran out.

Unexpectedly, everyone in the crowd leapt to their feet with their hands in the air. They were bursting with excited shouts and unending ③ complaints for Ethan. In this moment, all of Ethan's hard work and dedication was being rewarded with glory. Ethan's touchdown didn't win the game, but it will be ④ worth remembering. By now you're probably ⑤ wondering why.

● 제목 파악

05

다음 글의 제목으로 가장 적절한 것은?

Now, Ethan was finally getting the chance to step onto the grass. When the rival team dropped the ball, one of our players recovered it and quickly ran down the field with it. Ethan ran right after him to catch up. As our player got closer to the end zone, he saw Ethan behind him on his left. Instead of running straight ahead, the player kindly passed the ball to Ethan so that he could score a touchdown.

All eyes were on Ethan. With the ball in his hands, everything seemed to be moving in slow motion, like in a Hollywood movie. People kept their eyes on him as he made his way to the end zone. They saw him cross the goal line right before the clock ran out. Unexpectedly, everyone in the crowd leapt to their feet with their hands in the air. They were bursting with excited shouts and unending cheers for Ethan. In this moment, all of Ethan's hard work and dedication was being rewarded with glory. Ethan's touchdown didn't win the game, but it will be worth remembering.

① Ethan Scores a Touchdown despite the Boos from the Crowd
② A Miraculous Victory of Winston High Brought by Teamwork
③ Football Players Stressed Out by the Intense Competition
④ Ethan Becomes a Legend by Turning Crisis into Opportunity
⑤ Ethan Rewarded for His Dedication through the Final Touchdown!

출제 포인트 42.6% 정복!

리딩 본문[3]

14.9% 확률로 본문[3]에서 출제

본문[3] 적중 MAPPING

이것만 알아도 92.0% 맞힌다!

Well, Ethan is only five feet tall, and his legs unnaturally bend away from each other. ★It is difficult for him to walk, run, or move around. Because of his condition, he decided to leave his crowded high school in the big city. He moved to our school in the middle of his first year in high school. ★★That following summer, he asked the coach if he could join the football team as a sophomore. The coach wasn't sure at first, but in the end he allowed Ethan to come to practice. ★★★Regardless of his physical difficulties, Ethan worked just as hard as every other player on the team. ★Although he knew he would never be a valuable player in any of the team's games, he poured his heart and soul into practice every day.

내용 일치 〈출제 1위 유형〉

이 문단에서는 아래와 같은 세부 내용들이 내용 일치 문제로 출제되니 잘 기억해 두자. 특히, Ethan이 가진 신체적 어려움이 무엇인지 구체적으로 물어보거나, Ethan이 신체적 어려움에도 불구하고 다른 선수들만큼 열심히 했다는 내용이 자주 출제된다.

- Ethan은 키가 5피트(약 152.4cm)이며 다리가 부자연스럽게 바깥으로 구부러져 있다.
- Ethan은 움직이는 데 어려움이 있다.
- Ethan은 신체적 어려움 때문에 1학년 때 전학을 왔다.
- Ethan은 새로 전학 온 학교의 풋볼팀에 2학년으로서 들어가기를 원했다.
- 감독은 처음에는 Ethan이 풋볼팀에 들어오는 것을 망설였지만, 결국 허락했다.
- Ethan은 다른 선수들만큼 열심히 매일 연습했다.

지칭 추론 〈출제 2위 유형〉

대명사 he는 Ethan 또는 감독(the coach)을 지칭하는데, 문맥상 둘 중 누구를 지칭하는지 명확히 구분할 수 있어야 한다. 이 문단에서 Ethan과 관련된 내용은 다음과 같다. Ethan은 신체적 어려움 때문에 움직이는 것이 어려워 전학을 결정했고, 감독에게 풋볼팀에 들어갈 수 있는지 물었으며, 자신이 중요한 선수가 될 수 없음을 알았지만 열심히 연습했다. 한편, Ethan의 요청에 망설이다가 결국 풋볼팀 합류를 허락한 사람은 감독(the coach)임을 유의하자.

글의 순서 〈출제 3위 유형〉

이 문단의 전체적인 흐름은 다음과 같다.
Ethan의 신체적 어려움에 대한 설명 → (신체적 한계로 인해) 움직이는 것에 어려움이 있음 → (신체적 한계로 인해) 도시의 붐비는 고등학교를 떠나 전학 → 새 학교에서 풋볼팀에 들어가기를 요청 → 감독이 그를 받아들임 → 매일 열심히 연습함

출제 1위 문장 ★★★

Regardless of his physical difficulties, Ethan worked just as hard as every other player on the team.

[regardless of] 출제 공동 1위 (문장편-문장7 → p.81)
[as + 원급 + as] 출제 공동 1위 (문장편-문장7 → p.82)
[Ethan의 신체적 어려움] 출제 3위 (문장편-문장7 → p.82)

출제 2위 문장 ★★

That following summer, he asked the coach if he could join the football team as a sophomore.

[접속사 if 명사 역할 — 목적어] 출제 1위 (문장편-문장5 → p.79)
[전치사 as] 출제 2위 (문장편-문장5 → p.80)

출제 공동 3위 문장 ★

It is difficult for him to walk, run, or move around.

[It ~ (+ for + 목적격) + to-v] 출제 1위 (문장편-문장2 → p.76)
[어휘 difficult] 출제 2위 (문장편-문장2 → p.77)

출제 공동 3위 문장 ★

Although he knew he would never be a valuable player in any of the team's games, he poured his heart and soul into practice every day.

[접속사 although 부사 역할 — 양보] 출제 1위 (문장편-문장8 → p.83)
[어휘 valuable] 출제 2위 (문장편-문장8 → p.84)

문장1

문장 출제 확률: 0.4%

Well, Ethan is only five feet tall, and his legs unnaturally bend away from each other.

문장1에서 출제될 가능성은 0.4%이다. 다른 문장에 비해 출제 가능성이 낮은 편에 속한다.

문장2

문장 출제 확률: 2.0%

가주어 It / for+목적격 / 진주어 to부정사

It is difficult for him to walk, run, or move around.

어려운

출제 포인트

1위	2위
It ~ (+for+목적격) to-v	어휘 difficult
문장 내 출제 확률 82.4%	*문장 내 출제 확률 11.8%*
본문[3] 문장편 내 출제 확률 14.1%	*본문[3] 문장편 내 출제 확률 2.0%*

● It ~ (+for+목적격) to-v

문장2에서 출제될 가능성은 2.0%이다. 이 문장에서 출제가 된다면 82.4%의 확률로 〈It ~ (+for+목적격) to-v〉 구문을 묻는 어법 문제가 나올 수 있다. 이 구문은 주어 역할을 하는 to부정사(구)가 길 때 to부정사(구)를 문장의 뒤로 보내고 주어 자리에 가주어 It이 대신 위치하는 형태이다. 이때, to부정사의 의미상의 주어는 〈for+목적격〉으로 나타내는데, to부정사가 성질이나 성격을 나타내는 형용사(kind, generous 등)와 함께 쓰일 경우에는 의미상의 주어를 〈of+목적격〉으로 나타냄에 유의하자.

Q. 다음 글의 괄호 안에서 어법상 적절한 것은?

Well, Ethan is only five feet tall, and his legs unnaturally bend away from each other. (It / That) is difficult for him to walk, run, or move around. Because of his condition, he decided to leave his crowded high school in the big city. He moved to our school in the middle of his first year in high school.

정답 It

주어 역할을 하는 to부정사구(to walk, run, or move around)가 문장의 뒤로 보내진 형태이다. 이때 주어 자리에는 가주어 It이 대신 위치한다.

● 어휘 difficult

이 문장에서 11.8%의 확률로 형용사 difficult에 관한 어휘 문제가 나올 수 있다. Ethan은 신체적 한계로 인해 걷고, 뛰고, 움직이는 것이 '어렵다'는 내용으로, difficult가 쓰였다. 반의어 easy 등을 활용한 오답 선지가 출제된다.

Q. 다음 글의 괄호 안에서 문맥상 적절한 것은?

Well, Ethan is only five feet tall, and his legs unnaturally bend away from each other. It is (easy / difficult) for him to walk, run, or move around. Because of his condition, he decided to leave his crowded high school in the big city. He moved to our school in the middle of his first year in high school.

정답 difficult

앞 문장에서 Ethan은 작은 키와 부자연스럽게 구부러진 다리라는 신체적 한계를 가지고 있다고 했으므로, 걷고, 뛰고, 움직이는 게 '어렵다(difficult)'는 것이 문맥상 적절하다.

출제 포인트 44.1% 정복!

문장3

문장 출제 확률: 1.2%

Because of his condition, he **decided to leave** his **crowded** high school in the big city.

(Because of: ~ 때문에 / decide to-v: ~하기로 결정하다 / crowded: 붐비는, 복잡한)

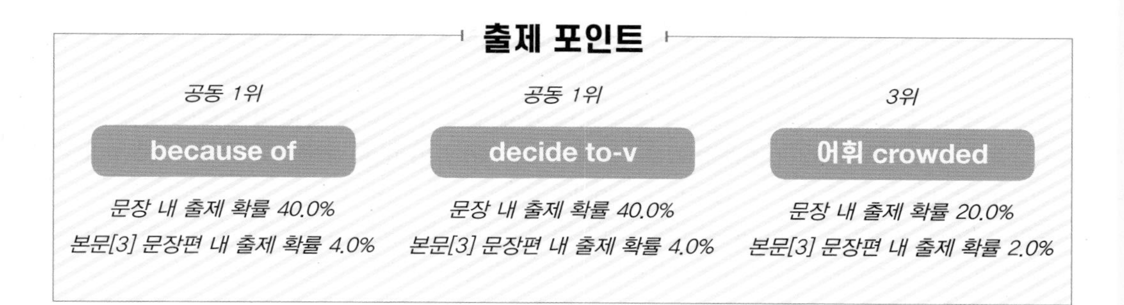

● because of

문장3에서 출제될 가능성은 1.2%이다. 이 문장에서 출제된다면, 40.0%의 확률로 because of 뒤에 명사 상당어구가 오는 것과 관련한 어법 문제가 나올 수 있다. because of는 '~ 때문에'라는 의미인 전치사이기 때문에, 의미는 같지만 뒤에 '주어+동사'의 절이 오는 접속사 as, since, because로 바꿔 쓸 수 없다. 한편, due to, owing to로는 바꿔 쓸 수 있다.

Q. 다음 글의 괄호 안에서 어법상 적절한 것은?

Well, Ethan is only five feet tall, and his legs unnaturally bend away from each other. It is difficult for him to walk, run, or move around. (Because / Because of) his condition, he decided to leave his crowded high school in the big city. He moved to our school in the middle of his first year in high school.

정답 Because of

because of는 명사 상당어구를 목적어로 취해 '~ 때문에'를 의미한다. 접속사 because는 '주어+동사'로 이루어진 완전한 절을 이끌기 때문에 어법상 적절하지 않다.

● decide to-v

이 문장에서 공동 1위로 출제 확률이 높은 것은 동사 decide의 목적어에 관한 어법 문제이다. '(~하기로) 결정하다'라는 뜻의 동사 decide는 목적어로 to부정사만을 취할 수 있다. 목적어 자리에 동명사는 올 수 없음에 유의하자.

Q. 다음 글의 (A)에 주어진 단어를 알맞게 배열해 문장을 완성하시오. (단, 필요시 단어를 변형할 수 있음)

Well, Ethan is only five feet tall, and his legs unnaturally bend away from each other. It is difficult for him to walk, run, or move around. Because of his condition, (A) (he / leave / decide) his crowded high school in the big city. He moved to our school in the middle of his first year in high school.

____

정답
he decided to leave
'(~하기로) 결정하다'를 의미하는 동사 decide는 to부정사를 목적어로 취한다.

● 어휘 crowded

20.0% 확률로 형용사 crowded에 관한 어휘 문제가 나올 수 있다. Ethan은 큰 도시의 '붐비는' 학교를 떠나 전학을 갔다. '붐비는, 복잡한'을 의미하는 형용사 역할의 과거분사 crowded는 큰 도시에서의 학교 생활을 묘사하는 데 쓰였다.

Q. 다음 글의 밑줄 친 ⓐ~ⓔ 중, 문맥상 바꿔 쓸 수 없는 것을 모두 고르시오.

Well, Ethan is only five feet tall, and his legs ⓐ unnaturally bend away from each other. It is ⓑ difficult for him to walk, run, or move around. Because of his condition, he decided to leave his ⓒ crowded high school in the big city. He moved to our school in the middle of his first year in high school. That following summer, he asked the coach if he could join the football team as a sophomore. The coach wasn't ⓓ sure at first, but in the end he allowed Ethan to come to practice. Regardless of his ⓔ physical difficulties, Ethan worked just as hard as every other player on the team. Although he knew he would never be a valuable player in any of the team's games, he poured his heart and soul into practice every day.

① ⓐ: abnormally ② ⓑ: hard ③ ⓒ: quiet
④ ⓓ: certain ⑤ ⓔ: psychological

정답 ③, ⑤
③ ⓒ: '붐비는, 복잡한'을 의미하는 형용사 crowded와 '조용한, 한산한'을 의미하는 형용사 quiet는 반의어 관계이므로, 바꿔 쓸 수 없다.
⑤ ⓔ: '신체적인'을 의미하는 형용사 physical과 '정신적인'을 의미하는 psychological은 형태상 유사하나 뜻이 다르므로, 바꿔 쓸 수 없다.

오답
① ⓐ: '부자연스럽게'를 의미하는 부사 unnaturally와 '비정상적으로'를 의미하는 부사 abnormally는 문맥상 바꿔 쓸 수 있다.
② ⓑ: '어려운'을 의미하는 형용사 difficult와 형용사 hard는 유의어 관계이다.
④ ⓓ: '확신하는'을 의미하는 형용사 sure과 형용사 certain은 유의어 관계이다.

문장4

문장 출제 확률: 0%

He moved to our school in the middle of his first year in high school.

문장4에서 출제될 가능성은 0%이다. 따라서 이 문장은 Ethan이 1학년 도중 전학을 왔다는 내용상 흐름만 잘 알아두고 넘어가자.

문장5

문장 출제 확률: 2.2%

접속사 if: ~인지 아닌지

That following summer, he asked the coach if he could join the football team as a sophomore.

전치사 as: ~로서

출제 포인트

1위	2위
접속사 if 명사 역할 – 목적어	전치사 as
문장 내 출제 확률 63.2%	*문장 내 출제 확률 10.5%*
본문[3] 문장편 내 출제 확률 12.1%	*본문[3] 문장편 내 출제 확률 2.0%*

● 접속사 if 명사 역할 – 목적어

문장5에서 출제될 가능성은 2.2%이다. 이 문장에서 출제가 된다면, 63.2%의 확률로 명사절 접속사 if에 관한 어법 문제가 나올 수 있다. 명사절 접속사 if는 '주어+동사'로 이루어진 완전한 절을 이끌어 '~인지 아닌지'를 의미하며, 접속사 whether로 바꿔 쓸 수 있다. 이 문장에서 접속사 if 이하는 4형식동사 ask의 직접목적어로, 불확실한 내용(2학년으로서 풋볼팀에 들어갈 수 있는지)을 말할 때 쓴다. 접속사 that은 확실한 내용과 함께 쓰므로, 본문의 if와 바꿔 쓸 수 없다. '만약 ~라면'을 의미하는 부사절 접속사 if와도 의미와 쓰임을 구별해야 한다.

Q. 다음 글의 빈칸에 들어갈 말로 가장 적절한 것은?

Well, Ethan is only five feet tall, and his legs unnaturally bend away from each other. It is difficult for him to walk, run, or move around. Because of his condition, he decided to leave his crowded high school in the big city. He moved to our school in the middle of his first year in high school. That following summer, he asked the coach ______________ he could join the football team as a sophomore. The coach wasn't sure at first, but in the end he allowed Ethan to come to practice.

① if ② unless ③ which ④ what ⑤ that

정답 ①

'(~을) 묻다'를 의미하는 4형식동사 ask의 직접목적어 자리로, '~인지 아닌지'를 의미하는 명사절 접속사 if 또는 whether이 불확실한 내용(2학년으로서 풋볼팀에 들어갈 수 있는지)을 이끄는 것이 적절하다. 접속사 that은 확실한 내용을 이끌 때 쓰므로 적절하지 않다.

● 전치사 as

전치사 as에 관한 문제 또한 10.5% 확률로 출제될 수 있다. 전치사 as는 자격(~로서) 등을 나타내는 전치사로, 명사 상당어구를 목적어로 취한다. 한편, 부사절 접속사 as는 '~할 때', '~하듯이' 등을 의미하며 '주어+동사'로 이루어진 절을 이끈다. 이 점에 유의하여 전치사 as와 접속사 as를 잘 구별하자.

Q. 다음 중, 밑줄 친 as와 쓰임이 같은 것은?

Well, Ethan is only five feet tall, and his legs unnaturally bend away from each other. It is difficult for him to walk, run, or move around. Because of his condition, he decided to leave his crowded high school in the big city. He moved to our school in the middle of his first year in high school. That following summer, he asked the coach if he could join the football team as a sophomore. The coach wasn't sure at first, but in the end he allowed Ethan to come to practice. Regardless of his physical difficulties, Ethan worked just as hard as every other player on the team. Although he knew he would never be a valuable player in any of the team's games, he poured his heart and soul into practice every day.

ⓐ As she was looking out the window, a man with a flower approached her.
ⓑ I had to tell him he was wrong as a parent and an adult.
ⓒ Trapped in the avalanche, she was on the verge of losing her hope as I was.

정답 ⓑ
본문의 밑줄 친 as와 ⓑ의 as는 명사(구)를 목적어로 취하며 '~로서'를 의미하는 전치사이다. 반면, ⓐ, ⓒ의 as는 뒤에 '주어+동사'로 이루어진 절이 오며, '~할 때', '~하듯이' 등을 의미하는 부사절 접속사이다.

출제 포인트 46.3% 정복!

문장6

문장 출제 확률: 0.7%

allow+목적어+to-v: ~가 …하도록 허락하다

The coach wasn't sure at first, but in the end he allowed Ethan to come to practice.

출제 포인트

1위

allow+목적어+to-v

문장 내 출제 확률 100%
본문[3] 문장편 내 출제 확률 6.1%

● allow+목적어+to-v

문장6에서 출제될 가능성은 0.7%이다. 이 문장에서 출제가 된다면 100%의 확률로 동사 allow의 목적격 보어에 관한 어법 문제가 나올 수 있다. 5형식동사 allow는 목적격 보어로 to부정사를 취해 '~가 …하도록 허락하다'라는 의미이다. 즉, 〈동사(allowed)+목적어(Ethan)+목적격 보어(to come)〉가 어법상 올바른 형태이므로, to부정사 to come을 come, coming 등의 잘못된 형태와 혼동하지 않도록 유의하자.

Q. 다음 글의 (A)에 주어진 단어를 알맞게 배열해 문장을 완성하시오. (단, 필요시 단어를 변형할 수 있음)

Well, Ethan is only five feet tall, and his legs unnaturally bend away from each other. It is difficult for him to walk, run, or move around. Because of his condition, he decided to leave his crowded high school in the big city. He moved to our school in the middle of his first year in high school. That following summer, he asked the coach if he could join the football team as a sophomore. The coach wasn't sure at first, but in the end (A) (he / Ethan / come / allow / to practice). Regardless of his physical difficulties, Ethan worked just as hard as every other player on the team. Although he knew he would never be a valuable player in any of the team's games, he poured his heart and soul into practice every day.

____

정답

he allowed Ethan to come to practice

해당 절은 등위접속사 but으로 앞 절과 병렬 연결되는 완전한 절이며, 과거 시제로 영작해야 한다. 5형식동사 allow는 목적격 보어로 to부정사를 취해 '~가 …하도록 허락하다'를 의미한다.

출제 포인트 46.8% 정복!

문장7

문장 출제 확률: 3.2%

~와 상관없이 / Ethan의 신체적 어려움

Regardless of his physical difficulties, Ethan worked just as hard as every other player on the team.

as+원급+as: ~만큼 …한[하게]

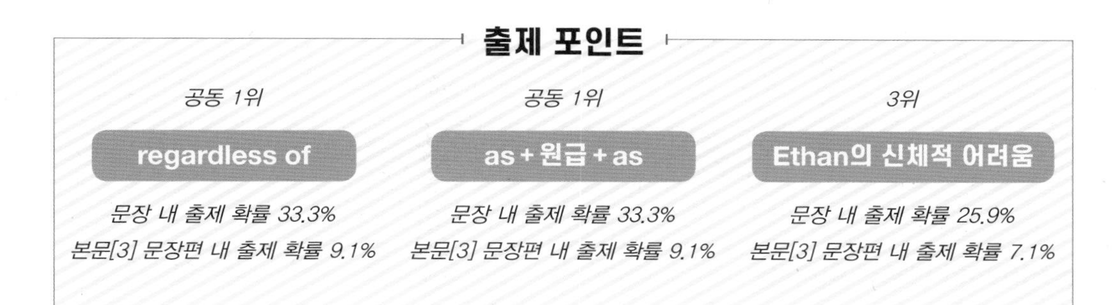

• regardless of

문장7에서 출제될 가능성은 3.2%이다. 이 문장에서 출제가 된다면, 33.3%의 확률로 전치사 regardless of가 명사 상당어구를 목적어로 취하는 어법 문제가 나올 수 있다. '~와 상관없이'를 의미하는 전치사 regardless of와 유사한 의미를 지니는 전치사는 despite(~에도 불구하고), in spite of(~에도 불구하고) 등이 있다. though, although, even though 등은 같은 의미를 나타내지만, '주어+동사'로 이루어진 완전한 절을 이끄는 접속사임을 유의하자.

Q. 다음 글의 괄호 안에서 어법상 적절한 것은?

Well, Ethan is only five feet tall, and his legs unnaturally bend away from each other. It is difficult for him to walk, run, or move around. Because of his condition, he decided to leave his crowded high school in the big city. He moved to our school in the middle of his first year in high school. That following summer,

정답 Regardless of

전치사 Regardless of는 명사 상당어구를 목적어로 취해 '~와 상관없이'를 의미한다. 접속사 Although는 '주어+동사'로 이루어진 완전한 절을 이끄는 접속사이므로 적절하지 않다.

he asked the coach if he could join the football team as a sophomore. The coach wasn't sure at first, but in the end he allowed Ethan to come to practice. (Regardless of / Although) his physical difficulties, Ethan worked just as hard as every other player on the team. Although he knew he would never be a valuable player in any of the team's games, he poured his heart and soul into practice every day.

● as+원급+as

이 문장에서 공동으로 출제 확률이 가장 높은 것은 〈as+원급+as〉 비교 표현에 관한 어법 문제이다. 〈as+원급+as〉 비교 표현은 종종 부사 just와 함께 쓰여 '~만큼 (꼭) …한[하게]'를 의미한다. 대부분의 부사는 '형용사+ly' 형태이지만, hard, long, early, fast 등은 형용사와 부사의 형태가 동일하다. -ly가 붙은 형태인 부사 hardly는 '거의 ~ 않다'라는 다른 의미를 지니므로 혼동하지 않도록 유의해야 한다. 한편, 부사 hard의 유의어로는 diligently, industriously, strenuously 등이 있으며, 반의어로는 lazily 등이 있다.

Q. 다음 글의 괄호 안에서 문맥상 적절한 것은?

Well, Ethan is only five feet tall, and his legs unnaturally bend away from each other. It is difficult for him to walk, run, or move around. Because of his condition, he decided to leave his crowded high school in the big city. He moved to our school in the middle of his first year in high school. That following summer, he asked the coach if he could join the football team as a sophomore. The coach wasn't sure at first, but in the end he allowed Ethan to come to practice. Regardless of his physical difficulties, Ethan worked just as (hard / hardly) as every other player on the team. Although he knew he would never be a valuable player in any of the team's games, he poured his heart and soul into practice every day.

정답 hard

문맥상 '열심히' 노력했다는 의미가 자연스러우므로, hard가 적절하다. hardly는 '거의 ~ 않다'라는 의미이다.

● Ethan의 신체적 어려움

Ethan의 신체적 어려움에 관한 문제 또한 18.5% 확률로 출제될 수 있다. Ethan은 5피트의 작은 키와 부자연스럽게 바깥으로 구부러진 다리라는 '신체적 어려움(physical difficulties)'을 지니고 있다. 그로 인해 움직임이 불편하지만 다른 모든 선수들만큼이나 매일 열심히 연습에 임했다. Ethan이 '정신적(mental, psychological)' 등의 다른 어려움이 아니라, '신체적' 어려움을 가지고 있다는 사실을 잘 알아두어야 한다. 그 두 가지 어려움이 어떤 것인지 또한 자세히 기억해두자.

Q. 다음 빈칸에 들어갈 말로 가장 적절한 것은?

Well, Ethan is only five feet tall, and his legs unnaturally bend away from each other. It is difficult for him to walk, run, or move around. Because of his condition, he decided to leave his crowded high school in the big city. He moved to our school in the middle of his first year in high school. That following summer, he asked the coach if he could join the football team as a sophomore. The coach wasn't sure at first, but in the end he allowed Ethan to come to practice. Regardless of his ______________, Ethan worked just as hard as every other

정답 ②

Ethan은 작은 키와 구부러진 다리라는 ② '신체적 어려움(physical difficulties)'으로 움직임이 불편하지만, 그것과 상관없이 그 팀의 다른 모든 선수들만큼이나 열심히 연습했다는 것이 문맥상 적절하다.

① 열정
③ 정신 질환
④ 팀 동료들의 지지
⑤ 부정적인 태도

player on the team. Although he knew he would never be a valuable player in any of the team's games, he poured his heart and soul into practice every day.

① passion ② physical difficulties ③ mental disorders
④ teammates' support ⑤ negative attitude

출제 포인트 49.1% 정복!

문장8

문장 출제 확률: 2.0%

접속사 although 부사 역할 – 양보 / 귀중한, 값진 / any of + 명사(구)

Although he knew he would never be a valuable player in any of the team's games, he poured his heart and soul into practice every day.

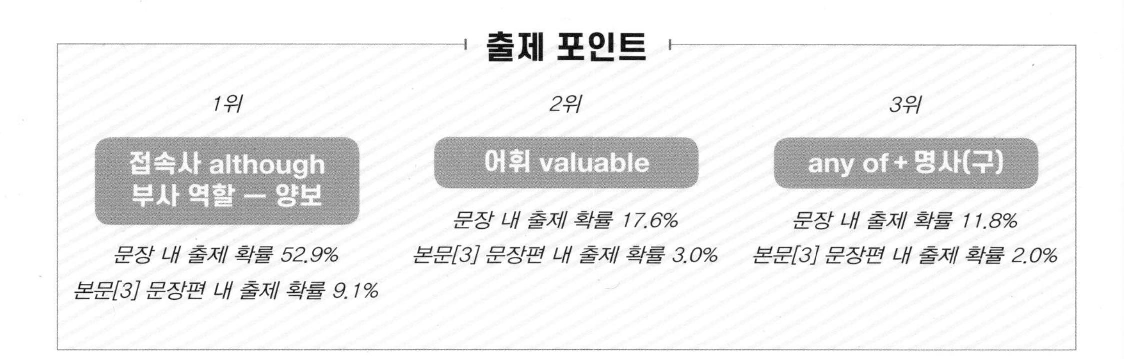

● 접속사 although 부사 역할 – 양보

문장8에서 출제될 가능성은 2.0%이다. 이 문장에서 출제가 된다면, 52.9%의 확률로 접속사 although에 관한 어법 문제가 나올 수 있다. 양보 부사절 접속사 although(~에도 불구하고)는 '주어+동사'로 이루어진 완전한 절을 이끌며, 접속사 though, even though 등과 바꿔 쓸 수 있다. 같은 의미를 갖는 despite, in spite of는 전치사로, 목적어로 명사 상당어구를 쓴다는 것도 함께 기억하자.

Q. 다음 글의 밑줄 친 부분 중, 어법상 적절하지 않은 것은?

Well, ① Ethan is only five feet tall, and his legs unnaturally bend away from each other. It is difficult for him to walk, run, or move around. Because of his condition, ② he decided to leave his crowded high school in the big city. He moved to our school in the middle of his first year in high school. That following summer, he asked the coach ③ if he could join the football team as a sophomore. The coach wasn't sure at first, but in the end he allowed Ethan to come to practice. Regardless of his physical difficulties, ④ Ethan worked just as hard as every other player on the team. ⑤ Despite he knew he would never be a valuable player in any of the team's games, he poured his heart and soul into practice every day.

정답 ⑤
뒤에 '주어(he)+동사(knew)'의 완전한 절이 왔으므로, 전치사 Despite은 옳지 않다. 접속사 Although, Though, Even though 등이 쓰여야 한다.

● 어휘 valuable

이 문장에서 두 번째로 출제 확률이 높은 것은 형용사 valuable에 관한 어휘 문제로, 17.6%의 확률로 출제될 수 있다. 형용사 valuable은 '귀중한, 값진'을 의미하는데, 유의어로는 invaluable, priceless, worthy 등이 있으며, 반의어로는 valueless, worthless 등이 있다. 특히, 접두사 in-과 접미사 -less로 인해 invaluable(귀중한)과 priceless(값을 매길 수 없는, 매우 귀중한)를 valuable의 반의어로 착각하지 않도록 유의하자.

Q. 다음 글의 밑줄 친 valuable과 문맥상 바꿔 쓸 수 있는 것을 모두 고르시오.

Well, Ethan is only five feet tall, and his legs unnaturally bend away from each other. It is difficult for him to walk, run, or move around. Because of his condition, he decided to leave his crowded high school in the big city. He moved to our school in the middle of his first year in high school. That following summer, he asked the coach if he could join the football team as a sophomore. The coach wasn't sure at first, but in the end he allowed Ethan to come to practice. Regardless of his physical difficulties, Ethan worked just as hard as every other player on the team. Although he knew he would never be a valuable player in any of the team's games, he poured his heart and soul into practice every day.

① invaluable ② valueless ③ worthless ④ useless ⑤ priceless

정답 ①, ⑤

형용사 valuable은 '귀중한, 값진'을 의미하므로, 유의어 관계인 invaluable이나 priceless로 바꿔 쓸 수 있다. 대개 반대되는 뜻을 더해주는 접두사 in-과 접미사 -less 때문에 반의어로 착각하지 않도록 유의한다.
② 가치 없는
③ 가치 없는
④ 쓸모없는

● any of + 명사(구)

〈any of + 명사(구)〉에 관한 어법 문제가 이 문장에서 11.8%의 확률로 출제될 수 있다. 한정사 any는 뒤에 한정사(정관사, 지시사, 소유격) 또는 대명사가 올 경우, 전치사 of와 함께 사용해야 한다. 여기서는 뒤에 the가 있으므로 any가 아니라 any of로 써야 한다.

Q. 다음 글의 괄호 안에서 어법상 적절한 것은?

Well, Ethan is only five feet tall, and his legs unnaturally bend away from each other. It is difficult for him to walk, run, or move around. Because of his condition, he decided to leave his crowded high school in the big city. He moved to our school in the middle of his first year in high school. That following summer, he asked the coach if he could join the football team as a sophomore. The coach wasn't sure at first, but in the end he allowed Ethan to come to practice. Regardless of his physical difficulties, Ethan worked just as hard as every other player on the team. Although he knew he would never be a valuable player in (any / any of) the team's games, he poured his heart and soul into practice every day.

정답 any of

한정사 any에 뒤이어 한정사(정관사, 지시사, 소유격) 또는 대명사가 올 경우, 전치사 of와 함께 any of로 써야 한다. 따라서 any of the team's games가 어법상 적절하다.

● Ethan의 열정

Ethan의 열정을 보여주는 부분을 빈칸으로 한 문제 역시 이 문장에서 11.8%의 확률로 출제될 수 있다. Ethan은 '자신이 팀의 어떤 경기에서도 절대 중요한 선수가 될 수 없다는 것(he would never be a valuable player in any of the team's games)'을 알았음에도 불구하고, '매일매일 연습에 열과 성을 다했다(poured his heart and soul into practice every day)'. 특히, 그의 태도와 관련된 표현으로는 동사 devote(쏟다), dedicate(바치다, 전념하다) 등이 있으니 잘 알아두자.

Q. 다음 빈칸에 들어갈 말로 가장 적절한 것은?

Well, Ethan is only five feet tall, and his legs unnaturally bend away from each other. It is difficult for him to walk, run, or move around. Because of his condition, he decided to leave his crowded high school in the big city. He moved to our school in the middle of his first year in high school. That following summer, he asked the coach if he could join the football team as a sophomore. The coach wasn't sure at first, but in the end he allowed Ethan to come to practice. Regardless of his physical difficulties, Ethan worked just as hard as every other player on the team. Although he knew he would never be a valuable player in any of the team's games, he ______________________.

① never came to practice after realizing his position in the team
② was jealous of his teammates who were the coach's favorites
③ devoted all of his energy to practice every day
④ poured his heart and soul into finding a cure for his disability
⑤ tried to go back to his crowded high school in the big city

정답 ③

양보의 의미(~에도 불구하고)를 나타내는 접속사 Although로 미루어 보아, Ethan은 자신이 팀에서 절대 중요한 선수가 될 수 없다는 것을 알았음에도 불구하고 '매일매일 연습에 전력을 다했다(devoted all of his energy to practice every day)'는 것이 문맥상 적절하다.

[원문 변형] poured his heart and soul into practice every day → devoted all of his energy to practice every day

① 팀에서 그의 위치를 깨달은 후로 연습에 결코 오지 않았다
② 감독이 가장 좋아하는 그의 팀 동료들을 질투했다
④ 그의 장애에 대한 치료법을 찾기 위해 심혈을 기울였다
⑤ 대도시에 있는 그의 붐비는 고등학교로 돌아가려고 노력했다

출제 포인트 50.6% 정복!

01

다음 빈칸에 들어갈 말로 가장 적절한 것은?

Well, Ethan is only five feet tall, and his legs unnaturally bend away from each other. It is difficult for him to walk, run, or move around. Because of his condition, he decided to leave his crowded high school in the big city. He moved to our school in the middle of his first year in high school. That following summer, he asked the coach if he could join the football team as a sophomore. The coach wasn't sure at first, but in the end he allowed Ethan to come to practice. ________________ his physical difficulties, Ethan worked just as hard as every other player on the team. Although he knew he would never be a valuable player in any of the team's games, he poured his heart and soul into practice every day.

① Whereas ② Regardless of
③ Instead of ④ Because of
⑤ Even though

02

다음 글의 (A), (B), (C)의 각 네모 안에서 어법상 적절한 것은?

Well, Ethan is only five feet tall, and his legs unnaturally bend away from each other. It is difficult for him (A) [walk / to walk], run, or move around. Because of his condition, he decided to leave his crowded high school in the big city. He moved to our school in the middle of his first year in high school. That (B) [followed / following] summer, he asked the coach if he could join the football team as a sophomore. The coach wasn't sure at first, but in the end he allowed Ethan to come to practice. Regardless of his physical difficulties, Ethan worked just as (C) [hard / harder] as every other player on the team. Although he knew he would never be a valuable player in any of the team's games, he poured his heart and soul into practice every day.

	(A)	(B)	(C)
①	walk	– followed	– hard
②	to walk	– following	– harder
③	walk	– following	– hard
④	to walk	– followed	– harder
⑤	to walk	– following	– hard

03

다음 글의 밑줄 친 if와 쓰임이 같은 것을 모두 고르시오.

Well, Ethan is only five feet tall, and his legs unnaturally bend away from each other. It is difficult for him to walk, run, or move around. Because of his condition, he decided to leave his crowded high school in the big city. He moved to our school in the middle of his first year in high school. That following summer, he asked the coach if he could join the football team as a sophomore. The coach wasn't sure at first, but in the end he allowed Ethan to come to practice. Regardless of his physical difficulties, Ethan worked just as hard as every other player on the team. Although he knew he would never be a valuable player in any of the team's games, he poured his heart and soul into practice every day.

① I'll consider it if my sister comes, too.
② He might sign the contract if they give him a raise.
③ I don't know if my mom will allow me to join you.
④ Would you have helped me if I hadn't asked you?
⑤ Let's find out if he was right.

04

다음 글의 밑줄 친 부분 중, 어법상 적절하지 않은 것은?

Well, Ethan is ① only five feet tall, and his legs unnaturally ② bend away from each other. It is difficult for him ③ walking, running, or moving around. ④ Because of his condition, he decided ⑤ to leave his crowded high school in the big city. He moved to our school in the middle of his first year in high school.

05

다음 글의 밑줄 친 부분 중, 문맥상 적절하지 않은 것은?

Well, Ethan is ① only five feet tall, and his legs ② unnaturally bend away from each other. It is difficult for him to walk, run, or move around. Because of his condition, he decided to leave his ③ crowded high school in the big city. He moved to our school in the middle of his first year in high school. That following summer, he asked the coach if he could join the football team as a sophomore. The coach wasn't ④ sure at first, but in the end he allowed Ethan to come to practice. Regardless of his ⑤ psychological difficulties, Ethan worked just as hard as every other player on the team. Although he knew he would never be a valuable player in any of the team's games, he poured his heart and soul into practice every day.

06

다음 글의 밑줄 친 ⓐ~ⓔ와 바꿔 쓸 수 있는 것은?

Well, Ethan is only five feet tall, and his legs unnaturally bend away from each other. ⓐ It is difficult for him to walk, run, or move around. Because of his condition, he decided to leave his crowded high school in the big city. He moved to our school in the middle of his first year in high school. That following summer, he asked the coach ⓑ if he could join the football team as a sophomore. The coach wasn't sure at first, but in the end he allowed Ethan ⓒ to come to practice. Regardless of his physical difficulties, Ethan worked just as ⓓ hard as every other player on the team. ⓔ Although he knew he would never be a valuable player in any of the team's games, he poured his heart and soul into practice every day.

① ⓐ: That
② ⓑ: whether
③ ⓒ: come
④ ⓓ: hardly
⑤ ⓔ: Despite

07

다음 빈칸에 들어갈 말로 적절한 것은?

Well, Ethan is only five feet tall, and his legs unnaturally bend away from each other. It is difficult ________ him to walk, run, or move around. Because of his condition, he decided to leave his crowded high school in the big city. He moved to our school in the middle of his first year in high school.

① of
② in
③ for
④ from
⑤ to

08

다음 빈칸에 들어갈 말로 적절한 것을 모두 고르시오.

Well, Ethan is only five feet tall, and his legs unnaturally bend away from each other. It is difficult for him to walk, run, or move around. Because of his condition, he decided to leave his crowded high school in the big city. He moved to our school in the middle of his first year in high school. That following summer, he asked the coach if he could join the football team as a sophomore. The coach wasn't sure at first, but in the end he allowed Ethan to come to practice. Regardless of his physical difficulties, Ethan worked just as hard as every other player on the team. ________ he knew he would never be a valuable player in any of the team's games, he poured his heart and soul into practice every day.

① Though
② Although
③ Even though
④ Despite
⑤ In spite of

09

다음 글의 밑줄 친 Regardless of와 바꿔 쓸 수 있는 것을 모두 고르시오.

Well, Ethan is only five feet tall, and his legs unnaturally bend away from each other. It is difficult for him to walk, run, or move around. Because of his condition, he decided to leave his crowded high school in the big city. He moved to our school in the middle of his first year in high school. That following summer, he asked the coach if he could join the football team as a sophomore. The coach wasn't sure at first, but in the end he allowed Ethan to come to practice. Regardless of his physical difficulties, Ethan worked just as hard as every other player on the team. Although he knew he would never be a valuable player in any of the team's games, he poured his heart and soul into practice every day.

① Nevertheless ② Despite
③ In spite of ④ Otherwise
⑤ Even though

10

다음 글의 밑줄 친 physical difficulties가 의미하는 2가지를 우리말로 쓰시오.

Well, Ethan is only five feet tall, and his legs unnaturally bend away from each other. It is difficult for him to walk, run, or move around. Because of his condition, he decided to leave his crowded high school in the big city. He moved to our school in the middle of his first year in high school. That following summer, he asked the coach if he could join the football team as a sophomore. The coach wasn't sure at first, but in the end he allowed Ethan to come to practice. Regardless of his physical difficulties, Ethan worked just as hard as every other player on the team. Although he knew he would never be a valuable player in any of the team's games, he poured his heart and soul into practice every day.

(1) ______________________

(2) ______________________

11

다음 글의 밑줄 친 ⓐ~ⓔ 중, 어법상 적절하지 않은 것을 찾아 기호를 쓰고, 전체를 바르게 고쳐 쓰시오.

Well, Ethan is only five feet tall, and his legs unnaturally bend away from each other. ⓐ It is difficult for him to walk, run, or move around. Because of his condition, he decided to leave his crowded high school in the big city. He moved to our school in the middle of his first year in high school. That following summer, he asked the coach ⓑ if he could join the football team as a sophomore. The coach wasn't sure at first, but in the end ⓒ he allowed Ethan to come to practice. Regardless of his physical difficulties, ⓓ Ethan worked just as hard as every other player on the team. ⓔ Although he knew he would never be a valuable player in any the team's games, he poured his heart and soul into practice every day.

(　　) → ______________________

____

12

다음 빈칸에 들어갈 말로 적절한 것을 모두 고르시오.

Well, Ethan is only five feet tall, and his legs unnaturally bend away from each other. It is difficult for him to walk, run, or move around. __________ his condition, he decided to leave his crowded high school in the big city. He moved to our school in the middle of his first year in high school. That following summer, he asked the coach if he could join the football team as a sophomore. The coach wasn't sure at first, but in the end he allowed Ethan to come to practice. Regardless of his physical difficulties, Ethan worked just as hard as every other player on the team. Although he knew he would never be a valuable player in any of the team's games, he poured his heart and soul into practice every day.

① As ② Since ③ Due to
④ Because ⑤ Because of

13

다음 글의 밑줄 친 (A)에 주어진 말을 알맞게 배열하시오. (단, 필요시 단어를 변형할 수 있음)

Well, Ethan is only five feet tall, and his legs unnaturally bend away from each other. (A) (to / walk, run, or move around / difficult / be / him / it / for). Because of his condition, he decided to leave his crowded high school in the big city. He moved to our school in the middle of his first year in high school.

____

____

14

다음 글의 밑줄 친 (A)에 주어진 말을 알맞게 배열하여 문장을 완성하시오. (단, 필요시 단어를 변형할 수 있음)

Well, Ethan is only five feet tall, and his legs unnaturally bend away from each other. It is difficult for him to walk, run, or move around. Because of his condition, he decided to leave his crowded high school in the big city. He moved to our school in the middle of his first year in high school. That following summer, he asked the coach if he could join the football team as a sophomore. The coach wasn't sure at first, but in the end he allowed Ethan to come to practice. Regardless of his physical difficulties, Ethan worked just as hard as every other player on the team. (A) (never / although / he / he / know / be / would / a valuable player) in any of the team's games, he poured his heart and soul into practice every day.

____

____

15

다음 글의 (A), (B), (C)의 각 네모 안에서 어법상 적절한 것은?

Well, Ethan is only five feet tall, and his legs unnaturally bend away from each other. (A) [It / That] is difficult for him to walk, run, or move around. Because of his condition, he decided (B) [leaving / to leave] his crowded high school in the big city. He moved to our school in the middle of his first year in high school. That following summer, he asked (C) [the coach / to the coach] if he could join the football team as a sophomore. The coach wasn't sure at first, but in the end he allowed Ethan to come to practice. Regardless of his physical difficulties, Ethan worked just as hard as every other player on the team. Although he knew he would never be a valuable player in any of the team's games, he poured his heart and soul into practice every day.

	(A)	(B)	(C)
①	It	– leaving	– the coach
②	It	– to leave	– the coach
③	It	– to leave	– to the coach
④	That	– leaving	– to the coach
⑤	That	– to leave	– the coach

본문[3]

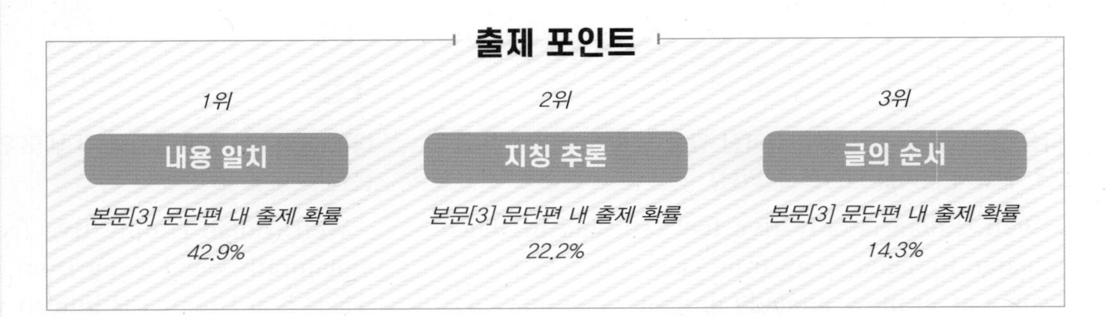

● 내용 일치

이 문단에서는 내용 일치 유형이 42.9%의 확률로 가장 많이 출제될 수 있다. 특히 Ethan의 '신체적 한계[어려움]'를 의미하는 여러 표현이 문제에서 등장하므로, '신체적(으로)'을 의미하는 형용사 physical과 부사 physically, 그리고 '한계' 또는 '어려움'을 의미하는 명사 limitation(s), difficulties, disabilities, disadvantages 등을 알아두어야 한다. 또한 Ethan은 불리한 신체 조건에도 불구하고 열정적인 태도를 가졌다는 사실도 기억하자.

1	Well, Ethan is only five feet tall, and his legs unnaturally bend away from each other.	15.5%
2	It is difficult for him to walk, run, or move around.	8.3%
3	Because of his condition, he decided to leave his crowded high school in the big city.	16.7%
4	He moved to our school in the middle of his first year in high school.	8.3%
5	That following summer, he asked the coach if he could join the football team as a sophomore.	11.9%
6	The coach wasn't sure at first, but in the end he allowed Ethan to come to practice.	15.5%
7	Regardless of his physical difficulties, Ethan worked just as hard as every other player on the team.	14.3%
8	Although he knew he would never be a valuable player in any of the team's games, he poured his heart and soul into practice every day.	9.5%

Q. 글의 내용과 일치하면 T, 일치하지 않으면 F에 표시하시오.

(1) Ethan은 시골에 있는 학교를 떠나기로 했다. (T / F)
(2) Ethan의 키는 5피트 정도이다. (T / F)
(3) 감독은 처음에는 Ethan이 풋볼팀에 들어오는 것을 망설였다. (T / F)
(4) Ethan은 다른 선수들보다 쉬운 훈련을 받았다. (T / F)
(5) Ethan은 3학년 때 풋볼팀에 들어가고 싶어 했다. (T / F)
(6) Ethan은 자신이 팀의 최고 선수라는 것을 알고 있었다. (T / F)
(7) Ethan은 움직이는 데 어려움이 있다. (T / F)
(8) Ethan은 고등학교 1학년 때 지금의 학교로 전학을 왔다. (T / F)
(9) Ethan wanted to leave his school in the big city due to his physical condition. (T / F)
(10) Ethan's legs are not straight. (T / F)
(11) The coach did not allow Ethan to join the team. (T / F)
(12) Ethan gave up on practice due to his physical problems. (T / F)
(13) Ethan expressed his interest in joining the football team in summer. (T / F)
(14) Ethan participated in the team's daily practice with his whole heart. (T / F)

정답

1	F	2	T	3	T
4	F	5	F	6	F
7	T	8	T	9	T
10	T	11	F	12	F
13	T	14	T	15	F
16	F				

(9) Ethan은 그의 신체적 상태 때문에 큰 도시에 있는 학교를 떠나고 싶어 했다.
(10) Ethan의 다리는 곧게 뻗어 있지 않다.
(11) 감독은 Ethan이 팀에 합류하는 것을 허락하지 않았다.
(12) Ethan은 신체적 문제 때문에 연습을 포기했다.
(13) Ethan은 여름에 풋볼팀에 합류하는 데 관심을 보였다.
(14) Ethan은 팀에서 매일 훈련하는 것에 진심으로 참여했다.
(15) Ethan은 매우 빠르게 달릴 수 있다.
(16) Ethan은 2학년 때 새 학교로 전학 갔다.

(15) Ethan can run very fast. (T / F)
(16) Ethan moved to new school in his second year. (T / F)

● 지칭 추론

이 문단에서 지칭 추론이 출제될 확률은 22.2%로, 두 번째로 높다. 이 문단의 대명사 he는 Ethan 또는 감독(the coach)을 지칭하는데, 문맥상 둘 중 누구를 지칭하는지 명확히 구분할 줄 알아야 한다. 이 문단에서 Ethan과 관련된 내용은 다음과 같다. 그는 신체적 어려움이 있어 움직이는 것이 어려우므로 전학을 결정했고, 감독에게 풋볼팀에 들어갈 수 있는지 물었으며, 자신이 중요한 선수가 될 수 없음을 알았지만 열심히 연습했다. Ethan의 요청에 망설이다가 결국 풋볼팀 합류를 허락한 사람은 감독(the coach)이다.

Q. 다음 글의 밑줄 친 부분 중, 가리키는 대상이 나머지 넷과 다른 것은?

Well, Ethan is only five feet tall, and his legs unnaturally bend away from each other. It is difficult for ① him to walk, run, or move around. Because of his condition, ② he decided to leave his crowded high school in the big city. He moved to our school in the middle of his first year in high school. That following summer, he asked the coach if he could join the football team as a sophomore. The coach wasn't sure at first, but in the end ③ he allowed Ethan to come to practice. Regardless of his physical difficulties, Ethan worked just as hard as every other player on the team. Although he knew ④ he would never be a valuable player in any of the team's games, he poured ⑤ his heart and soul into practice every day.

정답 ③
①, ②, ④, ⑤는 Ethan을 가리키는 반면, ③은 감독(the coach)을 가리킨다.

● 글의 순서

이 문단에서 글의 순서 유형이 출제될 확률은 14.3%로, 세 번째로 높다. 이 문단의 전체적인 흐름은 'Ethan의 신체적 어려움에 대한 설명 → (신체적 한계로 인해) 움직이는 것에 어려움이 있음 → (신체적 한계로 인해) 도시의 붐비는 고등학교를 떠나 전학 → 새 학교에서 풋볼팀에 들어가기를 요청 → 감독이 그를 받아들임 → 매일 열심히 연습함'이다. 문단 맨 앞에서 Ethan의 신체적 어려움에 대한 상세한 설명이 있은 후에야 그것을 일컫는 표현(his condition, physical difficulties 등)이 나옴에 유의해야 한다.

Q. 주어진 글 다음에 이어질 순서로 가장 적절한 것은?

Well, Ethan is only five feet tall, and his legs unnaturally bend away from each other. It is difficult for him to walk, run, or move around.

(A) That following summer, he asked the coach if he could join the football team as a sophomore. The coach wasn't sure at first, but in the end he allowed Ethan to come to practice.
(B) Because of his condition, he decided to leave his crowded high school in the big city. He moved to our school in the middle of his first year in high school.
(C) Regardless of his physical difficulties, Ethan worked just as hard as every other player on the team. Although he knew he would never be a valuable player in any of the team's games, he poured his heart and soul into practice every day.

________ – ________ – ________

정답 (B) – (A) – (C)
Ethan의 신체적 한계에 대한 서술에 뒤이어, (B) 그러한 그의 상태 때문에 전학을 갔고, (A) 이듬해 여름에 풋볼팀 연습을 시작했으며, (C) 자신의 신체적 한계에도 불구하고 다른 선수들만큼 열심히 연습했다는 내용이 이어지는 것이 흐름상 적절하다.

● 문장 삽입

이 문단에서 문장 삽입 유형은 11.1%의 확률로 출제될 수 있다. 전학 이후인 '이듬해 여름(That following summer)'에 Ethan이 풋볼팀에 합류하기를 요청했으며, 그 요청 이후 감독이 Ethan의 합류를 허락했고, Ethan은 풋볼팀에 합류한 이후 열심히 연습했다는 흐름을 기억하자.

Q. 글의 흐름으로 보아, 주어진 문장이 들어가기에 가장 적절한 곳은?

> The coach wasn't sure at first, but in the end he allowed Ethan to come to practice.

Well, Ethan is only five feet tall, and his legs unnaturally bend away from each other. (①) It is difficult for him to walk, run, or move around. (②) Because of his condition, he decided to leave his crowded high school in the big city. (③) He moved to our school in the middle of his first year in high school. (④) That following summer, he asked the coach if he could join the football team as a sophomore. (⑤) Regardless of his physical difficulties, Ethan worked just as hard as every other player on the team. Although he knew he would never be a valuable player in any of the team's games, he poured his heart and soul into practice every day.

정답 ⑤

'감독은 처음에 망설였지만 결국 Ethan이 연습에 오도록 허락했다'는 내용은 Ethan이 감독에게 2학년으로서 풋볼팀에 들어갈 수 있는지 물어본 직후인 ⑤에 위치하고, 뒤이어 그가 매일 열심히 연습했다는 내용이 이어지는 것이 흐름상 적절하다.

● 요약

이 문단에서 요약 유형은 4.8%의 확률로 출제될 수 있다. 이 문단은 Ethan이 작은 키와 부자연스럽게 구부러진 다리라는 신체적 어려움을 지니고 있지만, 그럼에도 불구하고 다른 모든 선수들만큼이나 열심히 매일 연습했다는 내용이다. 요약하면, '신체적 어려움에도 불구하고, Ethan은 다른 모든 선수들과 마찬가지로 매일 연습에 전념했다'는 것이 핵심 내용이다. '신체적 어려움'과 '~에도 불구하고', '전념했다' 등의 핵심 표현이 다른 표현으로 바뀌어 출제될 수 있으므로, 유사한 표현을 잘 알아두자.

Q. 글의 내용을 다음과 같이 요약할 때, 빈칸에 들어갈 말로 가장 적절한 것은?

Well, Ethan is only five feet tall, and his legs unnaturally bend away from each other. It is difficult for him to walk, run, or move around. Because of his condition, he decided to leave his crowded high school in the big city. He moved to our school in the middle of his first year in high school. That following summer, he asked the coach if he could join the football team as a sophomore. The coach wasn't sure at first, but in the end he allowed Ethan to come to practice. Regardless of his physical difficulties, Ethan worked just as hard as every other player on the team. Although he knew he would never be a valuable player in any of the team's games, he poured his heart and soul into practice every day.

> Ethan practiced as hard as every other player ______________.

① thanks to his unique upbringing
② with his physical advantages
③ regardless of his intelligence
④ despite his physical limitations
⑤ because of his mental disorders

정답 ④

> Ethan은 그의 신체적 한계에도 불구하고 다른 선수들만큼 열심히 연습했다.

Ethan이 작은 키와 부자연스럽게 구부러진 다리라는 신체적 한계를 지니고 있으며, 그럼에도 불구하고 다른 모든 선수들만큼이나 매일 열심히 연습했다는 내용의 글이다. 따라서 빈칸에는 despite his physical limitations(그의 신체적 한계에도 불구하고)가 적절하다.

① 그의 독특한 양육 덕분에
② 그의 신체적 이점을 가지고
③ 그의 지능과 무관하게
⑤ 그의 정신 질환 때문에

● 대의 파악

이 문단에서 대의 파악 문제가 출제될 확률은 3.2%이다. 이 문단은 Ethan이라는 한 소년이 자신의 신체적 한계에도 불구하고 다른 모든 선수들만큼이나 열심히 매일 연습했다는 내용이다. '신체적 어려움에 굴하지 않는 Ethan의 열정', '자신의 한계에 절대 굴복하지 않은 소년' 등이 주제나 제목이 될 수 있다.

Q. 다음 글의 주제로 가장 적절한 것은?

Well, Ethan is only five feet tall, and his legs unnaturally bend away from each other. It is difficult for him to walk, run, or move around. Because of his condition, he decided to leave his crowded high school in the big city. He moved to our school in the middle of his first year in high school. That following summer, he asked the coach if he could join the football team as a sophomore. The coach wasn't sure at first, but in the end he allowed Ethan to come to practice. Regardless of his physical difficulties, Ethan worked just as hard as every other player on the team. Although he knew he would never be a valuable player in any of the team's games, he poured his heart and soul into practice every day.

① the medical history of Ethan
② the history of high school football
③ benefits of moving to a new school
④ Ethan's passion despite physical challenges
⑤ difficulties of being a high school sports coach

정답 ④

Ethan이라는 한 소년이 자신의 신체적 어려움에도 불구하고 다른 모든 선수들만큼이나 열심히 매일 연습했다는 내용의 글이다. 따라서 글의 주제로 가장 적절한 것은 ④ '신체적 어려움에 굴하지 않는 Ethan의 열정'이다.
① Ethan의 병력
② 고등학교 풋볼의 역사
③ 새 학교로 전학가는 것의 이점
⑤ 고등학교 스포츠 감독으로서의 어려움

출제 포인트 56.3% 정복!

최중요 연습 문제

01

다음 글의 밑줄 친 문장을 통해 알 수 있는 것은?

Well, Ethan is only five feet tall, and his legs unnaturally bend away from each other. It is difficult for him to walk, run, or move around. Because of his condition, he decided to leave his crowded high school in the big city. He moved to our school in the middle of his first year in high school.

① Ethan is taller and faster than his peers.
② Ethan is able to move freely without any help.
③ Ethan has a few physical limitations.
④ Ethan has mental disorders.
⑤ Ethan is a very intelligent boy.

02

다음 글의 밑줄 친 부분 중, 가리키는 대상이 나머지 넷과 다른 것은?

Well, Ethan is only five feet tall, and ① his legs unnaturally bend away from each other. It is difficult for ② him to walk, run, or move around. Because of his condition, he decided to leave his crowded high school in the big city. He moved to our school in the middle of his first year in high school. That following summer, he asked the coach if ③ he could join the football team as a sophomore. The coach wasn't sure at first, but in the end ④ he allowed Ethan to come to practice. Regardless of his physical difficulties, Ethan worked just as hard as every other player on the team. Although he knew ⑤ he would never be a valuable player in any of the team's games, he poured his heart and soul into practice every day.

03

주어진 글 다음에 이어질 순서로 가장 적절한 것은?

Well, Ethan is only five feet tall, and his legs unnaturally bend away from each other.

(A) Regardless of his physical difficulties, Ethan worked just as hard as every other player on the team. Although he knew he would never be a valuable player in any of the team's games, he poured his heart and soul into practice every day.

(B) That following summer, he asked the coach if he could join the football team as a sophomore. The coach wasn't sure at first, but in the end he allowed Ethan to come to practice.

(C) It is difficult for him to walk, run, or move around. Because of his condition, he decided to leave his crowded high school in the big city. He moved to our school in the middle of his first year in high school.

① (A) – (C) – (B)
② (B) – (A) – (C)
③ (B) – (C) – (A)
④ (C) – (A) – (B)
⑤ (C) – (B) – (A)

04

글의 흐름으로 보아, 주어진 문장이 들어가기에 가장 적절한 곳은?

Because of his condition, he decided to leave his crowded high school in the big city.

Well, Ethan is only five feet tall, and his legs unnaturally bend away from each other. It is difficult for him to walk, run, or move around. (①) He moved to our school in the middle of his first year in high school. That following summer, he asked the coach if he could join the football team as a sophomore. (②) The coach wasn't sure at first, but in the end he allowed Ethan to come to practice. (③) Regardless of his physical difficulties, Ethan worked just as hard as every other player on the team. (④) Although he knew he would never be a valuable player in any of the team's games, he poured his heart and soul into practice every day. (⑤)

05

다음 글의 내용을 다음과 같이 요약할 때, 빈칸 (A), (B)에 들어갈 말로 가장 적절한 것은?

Well, Ethan is only five feet tall, and his legs unnaturally bend away from each other. It is difficult for him to walk, run, or move around. Because of his condition, he decided to leave his crowded high school in the big city. He moved to our school in the middle of his first year in high school. That following summer, he asked the coach if he could join the football team as a sophomore. The coach wasn't sure at first, but in the end he allowed Ethan to come to practice. Regardless of his physical difficulties, Ethan worked just as hard as every other player on the team. Although he knew he would never be a valuable player in any of the team's games, he poured his heart and soul into practice every day.

> Despite ____(A)____, Ethan ____(B)____ himself to practice every day just like every other player.

	(A)		(B)
①	bullying from his teammates	–	enabled
②	the coach's rejection	–	wanted
③	his physical disadvantages	–	dedicated
④	his psychological limitations	–	devoted
⑤	his parent's indifference	–	allowed

06

다음 글의 밑줄 친 ⓐ~ⓔ가 가리키는 대상을 잘못 연결한 것은?

Well, Ethan is only five feet tall, and ⓐ his legs unnaturally bend away from each other. It is difficult for ⓑ him to walk, run, or move around. Because of his condition, he decided to leave his crowded high school in the big city. He moved to our school in the middle of his first year in high school. That following summer, he asked the coach if ⓒ he could join the football team as a sophomore. The coach wasn't sure at first, but in the end ⓓ he allowed Ethan to come to practice. Regardless of his physical difficulties, Ethan worked just as hard as every other player on the team. Although ⓔ he knew he would never be a valuable player in any of the team's games, he poured his heart and soul into practice every day.

① ⓐ: Ethan's
② ⓑ: Ethan
③ ⓒ: the coach
④ ⓓ: the coach
⑤ ⓔ: Ethan

07

다음 글을 읽고 대답할 수 없는 질문은?

Well, Ethan is only five feet tall, and his legs unnaturally bend away from each other. It is difficult for him to walk, run, or move around. Because of his condition, he decided to leave his crowded high school in the big city. He moved to our school in the middle of his first year in high school. That following summer, he asked the coach if he could join the football team as a sophomore. The coach wasn't sure at first, but in the end he allowed Ethan to come to practice. Regardless of his physical difficulties, Ethan worked just as hard as every other player on the team. Although he knew he would never be a valuable player in any of the team's games, he poured his heart and soul into practice every day.

① How tall is Ethan?
② Why did Ethan decide to transfer to our school?
③ How did the coach first feel about Ethan's request to join the football team?
④ Did Ethan participate in the team's practice just like other players?
⑤ Why did the coach allow Ethan to join the football team?

08

글의 흐름으로 보아, 주어진 문장이 들어가기에 가장 적절한 곳은?

That following summer, he asked the coach if he could join the football team as a sophomore.

Well, Ethan is only five feet tall, and his legs unnaturally bend away from each other. (①) It is difficult for him to walk, run, or move around. Because of his condition, he decided to leave his crowded high school in the big city. (②) He moved to our school in the middle of his first year in high school. (③) The coach wasn't sure at first, but in the end he allowed Ethan to come to practice. (④) Regardless of his physical difficulties, Ethan worked just as hard as every other player on the team. Although he knew he would never be a valuable player in any of the team's games, he poured his heart and soul into practice every day. (⑤)

09

다음 글의 내용과 일치하지 않는 것을 모두 고르시오.

Well, Ethan is only five feet tall, and his legs unnaturally bend away from each other. It is difficult for him to walk, run, or move around. Because of his condition, he decided to leave his crowded high school in the big city. He moved to our school in the middle of his first year in high school. That following summer, he asked the coach if he could join the football team as a sophomore. The coach wasn't sure at first, but in the end he allowed Ethan to come to practice. Regardless of his physical difficulties, Ethan worked just as hard as every other player on the team. Although he knew he would never be a valuable player in any of the team's games, he poured his heart and soul into practice every day.

① 감독은 Ethan이 풋볼팀에 들어오도록 허락했다.
② Ethan은 자신이 경기에서 중요한 선수가 될 것이라고 확신했다.
③ Ethan은 다른 선수들만큼이나 열심히 연습에 참여했다.
④ Ethan은 2학년으로서 풋볼팀에 들어가기를 원했다.
⑤ Ethan은 큰 도시의 학교로 전학 왔다.

10

다음 글의 밑줄 친 부분 중, 가리키는 대상이 나머지 넷과 다른 것은?

Well, Ethan is only five feet tall, and his legs unnaturally bend away from each other. It is difficult for him to walk, run, or move around. Because of ① his condition, he decided to leave his crowded high school in the big city. ② He moved to our school in the middle of his first year in high school. That following summer, he asked the coach if he could join the football team as a sophomore. The coach wasn't sure at first, but in the end ③ he allowed Ethan to come to practice. Regardless of his physical difficulties, Ethan worked just as hard as every other player on the team. Although ④ he knew he would never be a valuable player in any of the team's games, ⑤ he poured his heart and soul into practice every day.

11

주어진 글 다음에 이어질 순서로 가장 적절한 것은?

Well, Ethan is only five feet tall, and his legs unnaturally bend away from each other. It is difficult for him to walk, run, or move around. Because of his condition, he decided to leave his crowded high school in the big city.

(A) The coach wasn't sure at first, but in the end he allowed Ethan to come to practice. Regardless of his physical difficulties, Ethan worked just as hard as every other player on the team.
(B) Although he knew he would never be a valuable player in any of the team's games, he poured his heart and soul into practice every day.
(C) He moved to our school in the middle of his first year in high school. That following summer, he asked the coach if he could join the football team as a sophomore.

① (A) – (C) – (B)
② (B) – (A) – (C)
③ (B) – (C) – (A)
④ (C) – (A) – (B)
⑤ (C) – (B) – (A)

12

다음 글의 제목으로 가장 적절한 것은?

Well, Ethan is only five feet tall, and his legs unnaturally bend away from each other. It is difficult for him to walk, run, or move around. Because of his condition, he decided to leave his crowded high school in the big city. He moved to our school in the middle of his first year in high school. That following summer, he asked the coach if he could join the football team as a sophomore. The coach wasn't sure at first, but in the end he allowed Ethan to come to practice. Regardless of his physical difficulties, Ethan worked just as hard as every other player on the team. Although he knew he would never be a valuable player in any of the team's games, he poured his heart and soul into practice every day.

① You Are Never Too Old to Learn
② The Boy Who Never Gave In to His Limitations
③ The Peaceful Life of Ethan Who Moved to a New School
④ The Football Coach Who Rescued a Boy in Trouble
⑤ The History of Most Valuable Players in Football

기타 연습 문제

1회 등장 포인트

● **숫자+단위명사 복수형+형용사**
부사 unnaturally
시제와 수 일치

> **Well, Ethan is only five feet tall, and his legs unnaturally bend away from each other.**

● **to부정사 병렬**

> **It is difficult for him to walk, run, or move around.**

● **능동태**

> **That following summer, he asked the coach if he could join the football team as a sophomore.**

● **시제와 수 일치, every other+단수명사**

> **Regardless of his physical difficulties, Ethan worked just as hard as every other player on the team.**

01

다음 글의 밑줄 친 ⓐ~ⓔ 중, 어법상 적절한 것을 고르시오.

Well, Ethan is ⓐ only five foot tall, and his legs unnaturally bend away from each other. It is difficult for him ⓑ to walk, run, or moving around. Because of his condition, he decided to leave his crowded high school in the big city. He moved to our school in the middle of his first year in high school. That following summer, he ⓒ was asked the coach if he could join the football team as a sophomore. The coach wasn't sure at first, but in the end he allowed Ethan to come to practice. ⓓ Regardless of his physical difficulties, Ethan worked just as hard as ⓔ every other players on the team. Although he knew he would never be a valuable player in any of the team's games, he poured his heart and soul into practice every day.

① ⓐ ② ⓑ ③ ⓒ ④ ⓓ ⑤ ⓔ

● **어휘 following, join, sophomore**

> **That following summer, he asked the coach if he could join the football team as a sophomore.**

● **어휘 pour**

> **Although he knew he would never be a valuable player in any of the team's games, he poured his heart and soul into practice every day.**

02

다음 글의 빈칸에 들어갈 말로 가장 적절한 것은?

Well, Ethan is only five feet tall, and his legs unnaturally bend away from each other. It is difficult for him to walk, run, or move around. Because of his condition, he decided to leave his crowded high school in the big city. He moved to our school in the middle of his first year in high school. That following summer, he asked the coach if he could join the football team as a ____________. The coach wasn't sure at first, but in the end he allowed Ethan to come to practice. Regardless of his physical difficulties, Ethan worked just as hard as every other player on the team. Although he knew he would never be a valuable player in any of the team's games, he poured his heart and soul into practice every day.

① coach ② sophomore ③ junior
④ senior ⑤ superior

03

다음 글의 밑줄 친 부분 중, 문맥상 적절하지 않은 것을 고르시오.

Well, Ethan is only five feet tall, and his legs unnaturally ① bend away from each other. It is difficult for him to walk, run, or move around. Because of his condition, he decided to leave his ② crowded high school in the big city. He moved to our school in the middle of his first year in high school. That following summer, he asked the coach if he could ③ leave the football team as a sophomore. The coach wasn't sure at first, but in the end he ④ allowed Ethan to come to practice. Regardless of his physical difficulties, Ethan worked just as hard as every other player on the team. Although he knew he would never be a valuable player in any of the team's games, he ⑤ put his heart and soul into practice every day.

04

다음 글의 밑줄 친 부분 중, 문맥상 낱말의 쓰임이 적절하지 않은 것은?

Ethan's touchdown didn't win the game, but it will be worth remembering. By now you're probably wondering why. Well, Ethan is only five feet tall, and his legs unnaturally bend away from each other. It is difficult for him to walk, run, or move around. Because of his condition, he decided to ① leave his crowded high school in the big city. He moved to our school in the middle of his first year in high school. That ② following summer, he asked the coach if he could ③ join the football team as a sophomore. The coach wasn't sure at first, but in the end he allowed Ethan to come to practice. Regardless of his ④ physical difficulties, Ethan worked just as ⑤ hardly as every other player on the team. Although he knew he would never be a valuable player in any of the team's games, he poured his heart and soul into practice every day.

● 무관한 문장

05

다음 글의 ①~⑤ 중, 전체 흐름과 관계 없는 문장은?

Well, Ethan is only five feet tall, and his legs unnaturally bend away from each other. It is difficult for him to walk, run, or move around. Because of his condition, he decided to leave his crowded high school in the big city. ① Any illness diagnosed in one's childhood is usually taken care of as soon as possible. ② He moved to our school in the middle of his first year in high school. That following summer, he asked the coach if he could join the football team as a sophomore. ③ The coach wasn't sure at first, but in the end he allowed Ethan to come to practice. ④ Regardless of his physical difficulties, Ethan worked just as hard as every other player on the team. ⑤ Although he knew he would never be a valuable player in any of the team's games, he poured his heart and soul into practice every day.

출제 포인트 57.5% 정복!

리딩 본문[4]

26.7% 확률로 본문[4]에서 출제

본문[4] 적중 MAPPING

이것만 알아도 95.9% 맞힌다!

Over time, however, Ethan became valuable to the team in different ways. His passion for the game was an inspiration to all his teammates. Because Ethan motivated and encouraged them, they became his most passionate fans. ★★★ Day in and day out, seeing Ethan's smile, positive attitude, and hard work lifted everyone's spirits. ★★ Right before every game, Ethan would always be in the middle of the group offering motivational words. He had a special talent for calming people down and bringing out the best in them. Ethan was also Winston High's loudest supporter. He always observed each play carefully from the sidelines. ★ Although he wasn't the one making the actual plays on the field, Ethan's mind was always right there with his teammates. Everyone could sense his love for football, and the coaches admired his commitment.

내용 일치 〈출제 1위 유형〉

본문[4]는 신체적 한계로 실제 경기에 뛸 수 없는 Ethan이 다른 방식으로 팀의 중요한 선수가 되었다는 내용이다. Ethan이 팀에서 어떤 역할을 했으며, 어떤 재능을 가지고 있었는지 구체적인 내용을 묻는 내용 일치 문제가 출제될 수 있다. Ethan의 태도, 선수들에게 전한 말, 경기 중에 한 역할 등의 내용을 약간 바꿔 틀린 선지로 출제될 수 있으니, 내용을 꼼꼼하게 파악해두자.

글의 순서 〈출제 2위 유형〉

본문[4]에서 순서를 묻는 문제가 나올 경우를 대비하여 문장1과 문장7을 눈여겨보자. 문장1에서, Ethan이 경기에서 중요한 선수가 될 수 없다는 본문[3]의 내용에 이어 연결어 however(그러나)와 함께 반대되는 내용, 즉 다른 방식으로 중요한 선수가 된다는 내용이 이어지고 있다. 본문[3]과 묶어서 순서를 묻는 문제가 출제될 수 있는 부분이다. 문장7은 Ethan의 성격과 행동을 나타내는 문장이 나열되는 부분으로, also(또한)를 근거로 순서 문제가 출제될 수 있다. 나열 부분의 순서를 묻는 문제는 고난도 문제이지만, 근거가 명확하기 때문에 고득점을 위해 미리 대비해두자.

대의 파악 〈출제 3위 유형〉

Ethan이 실제 경기를 뛰지 않고도 팀에서 중요한 선수로 자리매김할 수 있었던 방식들에 관한 글로, 제목, 요지, 주제, 교훈이나 속담 등을 묻는 대의 파악 문제가 출제될 수 있다. Ethan이 팀의 자극제이자 동기 부여자로서 어떻게 팀에 도움을 주었는지, 윈스턴 고등학교 팀이 Ethan을 어떻게 바라보는지에 관한 전반적인 내용을 이해해두자.

출제 1위 문장 ★★★

Day in and day out, seeing Ethan's smile, positive attitude, and hard work lifted everyone's spirits.

[동명사 명사 역할 — 주어] 출제 1위 (문장편 문장4 → p.107)
[어휘 positive] 출제 2위 (문장편 문장4 → p.108)
[본동사 찾기] 출제 3위 (문장편 문장4 → p.108)

출제 2위 문장 ★★

Right before every game, Ethan would always be in the middle of the group offering motivational words.

[분사구문 부사 역할 — 동시동작] 출제 1위 (문장편 문장5 → p.110)
[어휘 motivational] 출제 2위 (문장편 문장5 → p.110)

출제 3위 문장 ★

Although he wasn't the one making the actual plays on the field, Ethan's mind was always right there with his teammates.

[현재분사 형용사 역할 — 명사 수식] 출제 1위 (문장편 문장9 → p.116)
[접속사 although 부사 역할 — 양보] 출제 2위 (문장편 문장9 → p.117)
[빈도부사의 위치] 출제 3위 (문장편 문장9 → p.117)

문장1

문장 출제 확률: 2.9

Over time, however, Ethan became valuable to the team in different ways.

(however: 그러나(역접) / valuable: 중요한, 가치 있는)

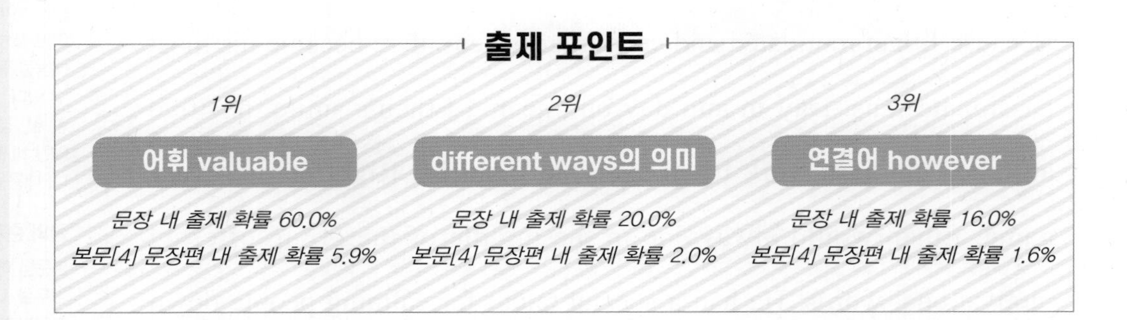

● 어휘 valuable

문장1이 출제될 가능성은 2.9%이다. 이 문장이 출제된다면, 어휘 valuable(중요한, 가치 있는)에 대해 묻는 문제가 60.0%로 출제 확률 1위이다. 그 중에서도 빈칸 유형과 형태가 비슷한 낱말, 유의어, 반의어를 활용한 문제가 많이 출제되었다. 본문[3]의 문장8에도 동일한 출제 포인트가 나왔으니, 다시 한번 복습해보자. 바꿔 쓸 수 있는 유의어로 invaluable(귀중한), priceless(귀중한), worthy(가치 있는) 등이 있으며, 반의어로는 valueless(가치 없는), worthless(쓸모없는) 등이 있다. 이들은 접두사 in-과 접미사 -less 때문에 혼동하기 쉬우니 정확히 구분해서 학습해두자.

Q. 다음 중, 밑줄 친 valuable과 바꿔 쓸 수 없는 것은?

Over time, however, Ethan became valuable to the team in different ways. His passion for the game was an inspiration to all his teammates.

① invaluable ② priceless ③ worthy ④ valueless

정답 ④

valuable은 '중요한, 가치 있는'의 의미를 가진 형용사로, invaluable, priceless, worthy 모두 '(가치를 매길 수 없이) 중요한, 매우 귀중한'의 의미를 가진 형용사이므로 바꿔 쓸 수 있다. 반면, valueless는 '가치 없는, 보잘것없는'의 의미를 가진 형용사로 반대 의미이다.

● different ways의 의미

이 문장에서 different ways가 의미하는 바에 대해 묻는 문제가 20.0%의 확률로 출제될 수 있다. 특히, different ways에 대해 우리말로 구체적으로 서술하라는 문제로 자주 출제되었으니, 우리말 해석까지도 정확하게 파악해두자.

Q. 다음 중, 글의 밑줄 친 different ways에 해당하지 않는 것은?

Ethan became valuable to the team in different ways. His passion for the game was an inspiration to all his teammates. Because Ethan motivated and encouraged them, they became his most passionate fans. Day in and day out, seeing Ethan's smile, positive attitude, and hard work lifted everyone's spirits. Right before every game, Ethan would always be in the middle of the group offering motivational words. He had a special talent for calming people down and

정답 ④

Ethan은 신체적인 한계로 인해 스스로 팀 경기에서 중요한 선수가 될 수 없다는 사실을 알았지만, 대신에 팀원들의 사기를 진작시키는 여러 행동을 하면서 팀의 중요한 선수가 되었다. 따라서 밑줄 친 different ways에 해당하지 않는 내용은 ④ '경기장에서 실제 경기에 출전하는 것'이다.

bringing out the best in them. Ethan was also Winston High's loudest supporter. He always observed each play carefully from the sidelines. Although he wasn't the one making the actual plays on the field, Ethan's mind was always right there with his teammates.

① Lifting all his teammates' spirits
② Offering motivational words to the players
③ Being an inspiration to all his teammates
④ Making the actual plays on the field

① 그의 모든 팀원들의 사기를 북돋우는 것
② 선수들에게 동기 부여의 말들을 전하는 것
③ 그의 모든 팀원들에게 영감을 주는 사람이 되는 것

● 연결어 however

이 문장에서 세 번째로 출제 확률(16.0%)이 높은 것은 연결어 however이다. 이 자리에 빈칸을 두고 알맞은 말을 고르는 문제로 나올 수 있다. however은 '그러나'의 의미로, 앞의 내용과 반대되는 내용을 연결하는 역접의 부사로, 보통은 문장 맨 앞에 오지만 콤마(,)를 활용해서 문장 중간에도 위치할 수 있다. 또한, however 대신에 쓸 수 있는 말인 still(그러나), yet(그러나), but(하지만), nonetheless(그럼에도 불구하고) 등으로 변형되어 출제될 수 있다는 점도 유의하자.

Q. 다음 글의 빈칸 (A), (B)에 들어갈 말을 〈보기〉에서 각각 찾아 쓰시오.

〈보기〉 for example / although / also / however / therefore

Regardless of his physical difficulties, Ethan worked just as hard as every other player on the team. Although he knew he would never be a valuable player in any of the team's games, he poured his heart and soul into practice every day. Over time, ____(A)____, Ethan became valuable to the team in different ways. His passion for the game was an inspiration to all his teammates. Day in and day out, seeing Ethan's smile, positive attitude, and hard work lifted everyone's spirits. Right before every game, Ethan would always be in the middle of the group offering motivational words. He had a special talent for calming people down and bringing out the best in them. Ethan was ____(B)____ Winston High's loudest supporter.

(A) ____________ (B) ____________

정답
(A) however (B) also
(A)의 앞에 Ethan이 신체적인 한계로 인해 팀 경기에 중요한 선수가 될 수 없음을 알았지만, 다른 방식으로 중요한 선수가 되었다는 반대의 내용이 나오기 때문에 (A)에는 however(그러나)가 적절하다. (B)의 경우, 앞에서 Ethan이 보여주는 행동들에 대해 열거하고 있으므로, 추가의 의미를 나타내는 also(또한)가 적절하다.

문장2

문장 출제 확률: 1.9%

His passion for the game was an inspiration to all his teammates.

(His passion: 열정 / was: 동사(수 일치) / inspiration: 영감[자극]을 주는 것[사람])

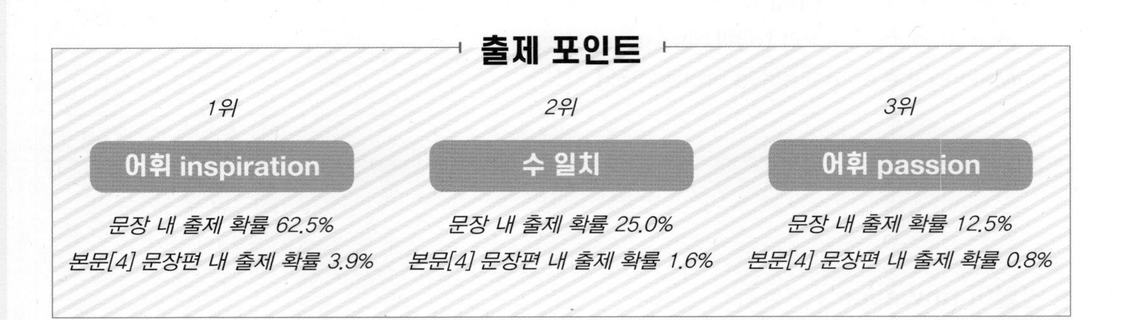

● 어휘 inspiration

문장2가 출제될 가능성은 1.9%이다. 그 중에서도 가장 높은 확률(62.5%)로 출제될 수 있는 포인트는 어휘 inspiration(영감[자극]을 주는 것[사람])이다. 밑줄 친 어휘의 적절성을 묻는 문제로, 반의어 interruption(방해), obstacle(방해)로 변형되어 출제되었으며, 철자가 비슷하여 혼동할 수 있는 어휘 aspiration(열망)이 오답 선지로 출제되기도 했다. 또한, 영영풀이 the stimulation or influence needed to create or achieve something(무언가를 창조하거나 성취하는 데 필요한 자극이나 영향력)에 대해 묻는 문제도 출제될 수 있으니 대비해두자.

Q. 다음 글의 빈칸에 들어가기에 적절한 단어를 〈보기〉에서 골라 쓰시오.

〈보기〉 difficulty / inspiration / imagination / aspiration / obstacle / talent

His passion for the game was a(n) ____________ to all his teammates. Because Ethan motivated and encouraged them, they became his most passionate fans. Day in and day out, seeing Ethan's smile, positive attitude, and hard work lifted everyone's spirits. Right before every game, Ethan would always be in the middle of the group offering motivational words.

____

정답 inspiration

빈칸 뒤에서 Ethan은 다른 선수들에게 좋은 기운을 북돋워주고 용기를 주는 말을 전달하며 긍정적인 태도와 강한 노력을 보여주었다고 했다. 따라서 경기에 대한 열정은 팀 선수 모두에게 '자극(inspiration)'이 되었다고 할 수 있다.

● 수 일치

문장2가 출제된다면, 주어와 동사의 수 일치에 대한 문제가 출제될 확률은 25.0%이다. 이 문장의 주어는 His passion으로 3인칭 단수이고, 전치사구 for the game은 주어를 수식하고 있으며, 동사는 3인칭 단수에 일치시킨 was이다. 실제 시험에서는 game을 games로 바꾸어 지문을 제시한 후, 동사의 수 일치를 묻는 문항이 출제되기도 했으므로, 주어를 정확하게 파악하고 있어야 한다.

Q. 다음 글의 밑줄 친 부분 중, 어법상 틀린 것은?

Over time, however, Ethan became ① valuable to the team in different ways. His passion for the games ② were an inspiration to all his teammates. Because Ethan motivated and ③ encouraged them, they became his most passionate fans.

정답 ②

문장의 동사인 be동사에 호응하는 주어는 the games가 아니라 His passion이다. 따라서 be동사의 복수형 were을 단수형 was로 고쳐야 한다.

Day in and day out, ④ seeing Ethan's smile, positive attitude, and hard work lifted everyone's spirits. Right before every game, Ethan would always be in the middle of the group ⑤ offering motivational words.

● 어휘 passion

문장2에서 어휘 passion에 대해 묻는 문제가 출제될 확률은 12.5%이다. Ethan이 경기에 출전하지 못하더라도 매일 열과 성을 다해 연습하는 모습을 그의 passion(열정)이라고 표현했으며, 비슷한 선지로 '노력(efforts, hard work)' 등으로 변형되어 출제될 수 있다. 또한, 영영풀이 a strong feeling of enthusiasm and interest towards something(무언가에 대한 강한 열정과 흥미)을 활용한 문제도 출제된 바 있으니, 함께 익혀두자.

Q. 다음 글에서 밑줄 친 (A), (B), (C)의 영영풀이를 올바르게 연결하시오.

Regardless of his physical (A) difficulties, Ethan worked just as hard as every other player on the team. Although he knew he would never be a valuable player in any of the team's games, he poured his heart and soul into practice every day. Over time, however, Ethan became valuable to the team in different ways. His (B) passion for the game was an inspiration to all his teammates. Because Ethan motivated and encouraged them, they became his most passionate (C) fans.

① a person who has a strong interest in and admiration for a particular sport, celebrity, activity, or product
② a state or condition of being hard, challenging, or troublesome
③ a strong feeling of enthusiasm and interest towards something

(A) ____________ (B) ____________ (C) ____________

정답
(A) ② (B) ③ (C) ①
(A) 어려움: ② 힘들거나, 도전적이거나, 까다로운 상태나 조건
(B) 열정: ③ 무언가에 대한 강한 열정과 흥미의 감정
(C) 팬: ① 특정 스포츠, 유명인, 활동, 또는 제품에 대해 강한 관심과 동경을 가지고 있는 사람

출제 포인트 61.2% 정복!

문장3

문장 출제 확률: 3.3% (총 851개의 출제 포인트 중 28회 출현, 45개 문장 중 10위)

접속사 because – 이유 / 동사1(병렬) / 동사2(병렬)

Because Ethan motivated and encouraged them, they became his most passionate fans.

encourage: 격려하다

출제 포인트

1위	2위	3위
접속사 because 부사 역할 – 이유	어휘 encourage	병렬 구조
문장 내 출제 확률 32.1%	문장 내 출제 확률 25.0%	문장 내 출제 확률 21.4%
본문[4] 문장편 내 출제 확률 3.5%	본문[4] 문장편 내 출제 확률 2.8%	본문[4] 문장편 내 출제 확률 2.4%

● 접속사 because 부사 역할 – 이유

문장3이 출제될 가능성은 3.3%이다. 이 문장에서 32.1%의 확률로 접속사 because(~ 때문에)에 대해 물어볼 수 있다. 특히, because of와 둘 중 적절한 것을 고르는 문제로 자주 출제되었는데, 뒤에 오는 문장의 구조를 보고 둘을 구분할 수 있어야 한다. because of는 전치사로, 뒤에 명사 상당어구가, because는 접속사이기 때문에 뒤에 절이 온다. 그 외에도 이유를 나타내는 접속사 since나 as로 변형되어 출제될 수 있다는 점도 유의하자.

Q. 다음 글의 밑줄 친 ⓐ~ⓓ 중, 어법상 틀린 것을 찾아 바르게 고치시오.

Over time, ⓐ however, Ethan became valuable to the team in different ways. His passion for the game was an inspiration to all his teammates. ⓑ Because of Ethan motivated and encouraged them, they became his most passionate fans. Day in and day out, ⓒ seeing Ethan's smile, positive attitude, and hard work lifted everyone's spirits. ⓓ Right before every game, Ethan would always be in the middle of the group offering motivational words.

(　　) ______________ → ______________

정답
ⓑ Because of
→ Because

because와 because of 모두 '~ 때문에'라는 같은 의미를 가졌으나, 전자는 접속사로 뒤에 절이 오고, 후자는 전치사로 뒤에 명사가 와야 한다. ⓑ 뒤에는 주어와 동사를 갖춘 절이 오므로 because of를 because로 고쳐야 한다.

● 어휘 encourage

문장3이 출제된다면, 어휘 encourage(격려하다)에 대해 묻는 문제가 나올 가능성이 25.0%이다. 특히, 반의어 discourage(낙담시키다)를 활용해서 밑줄 친 어휘의 적절성을 묻는 문제로 자주 출제되었다. 앞의 동사 motivate(자극하다)와 병렬 연결되어 비슷한 의미의 단어가 와야 한다는 점을 기억한다면 쉽게 맞힐 수 있다. 그 외에도 encourage를 대신하여 쓸 수 있는 단어 stimulate(자극하다), inspire(영감을 주다)로 변형되어 출제될 수 있으니 함께 알아두자.

Q. 다음 글의 괄호 안에 문맥상 들어갈 말로 적절한 것은?

Over time, however, Ethan became valuable to the team in different ways. His passion for the game was an inspiration to all his teammates. Because Ethan motivated and (encouraged / discouraged) them, they became his most passionate fans.

정답 encouraged

Ethan은 선수들에게 동기를 부여했다(motivate)고 했으므로, 이와 병렬을 이루어 '격려했다(encouraged)'는 것이 흐름상 자연스럽다.

● 병렬 구조

이 문장에서 종속절 내 동사의 병렬 구조에 대해 묻는 문제가 나올 가능성은 21.4%이다. 동사 encouraged에 밑줄을 치거나 형태를 encourage 또는 encouraging으로 변형하여 어법상 적절성을 묻는 문제가 나올 수 있다. 접속사 and에 의해 동사 motivated와 병렬 연결되어 과거 시제 encouraged로 써야 한다는 사실을 반드시 기억하자.

Q. 다음 글의 밑줄 친 우리말에 맞도록 〈보기〉의 단어를 모두 활용하여 영작하시오. (단, 필요시 단어 변형 및 추가 가능하며 6단어로 쓸 것)

〈보기〉 because / motivate / encourage

Over time, however, Ethan became valuable to the team in different ways. His passion for the game was an inspiration to all his teammates. Ethan은 그들에게 동기를 부여하고 격려했기 때문에, they became his most passionate fans.

____

정답
Because Ethan motivated and encouraged them

'~ 때문에'라는 이유를 나타내는 접속사 Because를 문두에 쓰고, Ethan과 them을 각각 주어와 목적어로 쓰며, 과거 시제이므로 동사 motivate와 encourage를 과거형으로 쓴다.

● 어휘 passionate

문장3에서 17.9%의 확률로 어휘 passionate에 대해 묻는 문제가 출제될 수 있다. 명사 passion이 앞 문장에서 이미 언급이 되어 passionate 자체를 묻는 문제보다는 같은 의미를 가진 enthusiastic(열정적인)으로 변형하여 출제될 가능성이 높기 때문에 맥락에서 쓰인 의미를 잘 알아두자.

Q. 다음 중, 밑줄 친 단어와 바꿔 쓸 수 있는 것으로 가장 적절한 것은?

Over time, however, Ethan became valuable to the team in different ways. His passion for the game was an inspiration to all his teammates. Because Ethan motivated and encouraged them, they became his most passionate fans. Day in and day out, seeing Ethan's smile, positive attitude, and hard work lifted everyone's spirits. Right before every game, Ethan would always be in the middle of the group offering motivational words.

① pessimistic ② enthusiastic ③ passive ④ indifferent

정답 ②
밑줄 친 passionate은 '열정적인, 열정이 가득 찬'의 의미로, enthusiastic(열정적인)과 바꿔 쓸 수 있다.
① 비관적인
③ 수동적인
④ 무관심한

출제 포인트 63.7% 정복!

문장4

문장 출제 확률: 4.9% (총 851개의 출제 포인트 중 42회 출현, 45개 문장 중 2위)

Day in and day out, seeing(동명사, 주어) Ethan's smile, positive(긍정적인) attitude, and hard work lifted(본동사) everyone's spirits.

출제 포인트

1위	2위	3위
동명사 명사 역할 – 주어	어휘 positive	본동사 찾기
문장 내 출제 확률 35.7%	문장 내 출제 확률 19.0%	문장 내 출제 확률 16.7%
본문[4] 문장편 내 출제 확률 5.9%	본문[4] 문장편 내 출제 확률 3.1%	본문[4] 문장편 내 출제 확률 2.8%

● 동명사 명사 역할 – 주어

문장4는 1과 본문 중 출제 순위 2위(4.9%)로, 반드시 알아두어야 하는 문장이다. 그 중에서도 주어 역할을 하는 동명사가 출제될 확률이 1위(35.7%)이다. 어법, 쓰임, 서술형, 문장 구조 변형 등 다양한 유형으로 출제되었으므로, 이 문장은 암기를 기본으로 하자.

Q. 다음 문장의 괄호 안에 알맞은 표현을 모두 고르시오.

Day in and day out, (see / saw / seeing / to see / seen) Ethan's smile, positive attitude, and hard work lifted everyone's spirits.

정답 seeing, to see
문장의 주어 자리이므로, 주어 역할을 하는 동명사 seeing 또는 to부정사 to see를 골라야 한다.

정답 ⑤

seeing과 ⑤의 offering은 문장의 주어인 동명사이다. ①, ②, ③은 'be v-ing'의 진행 시제를 나타낸다. ④는 목적어 him을 보충 설명하는 목적격 보어로, 진행의 상황을 강조하는 현재분사이다.
① 양쪽 팀 모두 공을 차지하기 위해 싸우고 있었다.
② 이쯤 되면 여러분은 아마 이유를 궁금해할 것이다.
③ 이제, Ethan은 마침내 잔디를 밟을 기회를 얻게 된 것이다.
④ 그들은 Ethan이 경기 종료 직전 골 라인을 넘어선 것을 보았다.
⑤ 의욕을 높이는 말을 해주는 것은 Ethan이 팀의 중심에 있게 했다.

Q. 다음 중, 글의 밑줄 친 부분과 쓰임이 같은 것은?

Over time, however, Ethan became valuable to the team in different ways. His passion for the game was an inspiration to all his teammates. Because Ethan motivated and encouraged them, they became his most passionate fans. Day in and day out, seeing Ethan's smile, positive attitude, and hard work lifted everyone's spirits.

① Both teams were fighting for the football.
② By now, you're probably wondering why.
③ Now, Ethan was finally getting the chance to step onto the grass.
④ They saw him crossing the goal line right before the clock ran out.
⑤ Offering motivational words made Ethan be in the middle of the group.

● 어휘 positive

문장4에서 두 번째로 출제 확률(19.0%)이 높은 포인트는 어휘 positive(긍정적인)이다. 반대의 의미를 가진 negative(부정적인), arrogant(오만한), pessimistic(비관적인) 등의 단어와 비교하는 문제로 출제되었으며, positive 대신 optimistic(낙관적인)으로 변형되어 출제된 적도 있으니, 반의어와 유의어 모두 잘 알아두자.

정답 positive

모두의 기운을 북돋은 Ethan에 관한 것을 나열한 부분으로, 미소(smile)와 노력(hard work)과 같은 맥락으로 '긍정적인(positive)' 자세가 모두의 기운을 북돋웠다는 흐름이 자연스럽다.
passive: 수동적인
negative: 부정적인
indifferent: 무관심한
pessimistic: 비관적인

Q. 다음 글의 빈칸에 들어가기에 적절한 단어를 〈보기〉에서 찾아 쓰시오.

〈보기〉 passive / positive / negative / indifferent / pessimistic

Over time, however, Ethan became valuable to the team in different ways. His passion for the game was an inspiration to all his teammates. Because Ethan motivated and encouraged them, they became his most passionate fans. Day in and day out, seeing Ethan's smile, ____________ attitude, and hard work lifted everyone's spirits. Right before every game, Ethan would always be in the middle of the group offering motivational words.

____

● 본동사 찾기

문장4가 출제된다면, 문장의 본동사를 찾는 문제가 출제될 가능성이 16.7%이다. 주어인 동명사구 seeing ~ hard work로 인해 주어와 동사를 찾는 것이 다소 복잡할 수 있기 때문에 출제하기에 매력적인 포인트라 할 수 있다. 동사 lifted 자리에는 to lift나 lift가 올 수 없으며, 수동형 was lifted도 쓸 수 없으니, 올바른 시제와 태인 lifted를 반드시 기억하자.

정답 lifted

문장의 주어는 동명사구 'seeing ~ work'이며, lift는 동사 자리이다. 글 전체적으로 과거 시제이므로 lifted로 변형해야 한다.

Q. 다음 글의 밑줄 친 lift를 어법에 알맞은 형태의 한 단어로 변형하여 쓰시오.

Because Ethan motivated and encouraged them, they became his most passionate fans. Day in and day out, seeing Ethan's smile, positive attitude, and hard work lift everyone's spirits. Right before every game, Ethan would always be in the middle of the group offering motivational words.

____

• 어휘 lift

동사로 쓰인 어휘 lift(북돋우다)는 어휘 문제로도 출제가 될 가능성이 11.9%이다. 특히, 반의어 discourage(낙담시키다), break(사기를 꺾다)와 구분하거나, 바꿔 쓸 수 있는 어휘 raise(북돋우다), encourage(격려하다)로 변형되어 문제가 나올 수 있다.

Q. 다음 중, 밑줄 친 lifted와 바꿔 쓸 수 없는 것은?

Day in and day out, seeing Ethan's smile and hard work lifted everyone's spirits.

① boosted ② encouraged ③ raised ④ broke

정답 ④

밑줄 친 lifted는 '(기분, 사기 등을) 북돋우다'의 의미로 쓰였으며, boost(북돋우다), encourage(격려하다), raise(올리다)로 바꿔 쓸 수 있다. break는 '사기를 꺾다'라는 의미로, lift의 반의어이므로 바꿔 쓸 수 없다.

• 어휘 attitude

이 문장에서 어휘 attitude(태도)에 대해 묻는 문제가 나올 확률은 7.1%로, 그 중에서도 올바른 영영풀이를 고르는 문제로 가장 많이 출제되었다. attitude의 영영풀이는 a feeling, opinion, or position about something or someone(무언가 또는 누군가에 대한 느낌, 의견이나 입장)으로, 눈에 익혀두자. 이외에도 철자가 비슷해 혼동할 수 있는 단어 aptitude(적성, 소질), altitude(고도)도 출제된 적이 있으니, 철자와 뜻을 정확하게 구분하여 외워두자.

Q. 다음 글의 괄호 (A), (B) 안에서 문맥에 맞는 낱말로 가장 적절한 것은?

Because Ethan motivated and encouraged them, they became his most passionate fans. Day in and day out, seeing Ethan's smile, positive (A) (altitude / aptitude / attitude), and hard work lifted everyone's spirits. Right before every game, Ethan would always be in the middle of the group offering motivational words. He had a special talent for calming people down and bringing out the (B) (worst / best / most) in them.

정답

(A) attitude (B) best

(A) 문맥상 Ethan이 팀 선수들에게 동기 부여를 하고, 격려를 해주는 모습을 통해 그의 긍정적인 '태도(attitude)'가 모두의 기운을 북돋워주었다는 내용이 자연스럽다.

altitude: 고도

aptitude: 적성, 소질

(B) Ethan은 사람들을 침착하게 하고 그들이 가진 '최고의(best)' 능력을 이끌어 내는 능력이 있다는 것이 문맥상 자연스럽다.

worst: 최악의

most: 대부분

• day in and day out

문장4가 출제된다면, '날이면 날마다'의 의미를 가진 표현 day in and day out도 출제될 가능성이 4.8%있다. 이 표현은 all the time(항상), on and on(줄곧, 계속하여) 등의 표현으로 바꿔 쓸 수 있다. Ethan이 매일 노력을 한다는 내용이 본문 초반부터 지속적으로 나오고 있으므로, 맥락을 이해하면서 의미를 기억해두자.

Q. 다음 글에서 밑줄 친 ⓐ~ⓓ의 해석으로 적절하지 않은 것은?

ⓐ Over time, however, Ethan became valuable to the team in different ways. His passion for the game was an inspiration to all his teammates. ⓑ Day in and day out, seeing Ethan's smile, positive attitude, and hard work lifted everyone's spirits. ⓒ Right before every game, Ethan would always be ⓓ in the middle of the group offering motivational words.

① ⓐ: 시간이 지나면서 ② ⓑ: 하루 걸러 한 번씩

③ ⓒ: ~의 바로 직전에 ④ ⓓ: ~의 중앙에

정답 ②

day in and day out은 '날이면 날마다'의 의미를 가진 표현이며, '하루 걸러 한 번씩'에 해당하는 표현은 every other day이다.

출제 포인트 67.5% 정복!

문장5

문장 출제 확률: 3.9% (총 851개의 출제 포인트 중 33회 출현, 45개 문장 중 5위)

Right before every game, Ethan would always be in the middle of the group offering motivational words.

offering: 분사구문 (동시동작) / motivational: 의욕을 높이는

출제 포인트

1위	2위
분사구문 부사 역할 — 동시동작	어휘 motivational
문장 내 출제 확률 51.5%	문장 내 출제 확률 27.3%
본문[4] 문장편 내 출제 확률 6.7%	본문[4] 문장편 내 출제 확률 3.5%

● 분사구문 부사 역할 - 동시동작

문장5가 출제될 가능성은 3.9%로, 전체 문장 중 출제 순위가 5위에 해당하는 빈출 문장이다. 그 중에서도 분사구문에 대해 묻는 문제가 출제될 확률은 51.5%로, 매우 중요한 문법 포인트라 할 수 있다. 분사구문에 해당하는 offering motivational words는 '의욕을 높이는 말을 전하면서'라는 뜻으로 동시동작을 나타낸다. 이 부분은 as he would offer motivational words로 바꿔 쓸 수 있다.

Q. 다음 글의 밑줄 친 부분 중, 어법상 틀린 것은?

His passion for the game ① was an inspiration to all his teammates. Because Ethan motivated and ② encouraged them, they became his most passionate fans. Day in and day out, ③ seeing Ethan's smile, positive attitude, and hard work lifted everyone's spirits. Right before every game, Ethan would always be in the middle of the group ④ offered motivational words. He had a special talent for calming people down and ⑤ bringing out the best in them.

정답 ④

④의 앞에는 주어(Ethan)와 동사(would ~ be)를 갖춘 완전한 절이므로, 문장을 수식하는 분사구문이 오는 것이 알맞다. 또한, offer의 주체가 Ethan이므로 능동을 나타내는 현재분사 형태 offering으로 분사구문을 써야 한다.

● 어휘 motivational

문장5가 출제된다면, 어휘 motivational에 대해 묻는 문제가 출제될 가능성은 27.3%로 2위를 차지하는 주요 출제 포인트이다. motivational(동기를 주는) 대신 encouraging(격려하는), inspiring(고무[격려]하는) 등으로 변형되어 출제될 수 있으며, 반의어 discouraging(낙담시키는), 혼동할 수 있는 어휘 motional(운동의)과 구분하는 문제가 출제될 수 있으니, 잘 기억해두자.

Q. 다음 글의 빈칸에 들어가기에 적절하지 않은 것은?

Ethan's passion for the game was an inspiration to all his teammates. Because Ethan motivated and encouraged them, they became his most passionate fans. Seeing Ethan's smile, positive attitude, and hard work lifted everyone's spirits. Right before every game, Ethan would always be in the middle of the group

정답 ②

Ethan은 팀에서 다른 선수들을 격려하고 동기 부여를 하는 역할을 해왔다는 내용이 앞에 언급되었다. 이러한 글의 흐름을 보아, 빈칸에는 '격려해주는, 자극을 주는' 등의 긍정적인 의미를 가진 단어가 적절하다.
① 고무[격려]하는
② 낙담시키는
③ 동기를 주는
④ 격려하는

offering ______________ words. He had a special talent for calming people down and bringing out the best in them.

① inspiring ② discouraging
③ motivational ④ encouraging

● 어휘 offer

어휘 offer에 대해 출제될 가능성은 6.1%로, Ethan은 팀 선수들을 격려하고 기운을 불어넣는 역할을 한다는 앞의 내용과 일맥상통하게 '동기 부여가 되는 말을 전해준다(offering)'는 내용이 담긴 부분이다. offer를 대신해서 비슷한 의미인 provide(제공하다), give(주다), supply(공급하다) 등으로 변형되어 출제된 경우가 많으므로, 유의어를 잘 알아두자. 또한, 올바른 영영풀이를 고르는 문제로도 출제될 가능성도 있으니, 영영풀이도 익혀 두자.

Q. 다음 글에서 밑줄 친 (A), (B), (C)의 영영풀이를 올바르게 연결하시오.

Because Ethan (A) encouraged them, they became his most passionate fans. (B) Day in and day out, seeing Ethan's smile, positive attitude, and hard work lifted everyone's spirits. Right before every game, Ethan would always be in the middle of the group (C) offering motivational words.

① repeatedly or consistently, day after day, without any significant breaks or interruptions
② to provide or supply something
③ to give someone support, confidence, or hope to do something

(A) ___________ (B) ___________ (C) ___________

정답
(A) ③ (B) ① (C) ②
(A) 용기를 북돋우다: ③ 누군가에게 지지, 자신감 또는 무언가를 할 수 있다는 희망을 주다
(B) 날이면 날마다: ① 큰 휴식이나 중단 없이 매일 반복적으로 또는 일관되게
(C) 제공하다: ② 어떤 것을 제공하거나 주다

● every[each]+단수명사

every 뒤에 오는 명사의 수에 대해 묻는 문제가 이 문장에서 출제될 가능성은 6.1%이다. every는 '모든', '매', '하나하나의'라는 의미를 가진 한정사로, 뒤에 항상 단수명사(game)가 와야 한다. 본문[3]의 문장7에서도 이 포인트가 등장하므로, 〈every[each]+단수명사〉를 암기해두자.

Q. 다음 문장에서 틀린 곳을 찾아 바르게 고쳐 쓰시오.

Right before every games, Ethan would be in the middle of the group offering motivational words.

______________ → ______________

정답
games → game
every는 '모든'의 의미를 가진 한정사로, 단수명사를 수식한다. 따라서 games를 단수형 game으로 고쳐야 한다.

● 빈칸 offering motivational words

문장5에서 출제될 수 있는 마지막 포인트는 빈칸 추론 유형이다. Ethan은 선수들을 격려하고 선수들에게 자극이 되는 존재라는 내용에 이어, 매 경기 직전마다 선수들에게 '의욕을 높이는 말을 전하면서(offering[providing] motivational[stimulating] words)' 팀의 중심이 되었다는 흐름이다. 본문에 나온 단어를 쓰지 않고 변형되는 경우가 많으므로, 내용을 정확하게 파악해두자.

Q. 다음 중, 글의 흐름상 빈칸에 들어갈 수 없는 것은?

Ethan's passion for the game was an inspiration to all his teammates. Because Ethan motivated and encouraged them, they became his most passionate fans. Day in and day out, seeing Ethan's smile, positive attitude, and hard work lifted everyone's spirits. Right before every game, Ethan would always be in the middle of the group ________________.

① giving motivational words to the players
② saying what inspired the players in the game
③ showing his physical difficulties to the audience

정답 ③
Ethan은 팀 선수들에게 자극이 되는 존재라는 전체적인 흐름으로 보아, 선수들에게 긍정적인 영향을 미쳤다는 내용이 적절하다. 따라서 ③ '관중들에게 신체적 어려움을 보이면서'라는 내용은 흐름에 어울리지 않는다.
① 선수들에게 동기 부여가 되는 말을 하면서
② 경기에 출전하는 선수들에게 영감을 주는 것을 말하면서

출제 포인트 70.5% 정복!

문장6

문장 출제 확률: 3.6% (총 851개의 출제 포인트 중 28회 출현, 45개 문장 중 8위)

동명사1 (전치사 for의 목적어) / 동명사2 (전치사 for의 목적어)

He had a special talent for calming people down and bringing out the best in them.

출제 포인트

1위

동명사 병렬 — 전치사의 목적어

문장 내 출제 확률 90.3%
본문[4] 문장편 내 출제 확률 11.0%

● 동명사 병렬 – 전치사의 목적어

문장6의 출제 순위는 8위(3.6%)로, 출제 가능성이 높다. 이 문장은 전치사 for의 목적어로 동명사가 온다는 점과, 등위접속사 and에 의해 동명사 calming과 bringing이 병렬 구조를 이루고 있다는 점이 핵심이다. and 뒤에 오는 bringing의 형태를 묻는 문법 문제나 주어진 원형을 알맞게 변형하는 서술형 문항이 자주 출제되었다.

Q. 다음 중, 밑줄 친 부분의 문법 설명으로 적절하지 않은 것은?

Over time, (a) however, Ethan became valuable to the team in different ways. (b) Because Ethan motivated and encouraged them, they became his most passionate fans. Day in and day out, (c) seeing Ethan's smile, positive attitude, and hard work lifted everyone's spirits. Right before every (d) game, Ethan would

정답 ⑤
(e) 등위접속사 and로 calming과 병렬 연결된 형태로 for의 목적어로 쓰인 동명사이다.

always be in the middle of the group offering motivational words. He had a special talent for calming people down and (e) bringing out the best in them.

① (a): 역접의 의미를 가진 부사
② (b): 이유를 나타내는 접속사
③ (c): 문장의 주어 역할을 하는 동명사
④ (d): 한정사 every의 수식을 받는 단수명사
⑤ (e): 결과를 나타내는 분사구문

Q. 밑줄 친 우리말에 맞게 〈보기〉의 단어를 알맞게 배열하시오. (단, 필요시 단어 변형 가능)

〈보기〉 people / the best / down / in / and / calm / them / bring out

He had a special talent for 사람들을 침착하게 하고 그들의 최선을 이끌어내는.

____

정답
calming people down and bringing out the best in them / calming down people and bringing out the best in them

앞에 전치사 for가 있으므로 〈보기〉의 동사를 동명사로 변형하여 단어를 배열해야 한다. for의 목적어에 해당하는 내용이 '침착하게 하다'와 '이끌어내다' 두 가지이므로, 등위접속사 and를 사용하여 병렬 구조를 이루도록 배열한다.

출제 포인트 73.1% 정복!

문장7

문장 출제 확률: 1.1%

Ethan was also Winston High's loudest supporter.
(also: 또한 / loudest: 가장 열정적인 / supporter: 지지자[옹호자])

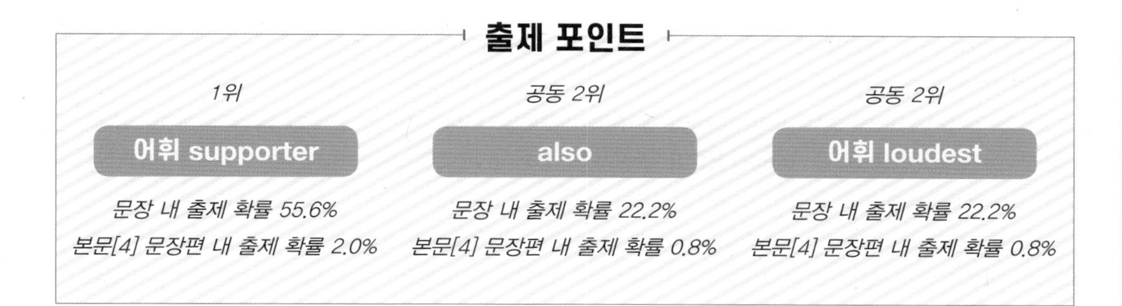

● 어휘 supporter

문장7이 출제될 가능성은 1.1%로 높지는 않지만, Ethan의 역할에 대한 내용이 나열되는 문장이므로 내용을 잘 파악해야 한다. 그 중에서도 1위를 차지한 포인트는 어휘 supporter이며, 이 문장이 출제된다면 55.6%의 확률로 supporter(지지자)와 관련한 문제가 나올 수 있다. 문맥에서 supporter의 의미를 추론하는 빈칸 문제나, opponent(반대자, 적), disrupter(방해가 되는 사람) 등의 반의어를 활용한 어휘 문제가 출제될 수 있다.

Q. 다음 글의 문맥상 괄호 안에 알맞은 단어를 고르시오.

Ethan was also Winston High's loudest (supporter / opponent). He always observed each play carefully from the sidelines. Although he wasn't the one making the actual plays on the field, Ethan's mind was always right there with his teammates.

정답 supporter

supporter는 '지지자, 옹호자'라는 뜻이고, opponent는 '반대자'라는 뜻이다. 다음 문장에서 'Ethan은 항상 사이드라인에서 플레이를 유심히 관찰하는, 경기장에서 실제 플레이를 하는 선수는 아니었을지라도, Ethan의 마음은 항상 같은 팀 선수들과 함께했다'고 했으므로, 가장 큰 '지지자, 옹호자'였다는 내용이 되어야 자연스럽다.

● also

문장7에서 22.2%로 두 번째로 출제 확률이 높은 것은 also로, 이 문장은 Ethan이 팀에서 하는 역할에 대해 추가적으로 덧붙이는 부분이다. 이러한 흐름을 보여주는 것이 also이다. also는 '또한, 게다가'의 의미로 글의 흐름에 단서가 되므로 위치를 잘 파악하고 있어야 한다. 이외에도, besides(게다가), moreover(더욱이), furthermore(게다가), in addition(게다가)으로 바뀌어 출제될 수 있다는 점도 유의하자.

Q. 다음 글의 빈칸에 들어갈 수 있는 말을 〈보기〉에서 모두 골라 쓰시오.

〈보기〉 Besides / Instead / However / Otherwise / For instance / Nevertheless / Therefore / Furthermore

Right before every game, Ethan would always be in the middle of the group offering motivational words. He had a special talent for calming people down and bringing out the best in them. ____________, Ethan was Winston High's loudest supporter. He always observed each play carefully from the sidelines.

____

정답
Besides, Furthermore
빈칸 뒤에는 앞 내용에 이어 Ethan이 팀에서 중요한 사람이 된 또 다른 방식이 추가적으로 제시되므로, 빈칸에는 '게다가'라는 의미의 'Besides, Furthermore'가 적절하다.

● 어휘 loudest

문장7이 출제된다면, 어휘 loudest에 대해 묻는 문제 역시 나올 확률이 22.2%이다. loudest는 supporter를 수식하는 형용사 loud의 최상급으로, '소리가 큰'의 의미보다는 문맥상 '가장 열정적인'의 뜻으로 해석하는 것이 자연스럽다. 따라서 enthusiastic(열렬한, 열광적인)으로 변형되어 출제될 수 있으니 의미를 잘 파악해두자.

Q. 다음 중, 문맥상 밑줄 친 ⓐ~ⓓ와 바꿔 쓸 수 없는 것은?

Over time, however, Ethan became ⓐ valuable to the team in different ways. His passion for the game was an ⓑ inspiration to all his teammates. Because Ethan motivated and encouraged them, they became his most passionate fans. Day in and day out, seeing Ethan's smile, positive attitude, and hard work ⓒ lifted everyone's spirits. Right before every game, Ethan would always be in the middle of the group offering motivational words. He had a special talent for calming people down and bringing out the best in them. Ethan was also Winston High's ⓓ loudest supporter.

① ⓐ: insignificant
② ⓑ: motivation
③ ⓒ: raised
④ ⓓ: most enthusiastic

정답 ①
valuable은 '가치 있는, 중요한'의 의미로 '하찮은'을 의미하는 insignificant가 아닌 significant(중요한)로 바꿔 쓸 수 있다.

출제 포인트 73.9% 정복!

문장8

문장 출제 확률: 1.3%

observe: 관찰하다 / 유심히, 신중하게 (부사)

He always observed each play carefully from the sidelines.

출제 포인트

1위	2위
어휘 observe	부사 carefully
문장 내 출제 확률 63.6%	문장 내 출제 확률 18.2%
본문[4] 문장편 내 출제 확률 2.8%	본문[4] 문장편 내 출제 확률 0.8%

● 어휘 observe

문장8이 출제될 가능성은 1.3%이다. 이 문장에서는 어휘 observe의 다양한 뜻을 묻거나, 문맥상 쓰인 의미를 묻는 문제로 나올 가능성이 63.6%로 가장 높다. observe는 '관찰하다', '준수하다', '(의식, 관습 등을) 지키다'라는 뜻을 가지고 있으며, 본문에서는 '관찰하다'의 뜻으로 사용되었다. 한편, observe와 철자가 비슷한 preserve(보존하다), reserve(예약하다), conserve(보존하다) 등과 구분하는 어휘 선택형 문제가 출제될 수 있으니 문제를 통해 미리 대비해두자.

Q. 다음 글의 (A), (B), (C)의 각 네모 안에서 문맥상 알맞은 말로 바르게 짝지어진 것은?

Day in and day out, seeing Ethan's smile, positive (A) [aptitude / attitude], and hard work lifted everyone's spirits. Right before every game, Ethan would always be in the middle of the group offering (B) [inspiring / discouraging] words. He had a special talent for calming people down and bringing out the best in them. Ethan was also Winston High's loudest supporter. He always (C) [observed / preserved] each play carefully from the sidelines. Although he wasn't the one making the actual plays on the field, Ethan's mind was always right there with his teammates.

	(A)	(B)	(C)
①	aptitude	inspiring	preserved
②	attitude	inspiring	observed
③	attitude	discouraging	observed
④	attitude	inspiring	preserved
⑤	aptitude	discouraging	preserved

정답 ②

(A) 문맥상 Ethan이 긍정적인 '태도(attitude)'를 지녔다는 내용이 자연스럽다.
aptitude: 적성

(B) 경기 직전에 Ethan이 '의욕을 높이는(inspiring)' 말을 했다는 내용이 자연스럽다.
discouraging: 낙담시키는

(C) Ethan이 경기에 참여하지 않고 사이드라인에서 풋볼 플레이를 '관찰했다(observed)'고 하는 것이 문맥상 자연스럽다.
preserve: 보존하다

● 부사 carefully

문장8이 시험에 출제된다면, 18.2%의 확률로 어휘 carefully에 대해서 물어볼 수 있다. carefully(유심히, 신중하게)의 영영풀이는 with close attention, paying attention to detail(세부사항에 집중하며 세심한 주의를 기울여)로 눈에 익혀두자. 한편, 단어의 형태를 묻는 문제도 나올 수 있는데, 동사 observed를 수식하기 때문에 형용사가 아니라 부사임을 확실하게 기억하자.

정답
He always observed each play carefully from the sidelines.
동사를 수식하는 것은 형용사가 아니라 부사이다. 따라서 형용사 careful을 부사 carefully로 고쳐야 옳다.

Q. 다음 문장에서 어법상 틀린 곳을 찾아 바른 문장으로 고쳐 쓰시오.

He always observed each play careful from the sidelines.

____

출제 포인트 74.7% 정복!

문장9

문장 출제 확률: 3.8% (총 851개의 출제 포인트 중 32회 출현, 45개 문장 중 7위)

접속사 Although: ~에도 불구하고 / 현재분사 – the one 수식

Although he wasn't the one making the actual plays on the field, Ethan's mind was always right there with his teammates.

빈도부사

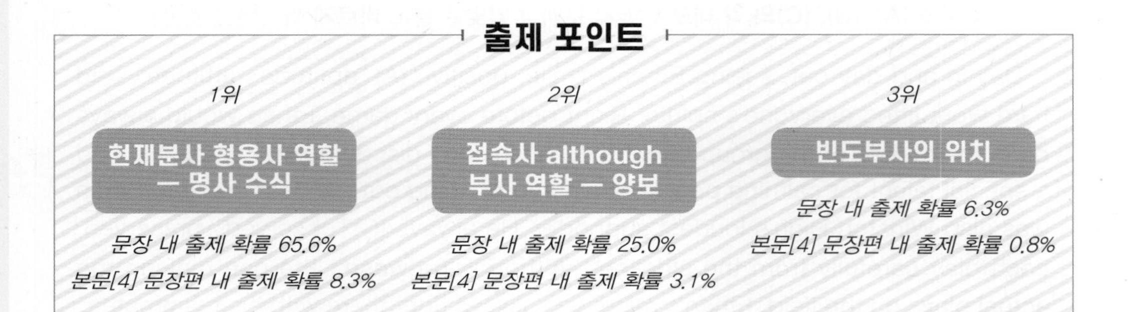

● 현재분사 형용사 역할 – 명사 수식

문장9가 1과에서 출제될 확률은 3.8%로, 전체 문장 중 7위에 해당하는 출제 가능성이 높은 문장에 해당한다. 그 중에서도 현재분사 making은 문장 내에서 출제될 확률이 65.6%이다. 본문[4]의 문장5와 문장6에서는 v-ing 형태가 각각 분사구문을 이끄는 부사 역할의 현재분사와 동명사로 쓰인 반면, 이 문장에서 making은 형용사 역할의 현재분사로, making the actual plays on the field가 앞에 나온 명사 the one을 수식하고 있다는 점을 반드시 기억하자. 현재분사(능동)인지 과거분사(수동)인지 구별하는 문제도 나올 수 있으니 형태를 잘 기억해두자.

정답 making
수식을 받는 명사와 분사의 관계가 능동이면 현재분사를, 수동이면 과거분사를 쓴다. make는 뒤에 목적어를 취하는 타동사로, 괄호 뒤에 the actual plays라는 목적어가 쓰였으므로, 괄호에는 능동의 현재분사 making이 와야 한다.

Q. 다음 문장의 괄호 안에서 어법상 알맞은 말을 고르시오.

Although he wasn't the one (making / made) the actual plays on the field, Ethan's mind was always right there with his teammates.

● 접속사 although 부사 역할 – 양보

문장9에서 두 번째로 출제 가능성이 높은 포인트는 25.0%의 출제 확률을 보이는 접속사 although이다. '~에도 불구하고'라는 양보의 의미를 갖는 접속사 although는 같은 의미인 though나 even though로 바뀌어 출제될 수 있으니 함께 알아두도록 하자. 이외에도, 의미는 같지만 전치사인 despite나 in spite of와 구별하는 문제로도 출제될 수 있으니, 각각의 접속사와 전치사를 잘 구별해서 기억해두자.

Q. 다음 문장의 괄호 안에서 어법상 알맞은 말을 고르시오.

(In spite of / Though) he wasn't the one making the actual plays on the field, Ethan's mind was always right there with his teammates.

정답 Though

in spite of와 though 둘 다 '~에도 불구하고'라는 뜻이지만, 전치사 in spite of 뒤에는 명사(구)가 오고, 접속사 though 뒤에는 '주어+동사'의 절이 온다. 여기서는 괄호 뒤에 'he wasn't ~'의 절이 오므로, 접속사 Though가 알맞다.

● 빈도부사의 위치

문장9가 출제된다면, 출제 가능성이 세 번째(6.3%)로 높은 포인트는 빈도부사의 위치이다. 빈도부사 always는 be동사 뒤나 조동사와 일반동사 사이에 위치한다는 점을 기억해두자. was always가 어법 문제 선지로 나오거나 문장의 어순 배열 및 영작 문제로 나올 수 있으니, 확실하게 외워두자.

Q. 밑줄 친 부분 중, 어법상 틀린 것은?

Over time, however, Ethan became valuable to the team in different ways. His passion for the game was an inspiration to all his teammates. ① Because Ethan motivated and encouraged them, they became his ② most passionate fans. Day in and day out, seeing Ethan's smile, positive attitude, and hard work lifted everyone's spirits. Right before every game, Ethan would always be in the middle of the group ③ offering motivational words. He had a special talent for calming people down and bringing out the best in them. Ethan was also Winston High's loudest supporter. He always observed each ④ play carefully from the sidelines. Although he wasn't the one making the actual plays on the field, Ethan's mind ⑤ always was right there with his teammates. Everyone could sense his love for football, and the coaches admired his commitment.

정답 ⑤

빈도부사는 be동사 뒤에 위치하므로, always was를 was always로 고쳐야 한다.

출제 포인트 77.6% 정복!

문장10

문장 출제 확률: 3.2%

Everyone could sense his love for football, and the coaches admired his commitment.

admire: 존경하다, 칭찬하다 헌신, 전념

출제 포인트

1위	2위
어휘 commitment	어휘 admire
문장 내 출제 확률 48.1%	문장 내 출제 확률 44.4%
본문[4] 문장편 내 출제 확률 5.1%	본문[4] 문장편 내 출제 확률 4.7%

● 어휘 commitment

본문[4]의 마지막 문장이 출제될 확률은 3.2%이다. 이 문장에서는 어휘 commitment가 출제될 가능성이 48.1%로 가장 높다. commitment(헌신, 전념)를 빈칸으로 하거나, 같은 뜻의 어휘 dedication(전념), devotion(전념)으로 바꾸어 적절성을 물어볼 수 있으니 문맥상 흐름과 의미를 파악해두자.

Q. 밑줄 친 부분과 바꿔 쓸 수 있는 단어를 〈보기〉에서 골라 쓰시오.

〈보기〉 difficulty / contentment / devotion / commission / reward

Everyone could sense his love for football, and the coaches admired his <u>commitment</u>.

____

정답 devotion

commitment는 '전념, 헌신'이라는 뜻으로, devotion(헌신)과 바꿔 쓸 수 있다.
difficulty: 어려움, 한계
contentment: 만족
commission: 수수료
reward: 보상

● 어휘 admire

문장10에서 출제 확률 2위(44.4%)를 차지한 포인트는 어휘 admire이다. admire는 '존경하다, 칭찬하다'라는 뜻으로, applaud(칭찬하다, 박수를 보내다), respect(존경하다, 존중하다) 등으로 바꿔 쓸 수 있다. 반의어로는 ignore(무시하다), overlook(간과하다, 못 본 체하다), neglect(경시하다) 등이 있다. admire 자리에 유의어 또는 반의어가 주어지고, 해당 어휘가 문맥상 적절한지를 묻는 문제가 주로 출제된다. 또한, 동사의 형태를 묻는 어법 문제로도 나올 수 있으니, 아래 문제를 통해 확인하자.

Q. 다음 글의 괄호에 문맥상 적절한 단어를 고르시오.

Although he wasn't the one making the actual plays on the field, Ethan's mind was always right there with his teammates. Everyone could sense his love for football, and the coaches (admired / neglected) his commitment.

정답 admired

모두가 그의 풋볼 사랑을 느꼈다는 앞 내용에 자연스럽게 이어지려면, 감독들이 Ethan의 헌신을 '존경하고 칭찬했다'는 내용이 되어야 한다. 따라서 '존경하다, 칭찬하다'라는 의미인 admire가 적절하다.
neglect: 무시하다, 경시하다

Q. 다음 문장에서 어법상 <u>틀린</u> 곳을 찾아 바르게 고쳐 쓰시오.

Everyone could sense his love for football, and the coaches admiring his commitment.

______________ → ______________

정답
admiring → admired

등위접속사 and로 두 개의 절이 연결된 형태로, 두 번째 절의 주어 the coaches에 이어지는 본동사가 필요하다. 앞 절의 시제에 맞춰 과거 시제 admired가 되어야 한다.

출제 포인트 80.1% 정복!

01

다음 글의 (A), (B), (C)의 각 네모 안에서 문맥에 맞는 낱말로 가장 적절한 것은?

Over time, however, Ethan became (A) [invaluable / valueless] to the team in different ways. His passion for the game was an (B) [imagination / inspiration] to all his teammates. Because Ethan motivated and encouraged them, they became his most passionate fans. Day in and day out, seeing Ethan's smile, positive attitude, and hard work lifted everyone's spirits. Right before every game, Ethan would always be in the middle of the group offering (C) [motivational / motional] words.

	(A)	(B)	(C)
①	invaluable	imagination	motional
②	valueless	imagination	motional
③	invaluable	imagination	motivational
④	valueless	inspiration	motional
⑤	invaluable	inspiration	motivational

02

다음 글의 밑줄 친 different ways에 해당하지 않는 것은?

Over time, however, Ethan became valuable to the team in <u>different ways</u>. His passion for the game was an inspiration to all his teammates. Because Ethan motivated and encouraged them, they became his most passionate fans. Day in and day out, seeing Ethan's smile, positive attitude, and hard work lifted everyone's spirits. Right before every game, Ethan would always be in the middle of the group offering motivational words. He had a special talent for calming people down and bringing out the best in them. Ethan was also Winston High's loudest supporter. He always observed each play carefully from the sidelines. Although he wasn't the one making the actual plays on the field, Ethan's mind was always right there with his teammates. Everyone could sense his love for football, and the coaches admired his commitment.

① 그의 팀 선수들에게 동기 부여하고 격려하기
② 긍정적인 태도와 노력으로 모두의 기운 북돋우기
③ 사람들을 침착하게 하고, 그들의 최고의 능력 끌어내기
④ 다른 선수의 헌신에 대해 높이 칭찬하기
⑤ 사이드라인에서 매 경기를 유심히 관찰하기

03

다음 글의 빈칸에 들어갈 말로 적절하지 않은 것을 모두 고르시오.

Regardless of his physical difficulties, Ethan worked just as hard as every other player on the team. Although he knew he would never be a valuable player in any of the team's games, he poured his heart and soul into practice every day.
______________, over time, Ethan became valuable to the team in different ways. His passion for the game was an inspiration to all his teammates. Because Ethan motivated and encouraged them, they became his most passionate fans. Day in and day out, seeing Ethan's smile, positive attitude, and hard work lifted everyone's spirits. Right before every game, Ethan would always be in the middle of the group offering motivational words. He had a special talent for calming people down and bringing out the best in them.

① Still ② Above all
③ However ④ Instead
⑤ Furthermore

04

다음 글의 (A), (B), (C)의 각 네모 안에서 어법상 맞는 표현으로 가장 적절한 것은?

Over time, however, Ethan became valuable to the team in different ways. His passion for the games (A) [was / were] an inspiration to all his teammates. Because Ethan motivated and encouraged them, they became his most passionate fans. Day in and day out, (B) [seeing / seen] Ethan's smile, positive attitude, and hard work lifted everyone's spirits. Right before every game, Ethan would always be in the middle of the group offering motivational words. He had a special talent for calming people down and (C) [bring / bringing] out the best in them. Ethan was also Winston High's loudest supporter. He always observed each play carefully from the sidelines.

	(A)		(B)		(C)
①	were	–	seen	–	bring
②	was	–	seen	–	bringing
③	were	–	seeing	–	bring
④	was	–	seeing	–	bringing
⑤	was	–	seeing	–	bring

05

다음 글의 빈칸에 들어가기에 가장 적절한 것은?

Over time, however, Ethan became valuable to the team in different ways. His passion for the game was an ______________ to all his teammates. Because Ethan motivated and encouraged them, they became his most passionate fans. Day in and day out, seeing Ethan's smile, positive attitude, and hard work lifted everyone's spirits. Right before every game, Ethan would always be in the middle of the group offering motivational words. He had a special talent for calming people down and bringing out the best in them. Ethan was also Winston High's loudest supporter. He always observed each play carefully from the sidelines. Although he wasn't the one making the actual plays on the field, Ethan's mind was always right there with his teammates.

① interruption ② imagination
③ independence ④ obstacle
⑤ inspiration

06

다음 글의 밑줄 친 우리말과 일치하도록 〈보기〉에 주어진 말을 알맞게 배열하시오. (단, 필요시 단어 변형 가능)

〈보기〉 everyone's spirits / and / positive / lift / see / Ethan's smile / attitude / hard work

Over time, however, Ethan became valuable to the team in different ways. His passion for the game was an inspiration to all his teammates. Because Ethan motivated and encouraged them, they became his most passionate fans. Day in and day out, <u>Ethan의 미소와 긍정적인 태도, 노력을 보는 것은 모두의 기운을 북돋웠다</u>. Right before every game, Ethan would always be in the middle of the group offering motivational words.

____

____

07

다음 글의 밑줄 친 부분 중, 어색한 것은?

Regardless of his physical difficulties, Ethan worked just ① <u>as hard as</u> every other player on the team. Although he knew he ② <u>would never be</u> a valuable player in any of the team's games, he poured his heart and soul into practice every day.

Over time, however, Ethan became valuable to the team in different ways. His passion for the game was an inspiration to all his teammates. ③ <u>Because of</u> Ethan motivated and encouraged them, they became his most passionate fans. ④ <u>Day in and day out</u>, seeing Ethan's smile, positive attitude, and hard work lifted everyone's spirits. Right before every game, Ethan would always be ⑤ <u>in the middle of the group</u> offering motivational words.

08

다음 중, 밑줄 친 ⓐ~ⓔ와 바꿔 쓸 수 있는 말로 적절하지 않은 것은?

Over time, however, Ethan became valuable to the team in ⓐ different ways. His ⓑ passion for the game was an inspiration to all his teammates. Because Ethan motivated and ⓒ encouraged them, they became his most passionate fans. Day in and day out, seeing Ethan's smile, positive attitude, and hard work ⓓ lifted everyone's spirits. Right before every game, Ethan would always be in the middle of the group offering ⓔ motivational words.

① ⓐ: other
② ⓑ: enthusiasm
③ ⓒ: obstructed
④ ⓓ: boosted
⑤ ⓔ: inspiring

09

다음 글의 밑줄 친 offering과 쓰임이 같은 것은?

Because Ethan motivated and encouraged them, they became his most passionate fans. Day in and day out, seeing Ethan's smile, positive attitude, and hard work lifted everyone's spirits. Right before every game, Ethan would always be in the middle of the group offering motivational words. He had a special talent for calming people down and bringing out the best in them. Ethan was also Winston High's loudest supporter. He always observed each play carefully from the sidelines.

① Ethan's touchdown will be worth remembering with glory.
② There is something better than being the best.
③ Lifting up those around us is also of great worth.
④ Getting closer to the end zone, he saw Ethan behind him.
⑤ Instead of running, the player passed the ball to him.

10

다음 글의 (A), (B), (C)의 각 네모 안에 들어갈 말로 바르게 짝지어진 것은?

Over time, however, Ethan became (A) [valuable / valuably] to the team in different ways. His passion for the game was an inspiration to all his teammates. Because Ethan motivated and (B) [encourage / encouraged] them, they became his most passionate fans. Day in and day out, seeing Ethan's smile, positive attitude, and hard work (C) [lifted / lifting] everyone's spirits.

	(A)	(B)	(C)
①	valuable	– encourage	– lifted
②	valuably	– encouraged	– lifted
③	valuable	– encouraged	– lifting
④	valuably	– encourage	– lifting
⑤	valuable	– encouraged	– lifted

11

다음 빈칸에 들어갈 수 없는 말을 모두 고르시오.

Over time, however, Ethan became valuable to the team in different ways. His passion for the game was an inspiration to all his teammates. Because Ethan motivated and encouraged them, they became his most passionate fans. Day in and day out, seeing Ethan's smile, positive attitude, and hard work lifted everyone's spirits. Right before every game, Ethan would always be in the middle of the group offering motivational words. He had a special talent for calming people down and bringing out the best in them. Ethan was also Winston High's loudest supporter. He always observed each play carefully from the sidelines. ____________ he wasn't the one making the actual plays on the field, Ethan's mind was always right there with his teammates. Everyone could sense his love for football, and the coaches admired his commitment.

① Despite ② Though
③ As if ④ Even if
⑤ Although

12

다음 글의 밑줄 친 observed와 같은 뜻으로 쓰인 것은?

Ethan was also Winston High's loudest supporter. He always observed each play carefully from the sidelines. Although he wasn't the one making the actual plays on the field, Ethan's mind was always right there with his teammates. Everyone could sense his love for football, and the coaches admired his commitment.

① Telescopes help us observe space in more detail.
② Most English people observe Christmas on December 25.
③ They observed 1 minute of silence in memory of the victims.
④ You'd better observe the rules unless you want to be expelled.
⑤ Observing your duty is as important as claiming your right.

13

다음 빈칸에 들어갈 말로 적절한 것을 모두 고르시오.

Although he knew he would never be a valuable player in any of the team's games, he poured his heart and soul into practice every day. Over time, however, Ethan became valuable to the team in different ways. His passion for the game was an inspiration to all his teammates. Because Ethan motivated and encouraged them, they became his most passionate fans. ____________, seeing Ethan's smile, positive attitude, and hard work lifted everyone's spirits. Right Before every game, Ethan would always be in the middle of the group offering motivational words.

① Day by day ② In the first place
③ In spite of this ④ At the moment
⑤ Day in and day out

14

다음 빈칸에 들어갈 말로 가장 적절한 것은?

Regardless of his physical difficulties, Ethan worked just as hard as every other player on the team. Although he knew he would never be a valuable player in any of the team's games, he poured his heart and soul into practice every day.

Over time, however, Ethan became valuable to the team in different ways. His passion for the game was an inspiration to all his teammates. Because Ethan motivated and encouraged them, they became his most passionate fans. Day in and day out, seeing Ethan's smile, ____________________, and hard work lifted everyone's spirits. Right before every game, Ethan would always be in the middle of the group offering motivational words. He had a special talent for calming people down and bringing out the best in them.

① arrogant attitude ② positive mindset
③ passive personality ④ indifferent standpoint
⑤ physical performance

15

다음 글의 (A), (B), (C)의 각 네모 안에서 문맥에 맞는 낱말로 가장 적절한 것은?

Regardless of his physical difficulties, Ethan worked just as hard as every other player on the team. Although he knew he would never be a valuable player in any of the team's games, he (A) [pulled / poured] his heart and soul into practice every day.

Over time, however, Ethan became (B) [priceless / worthless] to the team in different ways. His passion for the game was an inspiration to all his teammates. Because Ethan motivated and encouraged them, they became his most passionate fans. Day in and day out, seeing Ethan's smile, (C) [negative / positive] attitude, and hard work lifted everyone's spirits.

	(A)	(B)	(C)
①	pulled	– priceless	– negative
②	poured	– worthless	– positive
③	pulled	– worthless	– negative
④	poured	– priceless	– positive
⑤	pulled	– priceless	– positive

16

다음 글의 밑줄 친 부분 중, 문맥상 낱말의 쓰임이 적절하지 않은 것은?

Over time, however, Ethan became valuable to the team in different ways. His passion for the game was an inspiration to all his teammates. Because Ethan motivated and ① encouraged them, they became his most passionate fans. Day in and day out, seeing Ethan's smile, positive attitude, and hard work ② lifted everyone's spirits. Right before every game, Ethan would always be in the middle of the group offering ③ discouraging words. He had a special talent for ④ calming people down and bringing out the ⑤ best in them. Ethan was also Winston High's loudest supporter.

17

다음 글의 밑줄 친 우리말과 같은 뜻이 되도록 〈보기〉의 말을 알맞게 배열하시오. (단, 필요시 단어를 변형할 것)

Over time, however, Ethan became valuable to the team in different ways. His passion for the game was an inspiration to all his teammates. Because Ethan motivated and encouraged them, they became his most passionate fans. Day in and day out, seeing Ethan's smile, positive attitude, and hard work lifted everyone's spirits. Right before every game, Ethan would always be in the middle of the group offering motivational words. He had a special talent for calming people down and bringing out the best in them. Ethan was also Winston High's loudest supporter. He always observed each play carefully from the sidelines. 비록 그가 경기장에서 실제 경기를 뛰는 선수는 아니었을지라도, Ethan's mind was always right there with his teammates.

〈보기〉 be / he / the field / make / the one / the actual plays / on / not / though

____

____

18

다음 글의 (A), (B), (C)의 각 네모 안에서 어법상 맞는 표현으로 가장 적절한 것은?

Day in and day out, (A) [see / to see] Ethan's smile, positive attitude, and hard work lifted everyone's spirits. Right before every game, Ethan would always be in the middle of the group (B) [offer / offering] motivational words. He had a special talent for calming people down and (C) [bringing / to bring] out the best in them. Ethan was also Winston High's loudest supporter. He always observed each play carefully from the sidelines. Although he wasn't the one making the actual plays on the field, Ethan's mind was always right there with his teammates.

	(A)		(B)		(C)
①	see	–	offer	–	bringing
②	see	–	offering	–	to bring
③	to see	–	offer	–	bringing
④	to see	–	offering	–	bringing
⑤	to see	–	offering	–	to bring

19

다음 빈칸에 들어갈 말로 가장 적절한 것은?

Over time, however, Ethan became valuable to the team in different ways. His passion for the game was an inspiration to all his teammates. Because Ethan motivated and encouraged them, they became his most passionate fans. Day in and day out, seeing Ethan's smile, positive attitude, and hard work lifted everyone's spirits. Right before every game, Ethan would always be in the middle of the group offering motivational words. ______________, he had a special talent for calming people down and bringing out the best in them. Ethan was also Winston High's loudest supporter. He always observed each play carefully from the sidelines. Although he wasn't the one making the actual plays on the field, Ethan's mind was always right there with his teammates. Everyone could sense his love for football, and the coaches admired his commitment.

① Thus
② However
③ Moreover
④ For instance
⑤ Nevertheless

20

다음 중, 밑줄 친 motivational과 바꿔 쓸 수 있는 것을 모두 고르시오.

Over time, however, Ethan became valuable to the team in different ways. His passion for the game was an inspiration to all his teammates. Because Ethan motivated and encouraged them, they became his most passionate fans. Day in and day out, seeing Ethan's smile, positive attitude, and hard work lifted everyone's spirits. Right before every game, Ethan would always be in the middle of the group offering motivational words. He had a special talent for calming people down and bringing out the best in them.

① uplifting ② inspiring
③ hurtful ④ discouraging
⑤ sarcastic

21

다음 글의 밑줄 친 부분 중, 어법상 틀린 것은?

Over time, however, Ethan became ① valuable to the team in different ways. His passion for the game was an inspiration to all his teammates. Because Ethan motivated and encouraged them, they became his most passionate fans. Day in and day out, ② seeing Ethan's smile, positive attitude, and hard work lifted everyone's spirits. Right before every game, Ethan would always be in the middle of the group offering motivational words. He had a special talent for calming people down and bringing out the best in ③ them. Ethan was also Winston High's loudest supporter. He always observed each play carefully from the sidelines. Although he wasn't ④ the one making the actual plays on the field, Ethan's mind was always right there with his teammates. Everyone could sense his love for football, and the coaches ⑤ were admired his commitment.

22

다음 빈칸에 들어갈 말로 가장 적절한 것은?

Over time, Ethan became valuable to the team in different ways. His passion for the game was an inspiration to all his teammates. Because Ethan motivated and encouraged them, they became his most passionate fans. Day in and day out, seeing Ethan's smile, positive attitude, and hard work lifted everyone's spirits. Right before every game, Ethan would always be in the middle of the group offering motivational words. He had a special talent for calming people down and bringing out the best in them. Ethan was also Winston High's loudest ____________. He always observed each play carefully from the sidelines. Although he wasn't the one making the actual plays on the field, Ethan's mind was always right there with his teammates. Everyone could sense his love for football, and the coaches admired his commitment.

① opponent ② supporter ③ classmate
④ leader ⑤ disrupter

23

다음 글의 밑줄 친 부분 중, 문맥상 낱말의 쓰임이 적절하지 않은 것은?

Over time, however, Ethan became valuable to the team in different ways. His ① passion for the game was an inspiration to all his teammates. Because Ethan motivated and encouraged them, they became his most ② enthusiastic fans. Day in and day out, seeing Ethan's smile, positive attitude, and hard work lifted everyone's spirits. Right before every game, Ethan would always be in the middle of the group offering motivational words. He had a special talent for ③ offending people and bringing out the best in them. Ethan was also Winston High's loudest ④ supporter. He always observed each play carefully from the sidelines. Although he wasn't the one making the actual plays on the field, Ethan's mind was always right there with his teammates. Everyone could sense his love for football, and the coaches admired his ⑤ dedication.

24

다음 글의 밑줄 친 making과 쓰임이 같은 것은?

Day in and day out, seeing Ethan's smile, positive attitude, and hard work lifted everyone's spirits. Right before every game, Ethan would always be in the middle of the group offering motivational words. He had a special talent for calming people down and bringing out the best in them. Ethan was also Winston High's loudest supporter. He always observed each play carefully from the sidelines. Although he wasn't the one making the actual plays on the field, Ethan's mind was always right there with his teammates. Everyone could sense his love for football, and the coaches admired his commitment.

① He spends his weekends fishing at the lake.
② She enjoys watching movies in her free time.
③ She is good at expressing herself through dance.
④ The dog chasing after the squirrel is my dog.
⑤ They were excited about going to the concert later that evening.

25

다음 글의 밑줄 친 부분 중, 문맥상 낱말의 쓰임이 적절하지 않은 것은?

Although he knew he would never be a ① valuable player in any of the team's games, he poured his heart and soul into practice every day. Over time, however, Ethan became valuable to the team in ② different ways. His passion for the game was an inspiration to all his teammates. Because Ethan motivated and encouraged them, they became his most passionate fans. Day in and day out, seeing Ethan's smile, positive attitude, and hard work lifted everyone's spirits. Right before every game, Ethan would always be in the middle of the group offering motivational words. He had a special talent for ③ calming people down and bringing out the best in them. Ethan was also Winston High's loudest supporter. He always ④ observed each play carefully from the sidelines. Although he wasn't the one making the actual plays on the field, Ethan's mind was always right there with his teammates. Everyone could sense his love for football, and the coaches ⑤ overlooked his commitment.

26

다음 글의 밑줄 친 (a)~(e) 중, 어법상 적절하지 않은 것을 찾아 바르게 고치시오.

Day in and day out, (a) seeing Ethan's smile, positive attitude, and hard work lifted everyone's spirits. Right before every (b) games, Ethan would always be in the middle of the group (c) offering motivational words. He had a special talent for calming people down and (d) brings out the best in them. Ethan was also Winston High's (e) loudest supporter.

(　　) ____________ → ____________
(　　) ____________ → ____________

27

다음 중, 밑줄 친 ⓐ~ⓔ의 어법 설명으로 적절하지 않은 것은?

Over time, ⓐ however, Ethan became valuable to the team in different ways. His passion for the game ⓑ was an inspiration to all his teammates. Because Ethan motivated and encouraged them, they became his most passionate fans. Day in and day out, ⓒ seeing Ethan's smile, positive attitude, and hard work lifted everyone's spirits. Right before ⓓ every game, Ethan ⓔ would always be in the middle of the group offering motivational words.

① ⓐ: 역접의 의미를 가진 부사
② ⓑ: 3인칭 단수 과거형
③ ⓒ: 결과를 나타내는 분사구문
④ ⓓ: every+단수명사
⑤ ⓔ: 과거의 습관을 나타내는 조동사

28

다음 밑줄 친 부분 중, 쓰임이 나머지 넷과 다른 것은?

Day in and day out, ① seeing Ethan's smile, positive attitude, and hard work lifted everyone's spirits. Right before every game, Ethan would always be in the middle of the group offering motivational words. He had a special talent for calming people down and ② bringing out the best in them. Ethan was also Winston High's loudest supporter. He always observed each play carefully from the sidelines. Although he wasn't the one ③ making the actual plays on the field, Ethan's mind was always right there with his teammates. Everyone could sense his love for football, and the coaches admired his commitment.

For the past three years, Ethan has been schooling us all in the game of life. He always reminds us that everyone is important to a team's success, though their role on the team may be small. Instead of putting all his efforts into ④ trying to be the team's best player, he has done everything he can to make the team better. As Ethan has shown us, lifting up those around us is also of great worth. When we help others shine, their light will shine on us in return. Yes, sometimes there is something better than ⑤ being the best.

29

다음 글의 밑줄 친 부분을 분사구문을 활용하여 바꿔 쓰시오. (단, 3단어로 쓰시오.)

Over time, however, Ethan became valuable to the team in different ways. His passion for the game was an inspiration to all his teammates. Because Ethan motivated and encouraged them, they became his most passionate fans. Day in and day out, seeing Ethan's smile, positive attitude, and hard work lifted everyone's spirits. Right before every game, Ethan would always be in the middle of the group as he would offer motivational words.

____

30

다음 글의 밑줄 친 우리말과 같은 뜻이 되도록 〈보기〉에 주어진 말을 알맞게 배열하시오.

Over time, however, Ethan became valuable to the team in different ways. His passion for the game was an inspiration to all his teammates. Because Ethan motivated and encouraged them, they became his most passionate fans. Day in and day out, seeing Ethan's smile, positive attitude, and hard work lifted everyone's spirits. Right before every game, Ethan would always be in the middle of the group offering motivational words. He had a special talent for calming people down and bringing out the best in them. Ethan was also Winston High's loudest supporter. He always observed each play carefully from the sidelines. Although he wasn't the one making the actual plays on the field, Ethan의 마음은 항상 바로 그곳에서 같은 팀 선수들과 함께했다.

〈보기〉 teammates / his / there / with / right / was / Ethan's mind / always

____

____

본문[4]

출제 포인트

1위	공동 2위	공동 2위
내용 일치	**글의 순서**	**대의 파악**
본문[4] 문단편 내 출제 확률 58.3%	본문[4] 문단편 내 출제 확률 11.1%	본문[4] 문단편 내 출제 확률 11.1%

● 내용 일치

이 문단에서는 내용 일치 유형이 58.3%로 가장 많이 출제되었으며, 문장별 내용 일치 출제 비율은 아래와 같다. 'Ethan이 부정적인 태도를 지녔다', '실제로 경기를 뛰는 선수였다', 'Ethan의 역할이 팀의 동기 부여자가 아닌 전략가였다' 등으로 내용과 다른 문장이 문제로 출제될 수 있다. 아래 문장 빈출도를 확인하고, 선지로 출제될 수 있는 여러 문장을 살펴보자.

1	Over time, however, Ethan became valuable to the team in different ways.	3.8%
2	His passion for the game was an inspiration to all his teammates.	5.8%
3	Because Ethan motivated and encouraged them, they became his most passionate fans.	11.5%
4	Day in and day out, seeing Ethan's smile, positive attitude, and hard work lifted everyone's spirits.	23.1%
5	Right before every game, Ethan would always be in the middle of the group offering motivational words.	7.7%
6	He had a special talent for calming people down and bringing out the best in them.	11.5%
7	Ethan was also Winston High's loudest supporter.	1.9%
8	He always observed each play carefully from the sidelines.	13.5%
9	Although he wasn't the one making the actual plays on the field, Ethan's mind was always right there with his teammates.	9.6%
10	Everyone could sense his love for football, and the coaches admired his commitment.	11.5%

Q. 글의 내용과 일치하면 T, 일치하지 않으면 F에 표시하시오.

(1) Ethan은 경기를 직접 뛰는 대신에 유용한 전략들을 팀원들에게 공유했다. (T / F)
(2) 감독은 언제나 Ethan의 경기를 유심히 관찰하여 조언해 주었다. (T / F)
(3) Ethan의 경기 실적은 팀원들을 실망시켰다. (T / F)
(4) 팀원으로서 Ethan의 특기는 다른 사람들을 진정시키는 것이었다. (T / F)
(5) 모두가 팀에 대한 감독의 헌신과 열정을 칭찬했다. (T / F)
(6) Ethan은 언제나 열심히 경기를 뛰며 팀의 성공에 기여했다. (T / F)
(7) Ethan은 매일 연습 전후로 팀원들의 사기를 높이는 연설을 했다. (T / F)
(8) Ethan의 열정은 팀원들에게 동기를 부여했다. (T / F)
(9) Ethan은 남들과 같은 방식으로 팀에 중요한 선수가 되었다. (T / F)
(10) Ethan은 윈스턴 고등학교의 가장 열렬한 지지자였다. (T / F)

정답

1	F	2	F	3	F
4	T	5	F	6	F
7	F	8	T	9	F
10	T	11	F	12	F
13	F	14	T	15	F
16	F	17	F	18	F
19	T	20	F		

(11) Ethan의 부정적인 태도는 그의 팀원들과 감독들을 좌절시켰다.
(12) 감독은 사이드라인에서 Ethan의 플레이를 유심히 관찰했다.
(13) Ethan은 그의 팀원들이 한 실수들을 지적했다.
(14) Ethan 덕분에, 팀원들은 진정하고 최선을 다할 수 있었다.
(15) 감독은 Ethan의 경기장에서의 플레이에 대해 존경[감탄]을 보여주었다.
(16) Ethan은 그가 경기장에서 플레이를 할 때마다 최선을 다했다.

(17) Ethan은 매 게임 이후에 팀원들에게 동기 부여의 말을 해주곤 했다.
(18) Ethan은 풋볼 감독으로서 대단한 열정을 가지고 있었다.
(19) 결국, Ethan은 팀에서 가치 있게 여겨졌다.
(20) Ethan은 윈스턴 고등학교 풋볼 팀의 상대[적수]를 지지했다.

(11) Ethan's negative attitude discouraged his teammates and coaches. (T / F)
(12) The coaches carefully observed Ethan's play from the sidelines. (T / F)
(13) Ethan pointed out the mistakes his teammates made. (T / F)
(14) Thanks to Ethan, the teammates could calm down and do their best. (T / F)
(15) The coach showed his admiration for Ethan's play on the field. (T / F)
(16) Ethan did his best every time he was playing on the field. (T / F)
(17) Ethan would give inspiring words to his teammates after every game. (T / F)
(18) Ethan had a great passion as a football coach. (T / F)
(19) In the end, Ethan was considered valuable to the team. (T / F)
(20) Ethan supported the opponent of the Winston High school football team. (T / F)

정답 (B) - (A) - (C) - (D)
주어진 문장은 Ethan 스스로가 자신이 팀의 경기에서 가치 있는 선수가 될 수 없음을 알고 있었다는 내용이므로, Ethan이 '다른 방식으로(in different ways)' 팀에서 '가치 있게(valuable)' 되었다는 내용의 (B)와 역접의 연결어 however(그러나)과 함께 이어지는 게 자연스럽다. 그다음에, (B)에서 언급된 '다른 방식'을 구체적으로 서술한 (A)가 오고, 'also(또한)'와 함께 Ethan이 가치 있게 된 또 다른 방식을 덧붙이는 (C)가 이어진다. 마지막으로, 이러한 Ethan의 이야기를 통한 교훈을 도출하는 (D)가 이어지는 것이 자연스럽다.

● 글의 순서

이 문단에서는 글의 순서 문제가 11.1%로 대의 파악 문제와 함께 두 번째로 많이 출제되었다. 문장1의 however(그러나)과 문장7의 also(또한)를 근거로 순서 문제가 출제될 수 있다. however를 근거로 본문[3]과 [4]의 순서를 판단하는 문제는 자주 출제되었다. 단, 명확한 순서 배열 근거가 없이 단순 나열인 부분에서도 순서 배열 문제가 출제된 경우가 있기 때문에, 전체적인 글의 내용과 흐름을 파악해 둘 필요가 있다.

Q. 주어진 문장 다음에 이어질 내용을 순서대로 배열하시오.

Ethan knew he would never be a valuable player in any of the team's games.

(A) His passion for the game was an inspiration to all his teammates.
(B) Over time, however, Ethan became valuable to the team in different ways.
(C) Ethan was also Winston High's loudest supporter, always observing each play carefully from the sidelines.
(D) As Ethan has shown us, lifting up those around us is also of great worth.

________ – ________ – ________ – ________

정답 ②
Ethan이 실제 경기를 뛰는 선수가 아니었음에도 불구하고 팀에서 중요한 선수일 수 있었던 방식들을 기술한 글로, 글의 제목으로 가장 적절한 것은 ② '무엇이 Ethan으로 하여금 경기장에서 경기를 뛰지 않고도 가치 있게 만들었는가'이다.

● 대의 파악

이 문단에서는 대의 파악 유형이 11.1%로, 글의 순서 유형과 함께 두 번째로 많이 출제되었다. 'Ethan이 팀의 자극제이자 동기 부여자로서 팀에서 중요한 선수로 자리매김했다'는 핵심 내용이 제목, 요지, 주제, 교훈, 속담 등을 묻는 문제로 출제될 수 있다.

Q. 다음 글의 제목으로 가장 적절한 것은?

Over time, however, Ethan became valuable to the team in different ways. His passion for the game was an inspiration to all his teammates. Because Ethan motivated and encouraged them, they became his most passionate fans. Day in and day out, seeing Ethan's smile, positive attitude, and hard work lifted everyone's spirits. Right before every game, Ethan would always be in the middle of the group offering motivational words. He had a special talent for calming people down and bringing out the best in them. Ethan was also Winston High's loudest supporter. He always observed each play carefully from the sidelines.

Although he wasn't the one making the actual plays on the field, Ethan's mind was always right there with his teammates. Everyone could sense his love for football, and the coaches admired his commitment.

① The Advantages of Having an Inspiring Teacher
② What Made Ethan Valuable Without Playing the Game on the Field
③ The Influence of Encouragement on Performance of Football Players
④ How Ethan Overcame His Physical Difficulties To Be a Football Team Coach
⑤ A Natural Athlete Ethan Entering the Football Team of Winston High School

① 영감을 주는 선생님이 있는 것의 이점
③ 격려가 풋볼 선수들의 경기력에 미치는 영향
④ Ethan이 풋볼팀 코치가 되기 위해 신체적 어려움을 극복한 방법
⑤ 윈스턴 고등학교 풋볼팀에 들어간 타고난 운동선수 Ethan

무관한 문장

이 문단에서는 8.3%의 확률로 무관한 문장 유형이 출제되었다. 풋볼팀의 팀원으로서 Ethan이 중요해질 수 있었던 이유와 무관한 내용의 문장이 삽입되어 출제될 수 있으며, 원문에서 몇 개의 단어만 바꾸어 흐름과 맞지 않는 문장으로 출제될 수도 있다.

Q. 다음 글에서 전체 흐름과 관계가 없는 문장은?

Over time, Ethan became valuable to the team in different ways. His passion for the game was an inspiration to all his teammates. ① Because Ethan motivated and encouraged them, they became his most passionate fans. Day in and day out, seeing Ethan's smile, positive attitude, and hard work lifted everyone's spirits. ② Right before every game, Ethan would always be in the middle of the group offering motivational words. ③ He had a special talent for calming people down and bringing out the best in them. ④ Ethan was also careful enough not to show his frustration about his school life. ⑤ Although he wasn't the one making the actual plays on the field, Ethan's mind was always right there with his teammates. Everyone could sense his love for football, and the coaches admired his commitment.

정답 ④

Ethan이 어떻게 다른 방식으로 (풋볼) 팀에서 중요한 사람이 되었는지에 관한 글이다. Ethan이 자신의 학교 생활에 대한 좌절감을 보이지 않을 만큼 신중했다는 ④의 내용은 Ethan을 풋볼 팀의 팀원으로서 가치 있게 하는 특성으로 보기 어려우며, Ethan이 학교 생활에 좌절감을 가지고 있다는 부분은 늘 미소를 띠고 긍정적인 태도로 열심히 연습에 임했다는 Ethan에 대한 전반적인 설명과 상충된다. 따라서 정답은 ④이다.

요약

이 문단에서는 8.3%의 확률로 요약 유형이 출제되었다. 본문[4]는 신체적 한계로 실제 경기를 뛸 수 없었던 Ethan이 어떤 다른 방식들로 팀에서 중요한 선수가 되었는지를 설명하고 있으므로, 풋볼에 대한 Ethan의 열정, 팀원들에 대한 Ethan의 동기 부여, 팀에 대한 Ethan의 열렬한 지지와 헌신 등이 요약문 빈칸으로 출제될 수 있다.

Q. 다음 글의 내용을 한 문장으로 요약하고자 한다. 빈칸 (A), (B)에 들어갈 말로 가장 적절한 것은?

Over time, Ethan became valuable to the team in different ways. His passion for the game was an inspiration to all his teammates. Because Ethan motivated and encouraged them, they became his most passionate fans. Day in and day out, seeing Ethan's smile, positive attitude, and hard work lifted everyone's spirits.

Right before every game, Ethan would always be in the middle of the group offering motivational words. He had a special talent for calming people down and bringing out the best in them. Ethan was also Winston High's loudest supporter. He always observed each play carefully from the sidelines. Although he wasn't the one making the actual plays on the field, Ethan's mind was always right there with his teammates. Everyone could sense his love for football, and the coaches admired his commitment.

Although Ethan couldn't make the actual plays on the field, he became a valuable member by ______(A)______ others with his love for football and being an enthusiastic ______(B)______ of the team.

	(A)		(B)
①	defeating	–	fan
②	motivating	–	disrupter
③	changing	–	coach
④	persuading	–	follower
⑤	inspiring	–	supporter

정답 ⑤

Ethan이 어떻게 팀에서 중요한 선수가 되었는지에 관한 글로, Ethan이 긍정적인 태도와 열정으로 팀원들의 의욕을 높였으며, 팀의 가장 열렬한 지지자였다고 설명하고 있다. 따라서 (A)에는 inspiring, (B)에는 supporter가 적절하다.

Ethan은 경기장에서 실제 경기를 하지는 못했지만, 풋볼을 향한 그의 사랑으로 다른 사람들을 (A)고무시키고 팀의 열정적인 (B)지지자가 됨으로써 중요한 일원이 되었다.

① 좌절시킴 – 팬
② 동기를 부여함 – 방해꾼
③ 바꿈 – 감독
④ 설득함 – 추종자
⑤ 고무시킴 – 지지자

출제 포인트 83.3% 정복!

01

Ethan에 관한 다음 글의 내용과 일치하는 것은?

Over time, however, Ethan became valuable to the team in different ways. His passion for the game was an inspiration to all his teammates. Because Ethan motivated and encouraged them, they became his most passionate fans. Day in and day out, seeing Ethan's smile, positive attitude, and hard work lifted everyone's spirits. Right before every game, Ethan would always be in the middle of the group offering motivational words. He had a special talent for calming people down and bringing out the best in them. Ethan was also Winston High's loudest supporter. He always observed each play carefully from the sidelines. Although he wasn't the one making the actual plays on the field, Ethan's mind was always right there with his teammates. Everyone could sense his love for football, and the coaches admired his commitment.

① Ethan의 경기 실적은 팀원들을 실망시켰다.
② Ethan은 매일 연습 전후로 팀원들의 사기를 높이는 말을 했다.
③ Ethan의 특기는 다른 사람들을 진정시키는 것이었다.
④ Ethan의 매 경기를 감독이 유심히 관찰하고 조언해 주었다.
⑤ Ethan은 언제나 열심히 경기를 뛰며 팀의 성공에 기여했다.

02

다음 글의 내용과 일치하는 것은?

Over time, however, Ethan became valuable to the team in different ways. His passion for the game was an inspiration to all his teammates. Because Ethan motivated and encouraged them, they became his most passionate fans. Day in and day out, seeing Ethan's smile, positive attitude, and hard work lifted everyone's spirits. Right before every game, Ethan would always be in the middle of the group offering motivational words. He had a special talent for calming people down and bringing out the best in them. Ethan was also Winston High's loudest supporter. He always observed each play carefully from the sidelines. Although he wasn't the one making the actual plays on the field, Ethan's mind was always right there with his teammates. Everyone could sense his love for football, and the coaches admired his commitment.

① The teammates acknowledged Ethan's value as a member.
② Ethan always inspired his teammates right after the games.
③ Ethan made the actual plays on the field occasionally.
④ The coaches were good at calming people down.
⑤ The coaches carefully observed Ethan's play.

03

다음 글에서 전체 흐름과 관계 없는 문장은?

Day in and day out, seeing Ethan's smile, positive attitude, and hard work raised everyone's spirits. Right before every game, Ethan would always be in the middle of the group offering motivational words. ① He had a special talent for soothing people and bringing out the best in them. ② Ethan was also Winston High's loudest supporter. ③ He always observed each play carefully from the sidelines. ④ Although he wasn't the one making the actual plays on the field, Ethan's mind was always right there with his teammates. ⑤ Everyone could sense his desire for winning, and the coaches admired his ambition.

04

Ethan에 관한 다음 글의 내용과 일치하지 않는 것은?

Over time, however, Ethan became valuable to the team in different ways. His passion for the game was an inspiration to all his teammates. Because Ethan motivated and encouraged them, they became his most passionate fans. Day in and day out, seeing Ethan's smile, positive attitude, and hard work lifted everyone's spirits. Right before every game, Ethan would always be in the middle of the group offering motivational words. He had a special talent for calming people down and bringing out the best in them. Ethan was also Winston High's loudest supporter. He always observed each play carefully from the sidelines. Although he wasn't the one making the actual plays on the field, Ethan's mind was always right there with his teammates. Everyone could sense his love for football, and the coaches admired his commitment.

① 긍정적인 태도로 늘 노력하여 동료들에게 귀감이 되었다.
② 동료들이 경기에 들어가기 전에 응원의 말을 해 주었다.
③ 상대 팀이 연습하는 모습을 유심히 관찰하여 전략을 세웠다.
④ 경기장에서 실제로 경기를 뛰는 선수는 아니었다.
⑤ 윈스턴 고등학교 감독에게도 공에 대한 헌신을 인정받았다.

05

주어진 글 다음에 이어질 글의 순서로 가장 적절한 것은?

Ethan is only five feet tall, and his legs unnaturally bend away from each other. It is difficult for him to walk, run, or move around.

(A) Over time, however, Ethan became valuable to the team in different ways. His passion for the game was an inspiration to all his teammates. Because Ethan motivated and encouraged them, they became his most passionate fans.

(B) Because of his condition, he decided to leave his crowded high school in the big city. He moved to our school in the middle of his first year in high school. That following summer, he asked the coach if he could join the football team as a sophomore.

(C) The coach wasn't sure at first, but in the end he allowed Ethan to come to practice. Regardless of his physical difficulties, Ethan worked just as hard as every other player on the team. Although he knew he would never be a valuable player in any of the team's games, he poured his heart and soul into practice every day.

① (A) – (C) – (B)
② (B) – (A) – (C)
③ (B) – (C) – (A)
④ (C) – (A) – (B)
⑤ (C) – (B) – (A)

06

다음 글의 교훈으로 가장 적절한 것은?

Over time, however, Ethan became valuable to the team in different ways. His passion for the game was an inspiration to all his teammates. Because Ethan motivated and encouraged them, they became his most passionate fans. Day in and day out, seeing Ethan's smile, positive attitude, and hard work lifted everyone's spirits. Right before every game, Ethan would always be in the middle of the group offering motivational words. He had a special talent for calming people down and bringing out the best in them. Ethan was also Winston High's loudest supporter. He always observed each play carefully from the sidelines. Although he wasn't the one making the actual plays on the field, Ethan's mind was always right there with his teammates. Everyone could sense his love for football, and the coaches admired his commitment.

① 교사의 주의 깊은 관찰이 학생의 인생을 바꾼다.
② 때로는 잠시 멈춰 자신을 돌아볼 수 있어야 한다.
③ 아무리 작은 역할일지라도 팀의 성공에 있어 중요하다.
④ 어려운 사람들을 돕는 것은 지역 사회를 풍요롭게 만든다.
⑤ 인기를 얻는 것이 선천적인 재능을 타고 나는 것보다 낫다.

07

Ethan에 관한 다음 글의 내용과 일치하지 않는 것은?

Over time, however, Ethan became valuable to the team in different ways. His passion for the game was an inspiration to all his teammates. Because Ethan motivated and encouraged them, they became his most passionate fans. Day in and day out, seeing Ethan's smile, positive attitude, and hard work lifted everyone's spirits. Right before every game, Ethan would always be in the middle of the group offering motivational words. He had a special talent for calming people down and bringing out the best in them. Ethan was also Winston High's loudest supporter. He always observed each play carefully from the sidelines. Although he wasn't the one making the actual plays on the field, Ethan's mind was always right there with his teammates. Everyone could sense his love for football, and the coaches admired his commitment.

① Ethan's hard work inspired other teammates.
② Ethan's presence raised the teammates' morale.
③ Ethan always watched his team's plays attentively.
④ The coaches allowed Ethan to make every actual play.
⑤ The coaches respected Ethan for his dedication to the team.

08

주어진 글 (A)에 이어질 내용을 순서에 맞게 배열한 것으로 가장 적절한 것은?

(A) Ethan is only five feet tall, and his legs unnaturally bend away from each other. It is difficult for him to walk, run, or move around. Because of his condition, he decided to leave his crowded high school in the big city. He moved to our school in the middle of his first year in high school. That following summer, he asked the coach if he could join the football team as a sophomore.

(B) Ethan was also Winston High's loudest supporter. He always observed each play carefully from the sidelines. Although he wasn't the one making the actual plays on the field, Ethan's mind was always right there with his teammates. Everyone could sense his love for football, and the coaches admired his commitment.

(C) The coach wasn't sure at first, but in the end he allowed Ethan to come to practice. Regardless of his physical difficulties, Ethan worked just as hard as every other player on the team. Although he knew he would never be a valuable player in any of the team's games, he poured his heart and soul into practice every day. Over time, however, Ethan became valuable to the team in different ways.

(D) His passion for the game was an inspiration to all his teammates. Because Ethan motivated and encouraged them, they became his most passionate fans. Day in and day out, seeing Ethan's smile, positive attitude, and hard work lifted everyone's spirits. Right before every game, Ethan would always be in the middle of the group offering motivational words. He had a special talent for calming people down and bringing out the best in them.

① (B) – (D) – (C)
② (C) – (B) – (D)
③ (C) – (D) – (B)
④ (D) – (B) – (C)
⑤ (D) – (C) – (B)

09

다음 글의 내용과 일치하는 것은?

Over time, however, Ethan became valuable to the team in different ways. His passion for the game was an inspiration to all his teammates. Because Ethan motivated and encouraged them, they became his most passionate fans. Day in and day out, seeing Ethan's smile, positive attitude, and hard work lifted everyone's spirits. Right before every game, Ethan would always be in the middle of the group offering motivational words. He had a special talent for calming people down and bringing out the best in them. Ethan was also Winston High's loudest supporter. He always observed each play carefully from the sidelines. Although he wasn't the one making the actual plays on the field, Ethan's mind was always right there with his teammates. Everyone could sense his love for football, and the coaches admired his commitment.

① Ethan was so loud that he distracted the players on the field.
② Ethan was jealous of his teammates for making the actual plays.
③ Ethan recorded each play from the sidelines to spot the team's weakness.
④ Ethan gave inspiring words to his teammates before every game.
⑤ Some teammates were uncomfortable about Ethan's presence.

10

다음 글의 내용을 한 문장으로 요약하고자 한다. 빈칸 (A), (B)에 들어갈 말로 가장 적절한 것은?

Over time, Ethan became valuable to the team in different ways. His passion for the game was an inspiration to all his teammates. Because Ethan motivated and encouraged them, they became his most passionate fans. Day in and day out, seeing Ethan's smile, positive attitude, and hard work lifted everyone's spirits. Right before every game, Ethan would always be in the middle of the group offering motivational words. He had a special talent for calming people down and bringing out the best in them. Ethan was also Winston High's loudest supporter. He always observed each play carefully from the sidelines. Although he wasn't the one making the actual plays on the field, Ethan's mind was always right there with his teammates. Everyone could sense his love for football, and the coaches admired his commitment.

Ethan's ______(A)______ for football and positive attitude motivated the teammates, making him ______(B)______ to the team without actually playing the game.

	(A)		(B)
①	fear	–	valuable
②	obsession	–	a threat
③	confidence	–	devoted
④	passion	–	invaluable
⑤	authority	–	loyal

11

다음 글에서 Ethan의 역할로 적절한 것은?

Over time, Ethan became valuable to the team in different ways. His passion for the game was an inspiration to all his teammates. Because Ethan motivated and encouraged them, they became his most passionate fans. Day in and day out, seeing Ethan's smile, positive attitude, and hard work lifted everyone's spirits. Right before every game, Ethan would always be in the middle of the group offering motivational words. He had a special talent for calming people down and bringing out the best in them. Ethan was also Winston High's loudest supporter. He always observed each play carefully from the sidelines. Although he wasn't the one making the actual plays on the field, Ethan's mind was always right there with his teammates. Everyone could sense his love for football, and the coaches admired his commitment.

① competitor ② recruiter
③ strategist ④ motivator
⑤ disrupter

12

다음 글의 내용과 일치하는 것은?

Over time, however, Ethan became valuable to the team in different ways. His passion for the game was an inspiration to all his teammates. Because Ethan motivated and encouraged them, they became his most passionate fans. Day in and day out, seeing Ethan's smile, positive attitude, and hard work lifted everyone's spirits. Right before every game, Ethan would always be in the middle of the group offering motivational words. He had a special talent for calming people down and bringing out the best in them. Ethan was also Winston High's loudest supporter. He always observed each play carefully from the sidelines. Although he wasn't the one making the actual plays on the field, Ethan's mind was always right there with his teammates. Everyone could sense his love for football, and the coaches admired his commitment.

① Ethan turned out to be neglected by the coaches.
② Ethan voluntarily shared diverse strategies to his teammates.
③ Thanks to Ethan, the teammates could calm down and do their best.
④ It was not that Ethan always went to watch his team's play.
⑤ The coach showed his admiration for Ethan's play on the field.

100점 맞고 싶다면!

기타 연습 문제

1회 등장 포인트

● **빈도부사의 위치:** 조동사 뒤, 일반동사 앞

> **Right before every game, Ethan would always be in the middle of the group offering motivational words.**

> **He always observed each play carefully from the sidelines.**

01

다음 밑줄 친 부분 중, 어법상 틀린 것을 고르면?

Over time, however, Ethan became ① valuable to the team in different ways. His passion for the game ② was an inspiration to all his teammates. Because Ethan motivated and encouraged them, they became his most passionate fans. Day in and day out, seeing Ethan's smile, positive attitude, and hard work lifted everyone's spirits. Right before every game, Ethan ③ would always be in the middle of the group offering motivational words. He had a special talent for ④ calming people down and bringing out the best in them. Ethan was also Winston High's loudest supporter. He always ⑤ observing each play carefully from the sidelines. Although he wasn't the one making the actual plays on the field, Ethan's mind was always right there with his teammates. Everyone could sense his love for football, and the coaches admired his commitment.

● **every[each]+단수명사**

> **He always observed each play carefully from the sidelines.**

02

다음 문장에서 밑줄 친 부분을 바르게 고쳐 문장 전체를 쓰시오.

He observed always each plays carefully from the sidelines.

→ ______________________________

____

● **문장 삽입**

03

글의 흐름으로 보아, 주어진 문장이 들어가기에 가장 적절한 곳을 고르시오.

> Over time, however, Ethan became valuable to the team in different ways.

That following summer, Ethan asked the coach if he could join the football team as a sophomore. The coach wasn't sure at first, but in the end he allowed Ethan to come to practice. Regardless of his physical difficulties, Ethan worked just as hard as every other player on the team. (①) Although he knew he would never be a valuable player in any of the team's games, he poured his heart and soul into practice every day. (②) His passion for the game was an inspiration to all his teammates. Because Ethan motivated and encouraged them, they became his most passionate fans. (③) Day in and day out, seeing Ethan's smile, positive attitude, and hard work lifted everyone's spirits. Right before every game, Ethan would always be in the middle of the group offering motivational words. (④) He had a special talent for calming people down and bringing out the best in them. Ethan was also Winston High's loudest supporter. He always observed each play carefully from the sidelines. (⑤) Although he wasn't the one making the actual plays on the field, Ethan's mind was always right there with his teammates. Everyone could sense his love for football, and the coaches admired his commitment.

● **어휘 talent**

> **He had a special talent for calming people down and bringing out the best in them.**

● 어휘 field

Although he wasn't the one making the actual plays on the field, Ethan's mind was always right there with his teammates.

04

〈보기〉의 영영풀이에 해당하는 단어를 본문에서 찾아 쓰시오.

〈보기〉 an area usually covered with grass used for playing sports

Over time, however, Ethan became valuable to the team in different ways. His passion for the game was an inspiration to all his teammates. Because Ethan motivated and encouraged them, they became his most passionate fans. Day in and day out, seeing Ethan's smile, positive attitude, and hard work lifted everyone's spirits. Right before every game, Ethan would always be in the middle of the group offering motivational words. He had a special talent for calming people down and bringing out the best in them. Ethan was also Winston High's loudest supporter. He always observed each play carefully from the sidelines. Although he wasn't the one making the actual plays on the field, Ethan's mind was always right there with his teammates. Everyone could sense his love for football, and the coaches admired his commitment.

____

● 문장 변형

Ethan의 팀에서의 역할이 중요했음을 말하면서 그의 자질과 가치를 첨언하는 부분에서, 적절한 연결어를 추가하는 등의 문장 변형 문제가 출제될 수 있다.

05

다음 빈칸에 들어갈 말로 가장 적절한 것은?

Although Ethan knew he would never be a valuable player in any of the team's games, he poured his heart and soul into practice every day. Over time, however, Ethan became valuable to the team in different ways. His passion for the game was an inspiration to all his teammates. Because Ethan motivated and encouraged them, they became his most passionate fans. Day in and day out, seeing Ethan's smile, positive attitude, and hard work lifted everyone's spirits. Right before every game, Ethan would always be in the middle of the group offering motivational words. ____________, he had a special talent for calming people down and bringing out the best in them. Ethan was also Winston High's loudest supporter. He always observed each play carefully from the sidelines. Although he wasn't the one making the actual plays on the field, Ethan's mind was always right there with his teammates. Everyone could sense his love for football, and the coaches admired his commitment.

① Unfortunately ② Therefore
③ In addition ④ Even so
⑤ However

출제 포인트 84.2% 정복!

리딩 본문[5]

15.8% 확률로 본문[5]에서 출제

본문[5] 적중 MAPPING

이것만 알아도 94.2% 맞힌다!

For the past three years, Ethan has been schooling us all in the game of life. ★He always reminds us that everyone is important to a team's success, though their role on the team may be small. ★★★Instead of putting all his efforts into trying to be the team's best player, he has done everything he can to make the team better. ★★As Ethan has shown us, lifting up those around us is also of great worth. When we help others shine, their light will shine on us in return. Yes, sometimes there is something better than being the best.

대의 파악 〈출제 1위 유형〉

1과의 마지막 부분으로, Ethan이 최고의 선수가 되고자 노력하기 보다는 팀을 더 좋게 만드는 방향으로 노력했다는 내용으로 글을 마무리 짓고 있다. '팀원들의 기운을 북돋고 모두의 역할이 소중하다는 것을 상기시켜주는' Ethan의 행동이 팀원들과 우리에게 어떤 교훈을 주는지 생각해보자.

요약 〈출제 2위 유형〉

본문[5]는 다른 사람을 빛나게 하는 것이 자신을 빛나게 하는 것이라는 주제로 글을 마무리 한다. 이 본문에서 '최고의 선수가 되는 것'과 '팀을 더 좋게 만들기 위해 노력하는 것'이 서로 대조를 이루고 있으므로, 이에 주목하여 글을 요약해보도록 하자.

내용 일치 〈출제 3위 유형〉

내용 일치 유형 문제에서는 글의 세부적인 내용에 유의해야 한다. 본문[5]에서는 아래 내용들을 숙지하되, Ethan이 자신보다 다른 사람을 빛나도록 하는 데 노력을 기울였다는 사실을 기억하도록 하자.

- Ethan은 3년동안 팀에 있었다.
- Ethan은 작은 역할이라도 팀의 성공을 위해 중요하다는 것을 일깨워 주었다.
- Ethan은 최고가 되기 위해 노력하기 보다, 주변 사람들의 기운을 북돋아 주었다.
- 최고가 되는 것이 전부는 아니다.

출제 1위 문장 ★★★

Instead of putting all his efforts into trying to be the team's best player, he has done everything he can to make the team better.

[동명사 명사 역할 – 전치사의 목적어] 출제 1위 (문장편–문장3 → p.143)
[to부정사의 부사적 용법 – 목적] 출제 2위 (문장편–문장3 → p.144)
[목적격관계대명사 생략] 출제 3위 (문장편–문장3 → p.144)

출제 2위 문장 ★★

As Ethan has shown us, lifting up those around us is also of great worth.

[동명사 명사 역할 – 주어] 출제 1위 (문장편–문장4 → p.146)
[of + 추상명사] 출제 2위 (문장편–문장4 → p.146)
[수 일치] 출제 3위 (문장편–문장4 → p.146)

출제 3위 문장 ★

He always reminds us that everyone is important to a team's success, though their role on the team may be small.

[접속사 that 명사 역할 – 목적어] 출제 1위 (문장편–문장2 → p.141)
[대조 어휘 small vs. important] 출제 2위 (문장편–문장2 → p.141)

문장1

문장 출제 확률: 2.1%

For the past three years, Ethan has been schooling us all in the game of life.

(현재완료 진행: has been schooling)

출제 포인트

1위

현재완료 진행

문장 내 출제 확률 100%
본문[5] 문장편 내 출제 확률 11.7%

● 현재완료 진행

본문[5]의 문장1에서 출제될 가능성은 2.1%이다. 이 문장에서 출제가 된다면 100%의 확률로 현재완료 진행 〈have/has been v-ing〉의 형태를 묻는 어법 문제가 나올 수 있다. 현재완료 진행형은 현재완료(have/has p.p.)와 진행형(be v-ing)이 합쳐진 것으로, 과거의 사건이 현재까지 이어지고 있음을 나타내며, '~해오고 있다'로 해석된다. 여기서는 been 뒤의 형태가 schooled가 아니라는 점도 눈여겨 봐두자.

Q. 다음 괄호 안에서 올바른 것을 고르시오.

For the past three years, Ethan (has been schooling / has been schooled) us all in the game of life.

정답
has been schooling
문맥상 Ethan이 과거 3년 전부터 지금까지 우리 모두를 '가르쳐오고 있는' 것이므로, 현재완료 진행 〈have/has been v-ing〉의 형태 has been schooling이 오는 것이 적절하다.

출제 포인트 85.9% 정복!

문장2

문장 출제 확률: 2.8%

He always reminds us that everyone is important to a team's success, though their role on the team may be small.

(접속사 명사 역할 – 목적어: that / 대조 어휘: important, small)

출제 포인트

1위

접속사 that 명사 역할 — 목적어

문장 내 출제 확률 29.2%
본문[5] 문장편 내 출제 확률 4.5%

2위

대조 어휘 small vs. important

문장 내 출제 확률 20.8%
본문[5] 문장편 내 출제 확률 3.2%

● 접속사 that 명사 역할 – 목적어

문장2에서 출제될 가능성은 2.8%이다. 이 문장에서 출제가 된다면, 29.2%의 확률로 접속사 that 자리에 관계대명사 which, what과 선별하는 어법 문제가 나올 수 있다. 접속사 that은 ① 완전한 절을 이끌고, ② 선행사가 없으며, ③ 동사 remind의 직접목적어 역할을 하는 명사절을 이끈다. 관계대명사 which와 what은 뒤에 불완전한 절이 오므로, 해당 자리에 들어갈 수 없다는 점에 유의하자.

Q. 다음 글의 밑줄 친 that과 쓰임이 같은 것을 고르시오.

For the past three years, Ethan has been schooling us all in the game of life. He always reminds us that everyone is important to a team's success, though their role on the team may be small. Instead of putting all his efforts into trying to be the team's best player, he has done everything he can to make the team better. As Ethan has shown us, lifting up those around us is also of great worth. When we help others shine, their light will shine on us in return. Yes, sometimes there is something better than being the best.

① That was the first moment that I saw her.
② I know a man that speaks three languages.
③ That tie doesn't agree with that suit.
④ Everybody thinks that he is a genius.
⑤ Why don't you wear the dress that I bought you?

정답 ④

글과 ④의 that은 각각 reminds와 thinks의 직접목적어인 명사절을 이끄는 접속사이다.

오답

①은 '그것'이라는 의미인 지시대명사, ②는 a man을 선행사로 하는 주격관계대명사, ③은 뒤의 명사 tie를 수식하는 '그, 저'라는 의미인 지시형용사, ⑤는 the dress를 선행사로 하는 목적격관계대명사이다.

① 그게 내가 그녀를 처음 본 순간이었다.
② 나는 3개 국어를 할 줄 아는 한 남자를 안다.
③ 그 넥타이는 그 양복과 어울리지 않는다.
④ 모두가 그를 천재라고 생각한다.
⑤ 내가 사준 드레스를 입는 게 어때요?

● 대조 어휘 small vs. important

문장2는 '역할이 작더라도 모두가 팀의 성공을 위해 중요하다'는 1과의 교훈을 서술하고 있다. 이 문장에서 출제가 된다면 20.8%의 확률로, 이 교훈의 핵심을 담고 있는 어휘 small과 important를 묻는 문제가 나올 수 있다. 이때, 팀에서의 역할이 '작다(small)'는 부분과 모두가 '중요하다(important)'는 부분이 대조를 이루고 있음에 주목하자. small과 바꿔 쓸 수 있는 유의어로는 minor, insignificant 등을, important와 바꿔 쓸 수 있는 유의어로 crucial, significant 등을 함께 기억하자.

Q. 다음 글의 밑줄 친 부분 중, 문맥상 낱말의 쓰임이 적절하지 않은 것은?

For the past three years, Ethan has been schooling us all in the game of life. He always ① reminds us that everyone is important to a team's success, though their role on the team may be ② huge. Instead of putting all his efforts into trying to be the team's best player, he has done everything he can to make the team ③ better. As Ethan has shown us, lifting up those around us is also of great worth. When we help others shine, their light will shine on us in ④ return. Yes, sometimes there is something better than being the ⑤ best.

정답 ②

'~에도 불구하고'라는 의미인 양보의 접속사 though가 쓰였으므로, 팀에서 맡은 역할이 '작을지라도' 모두가 팀의 성공을 위해 '중요하다'는 내용이 이어지는 것이 문맥상 자연스럽다. 따라서, ② huge(거대한)가 아닌 small(작은), minor(사소한) 등이 되어야 한다.

정답 ②

despite는 '~임에도 불구하고'의 의미인 전치사로 뒤에 명사(구)가 이어져야 한다. 해당 문장에서는 주어(their role)와 동사(may be)로 이루어진 완전한 절이 이어지므로, 전치사가 아닌 접속사나 although, even though가 되어야 한다.

오답

① 〈for + 기간〉
③ 현재완료
④ 단수 취급하는 동명사 주어
⑤ 전치사(than) + 동명사

● 접속사 though – 양보

이 문장에서 출제가 된다면 16.7%의 확률로 접속사 though를 물어보는 문제가 나올 수 있다. though는 '~임에도 불구하고'라는 양보의 의미를 가진 접속사이고, 동일한 의미의 접속사 although, even though로 바꿔 쓸 수 있다. 의미는 같지만 전치사인 despite나 in spite of로는 바꿔 쓸 수 없다는 점에 유의하자.

Q. 다음 글의 밑줄 친 부분 중, 어법상 틀린 것은?

① For the past three years, Ethan has been schooling us all in the game of life. He always reminds us that everyone is important to a team's success, ② despite their role on the team may be small. Instead of putting all his efforts into trying to be the team's best player, he ③ has done everything he can to make the team better. As Ethan has shown us, lifting up those around us ④ is also of great worth. When we help others shine, their light will shine on us in return. Yes, sometimes there is something better than ⑤ being the best.

정답 ②

everyone은 단수 취급을 하므로, 이에 맞게 단수동사 is가 되어야 한다.

오답

① 동사 remind: 3인칭 단수, 능동태
③ -thing으로 끝나는 명사를 선행사로 하는 목적격 관계대명사 that
④ 주절의 주어인 동명사 lifting
⑤ 〈help + 목적어 + to-v/동사원형〉

● 시제와 수 일치

이 문장에서는 16.7%의 확률로 시제 및 수 일치 문제가 출제될 수 있다. 주절의 동사 remind는 주어 he에 맞추어 reminds로 쓴다. 한편, 목적어절의 주어 eveyone은 '모든 사람'이라는 뜻을 가지고 있지만 단수 취급하므로 단수동사 is를 써야 한다는 것도 기억하자.

Q. 다음 글의 밑줄 친 부분 중, 어법상 틀린 것은?

For the past three years, Ethan has been schooling us all in the game of life. He always ① reminds us that everyone ② are important to a team's success, though their role on the team may be small. Instead of putting all his efforts into trying to be the team's best player, he has done everything ③ that he can to make the team better. As Ethan has shown us, ④ lifting up those around us is also of great worth. When we help others ⑤ to shine, their light will shine on us in return. Yes, sometimes there is something better than being the best.

정답 ③

'최고'의 선수가 되는 것보다는 '더 좋은' 팀을 만드는 것이 필요하다고 강조하고 있다. 이런 맥락에서 빈칸에 들어갈 말로 가장 적절한 것은 ③ '모두가 팀의 성공에 중요하다'이다.

● 빈칸 everyone is important to a team's success

이 문장에서는 8.3%의 확률로 빈칸 유형의 문제가 출제될 수 있다. 1과 전체의 교훈이라고 볼 수 있는 '역할이 작더라도 모두가 팀의 성공을 위해 중요하다'는 부분을 서술하고 있다. '팀에 기여하는 역할이 작다'라는 부분과, 그럼에도 불구하고 '모두가 팀의 성공을 위해서 중요하다'는 부분이 빈칸으로 출제될 가능성이 높으니 꼭 암기하자.

Q. 다음 빈칸에 들어갈 말로 가장 적절한 것은?

For the past three years, Ethan has been schooling us all in the game of life. He always reminds us that ______________________________, though their role on the team may be small. Instead of putting all his efforts into trying to be the team's best player, he has done everything he can to make the team better. As Ethan has shown us, lifting up those around us is also of great worth. When we help others shine, their light will shine on us in return. Yes, sometimes there is something better than being the best.

① the team only needs its star players
② the players must score a goal for their team
③ everyone is important to a team's success
④ players come in all shapes and sizes
⑤ individual players are more important than the team

① 팀은 오직 스타 선수들만 필요하다
② 선수들은 그들의 팀을 위해 반드시 득점해야 한다
④ 선수들은 체형과 신체 사이즈가 모두 다르다
⑤ 선수 개개인이 팀보다 더 중요하다

출제 포인트 87.9% 정복!

문장3

문장 출제 확률: 4.9% (총 851개의 출제 포인트 중, 42회 출현, 45개 문장 중 3위)

Instead of putting all his efforts into trying to be the team's best player, he has done everything (he can) to make the team better.

putting: 동명사(전치사의 목적어) / trying: 동명사(전치사의 목적어) / (that) / to make: to부정사의 부사적 용법 – 목적

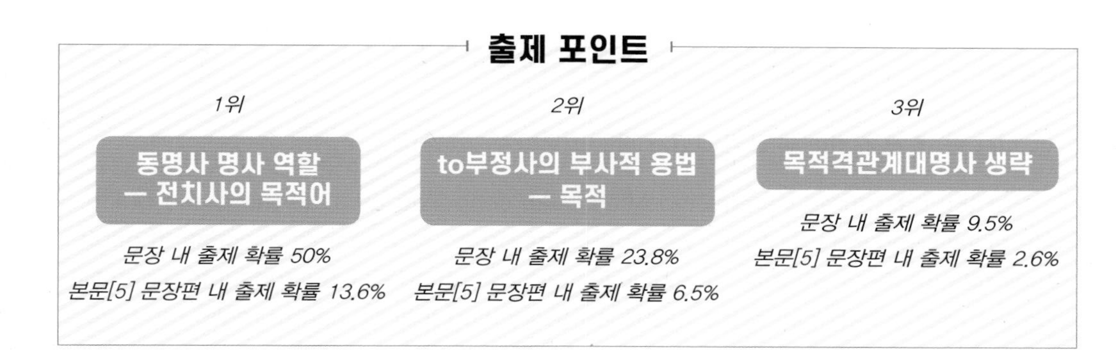

출제 포인트

1위	2위	3위
동명사 명사 역할 – 전치사의 목적어	to부정사의 부사적 용법 – 목적	목적격관계대명사 생략
문장 내 출제 확률 50%	문장 내 출제 확률 23.8%	문장 내 출제 확률 9.5%
본문[5] 문장편 내 출제 확률 13.6%	본문[5] 문장편 내 출제 확률 6.5%	본문[5] 문장편 내 출제 확률 2.6%

● 동명사 명사 역할 – 전치사의 목적어

문장3에서 출제될 가능성은 4.9%이다. 이 문장에서 출제가 된다면 50%의 확률로 전치사 뒤 동명사의 형태를 물어보는 문제가 나올 수 있다. 전치사의 목적어로는 명사가 와야 하므로, 동사를 동명사로 바꿔야 한다. 이 문장에서는 전치사 Instead of와 into 뒤의 putting과 trying에 주목하자.

Q. 다음 괄호 안에 동사를 알맞은 형태로 바꿔 쓰시오.

Instead of ____________(put) all his efforts into ____________(try) to be the team's best player, he has done everything he can to make the team better.

정답 putting, trying

전치사의 목적어로는 명사가 와야 하므로, 동사의 형태를 동명사(v-ing)로 바꿔야 한다. 따라서, 빈칸에는 동명사 putting과 trying이 오는 것이 적절하다.

● to부정사의 부사적 용법 – 목적

이 문장에서는 23.8%의 확률로, '목적'을 나타내는 부사적 용법의 to부정사에 관한 문제가 출제될 수 있다. 여기서 to make the team better는 '팀을 더 좋게 만들기 위해'라는 뜻이다.

Q. 다음 글의 밑줄 친 (a)~(e) 중, 〈보기〉의 밑줄 친 to부정사와 쓰임이 같은 것을 모두 고르시오.

〈보기〉 They had to run to catch the bus.

For the past three years, Ethan has been schooling us all in the game of life. He always reminds us that every member is important (a) to achieve success, though their role on the team may be small. Instead of putting all his efforts into trying to be the team's best player, he has done everything he can (b) to make the team better. As Ethan has shown us, (c) to lift up those around us is also of great worth. When we help others (d) to shine, their light will shine on us in return. Yes, sometimes there is something better than being the best.

① (a) ② (b) ③ (c) ④ (d)

정답 ①, ②

〈보기〉의 to catch는 '잡기 위해서'의 의미로 '목적'을 나타내는 to부정사의 부사적 용법으로 쓰였다.
(a), (b) 부사적 용법 (목적)
(c) 명사적 용법 (주어)
(d) 명사적 용법 (목적격 보어)

● 목적격관계대명사의 생략

이 문장에서는 9.5%의 확률로 목적격관계대명사의 생략과 관련된 어법 문제가 출제될 수 있다. he can은 목적격관계대명사절로, everything 뒤에 관계대명사 that이 생략된 형태로 볼 수 있다.

Q. 다음 중, 밑줄 친 that과 쓰임이 같지 않은 것을 모두 고르시오.

For the past three years, Ethan has been schooling us all in the game of life. He always reminds us that everyone is important to a team's success, though their role on the team may be small. Instead of putting all his efforts into trying to be the team's best player, he has done everything that he can to make the team better. As Ethan has shown us, lifting up those around us is also of great worth. When we help others shine, their light will shine on us in return. Yes, sometimes there is something better than being the best.

① The man that won an award in the contest is my friend.
② The building that you can see is my school.
③ Is this book that your sister bought you?
④ This is a building that is located in Busan.
⑤ She is the singer that I like the most.

정답 ①, ④

본문의 that은 everything을 선행사로 하는 목적격관계대명사이다.

오답

①, ④: 각각 The man과 a building을 선행사로 하는 주격관계대명사

① 대회에서 상을 받은 남자는 내 친구이다.
② 당신이 볼 수 있는 건물은 우리 학교입니다.
③ 이것이 네 언니가 네게 사준 책이니?
④ 이것은 부산에 위치한 건물입니다.
⑤ 그녀는 내가 가장 좋아하는 가수이다.

● try to-v

이 문장에서는 4.8%의 확률로 try의 목적어 문제가 출제될 수 있다. try는 목적어로 to부정사와 동명사 모두를 쓸 수 있지만, 의미 차이가 있다. 〈try v-ing〉는 '(시험 삼아) 한번 ~해보다'라는 의미인 반면, 〈try to-v〉는 '~하기 위해 노력하다'라는 의미이다. Ethan은 팀에서 최고의 선수가 '되기 위해 노력하는' 대신 팀을 더 좋게 만들기 위한 일들을 했다는 내용으로, try의 목적어로 to부정사 to be가 왔다.

Q. 다음 글의 괄호 안에 주어진 단어를 활용하여 빈칸에 알맞은 말을 쓰시오.

For the past three years, Ethan has been schooling us all in the game of life. He always reminds us that everyone is important to a team's success, though their role on the team may be small. Instead of putting all his efforts into ______________(try, be) the team's best player, he has done everything he can to make the team better. As Ethan has shown us, lifting up those around us is also of great worth. When we help others shine, their light will shine on us in return. Yes, sometimes there is something better than being the best.

정답 trying to be

문맥상 '팀의 최고의 선수가 되기 위해 노력하는 것 대신에'라는 의미가 되어야 하므로, try의 목적어로 to부정사를 써야 한다. 한편, 앞에 전치사 into가 있으므로 동명사 trying을 써야 한다.

● 어휘 better

이 문장에서는 4.8%의 확률로 핵심 어휘 better을 변형한 문제가 출제될 수 있다. 문맥상 Ethan이 해온 일들은 자신을 최고의 선수로 만들기 위한 것이 아니라, 팀을 '더 좋게' 만들기 위한 것이므로, make의 목적격 보어로 형용사 good의 비교급인 better을 썼다. 이때, 반의어인 worse가 오답 선지로 출제될 수 있다.

Q. 다음 글의 빈칸 (A), (B)에 들어갈 말로 가장 적절한 것을 본문에서 찾아 쓰시오.

For the past three years, Ethan has been schooling us all in the game of life. He always reminds us that everyone is important to a team's success, though their role on the team may be small. Instead of putting all his efforts into trying to be the team's ____(A)____ player, he has done everything he can to make the team ____(B)____. As Ethan has shown us, lifting up those around us is also of great worth. When we help others shine, their light will shine on us in return. Yes, sometimes there is something better than being the best.

(A) ______________ (B) ______________

정답

(A) best (B) better

문맥상 자신이 '최고의' 선수가 되려고 노력하는 것보다 '더 나은' 팀을 만들기 위해 노력했다는 내용이 되어야 자연스럽다. 따라서, (A)와 (B)에는 각각 best와 better이 적절하다.

출제 포인트 91.5% 정복!

문장4

문장 출제 확률: 3.9% (총 851개의 출제 포인트 중, 33회 출현, 45개 문장 중 5위)

As Ethan has shown us, lifting up those around us is also of great worth.

(lifting: 동명사 명사 역할 – 주어 / is: 수 일치 / of great worth: of+추상명사)

출제 포인트

1위	2위	3위
동명사 명사 역할 – 주어	of+추상명사	수 일치
문장 내 출제 확률 33.3%	*문장 내 출제 확률 30.3%*	*문장 내 출제 확률 18.2%*
본문[5] 문장편 내 출제 확률 7.1%	*본문[5] 문장편 내 출제 확률 6.5%*	*본문[5] 문장편 내 출제 확률 3.9%*

● 동명사 명사 역할 - 주어

문장4에서 출제될 가능성은 3.9%이다. 이 문장에서 출제가 된다면 33.3%의 확률로 동명사 주어인 lifting을 묻는 문제가 나올 수 있다. 동사가 문장에서 주어 역할을 하기 위해서는 동명사 또는 to부정사의 형태로 바뀌어야 한다. 또한, 주어로 쓰인 동명사는 3인칭 단수 취급하므로, 이 문장의 본동사는 3인칭 단수동사 is가 쓰였다.

Q. 다음 글의 밑줄 친 부분 중, 어법상 틀린 것은?

Ethan was also Winston High's ① loudest supporter. He always observed each ② play carefully from the sidelines. Although he wasn't the one making the actual plays on the field, Ethan's mind was always right there with his teammates. Everyone could sense his love for football, and the coaches admired his commitment.

For the past three years, Ethan has been schooling us all in the game of life. He always reminds us ③ that everyone is important to a team's success, though their role on the team may be small. Instead of putting all his efforts into ④ trying to be the team's best player, he has done everything he can to make the team better. As Ethan has shown us, ⑤ lifted up those around us is also of great worth. When we help others shine, their light will shine on us in return. Yes, sometimes there is something better than being the best.

정답 ⑤

As Ethan has shown us는 부사절이고, 밑줄 친 부분은 주절의 주어 자리이다. 따라서, 동명사 lifting이나 to부정사 to lift의 형태가 되어야 한다.

오답

① supporter를 수식하는 형용사 loud의 최상급
② each + 단수명사
③ 명사절을 이끄는 목적격 관계대명사 that
④ 전치사의 목적어로 쓰인 동명사

● of + 추상명사

이 문장에서는 30.3%의 확률로 〈전치사 + 추상명사〉를 묻는 문제가 출제될 수 있다. 〈전치사 + 추상명사〉는 형용사의 역할을 하며, of (great) worth는 '(큰) 가치가 있는'이라는 의미이다. worth 이외에도 value(가치), significance(중요성) 등의 명사를 쓸 수도 있다. 또한, 〈전치사 + 추상명사〉를 형용사로 바꿔 (greatly) worthy로 쓸 수 있다는 것도 알아두자.

Q. 다음 괄호 안에서 알맞은 것을 고르시오.

As Ethan has shown us, lifting up those around us is also of great (worth / worthy).

정답 worth

〈전치사 + 추상명사〉는 형용사 역할을 한다. 괄호 앞에 전치사 of가 쓰였으므로, 형용사 worthy가 아닌 명사 worth가 옳다.

● 수 일치

이 문장에서는 18.2%의 확률로 동명사 주어와 동사의 수 일치를 묻는 문제가 출제될 수 있다. 주어로 쓰인 동명사 lifting은 3인칭 단수 취급하므로, 3인칭 단수동사의 현재형 is가 쓰였다. 바로 앞의 복수명사 us를 보고 동사를 are로 쓰지 않도록 주의하자.

Q. 다음 괄호 안에서 알맞은 것을 고르시오.

As Ethan has shown us, lifting up those around us (is / are) also of great worth.

정답 is

동명사구 lifting up those around us가 주어이므로, 3인칭 단수 취급하여 is가 알맞다.

● 빈칸 lifting up those around us is also of great worth

이 문장에서는 9.1%의 확률로 빈칸 추론 문제가 출제될 수 있다. Ethan이 팀원들을 응원하고 격려하면서 주변을 빛내는 역할을 했다는 내용의 본문[4]를 바탕으로, 본문[5]에서는 '다른 사람의 기운을 북돋아 주는 행동도 중요하다(lifting up those around us is also great worth)'고 말하고 있다. 해당 부분이 다른 표현으로 변형되어 출제될 수 있으니 의미를 잘 파악해두자.

Q. 다음 빈칸에 들어갈 말로 가장 적절한 것은?

For the past three years, Ethan has been schooling us all in the game of life. He always reminds us that everyone is important to a team's success, though their role on the team may be small. Instead of putting all his efforts into trying to be the team's best player, he has done everything he can to make the team better. As Ethan has shown us, ______________________________. When we help others shine, their light will shine on us in return. Yes, sometimes there is something better than being the best.

① practicing by yourself is also of great value
② being the team's best player can be a source of fame
③ suppressing others is sometimes highly valuable
④ spending your time in school is always worth it
⑤ lifting up those around us is also of great worth

정답 ⑤

빈칸 뒤에서 우리가 남들이 빛나도록 도우면 우리도 빛날 것이라고 했으므로, 맥락상 빈칸에는 ⑤ 'lifting up those around us is also of great worth(우리 주변 사람들의 기운을 북돋아 주는 것 역시 큰 가치가 있다)'가 가장 적절하다.
① 혼자서 연습하는 것도 큰 가치가 있다
② 팀에서 최고의 선수가 되는 것은 인기의 원천이 될 수 있다
③ 다른 사람들을 억압하는 것은 때때로 매우 가치가 있다
④ 학교에서 시간을 보내는 것은 항상 가치가 있다

● 어휘 lift up

이 문장에서는 6.1%의 확률로 핵심 어휘 lift up을 묻는 문제가 출제될 수 있다. Ethan이 팀원들을 응원하고 격려함을 lift up(~을 정신적으로 고양시키다)이라는 어휘를 써서 나타냈다. 이와 비슷한 의미인 motivate(동기 부여하다), encourage(장려하다), cheer up(응원하다) 등으로 바꿔 쓸 수 있으며, 반의어로는 discourage(낙담시키다) 등이 있다.

Q. 다음 글의 밑줄 친 lifting up과 바꿔 쓸 수 있는 것을 모두 고르시오.

For the past three years, Ethan has been schooling us all in the game of life. He always reminds us that everyone is important to a team's success, though their role on the team may be small. Instead of putting all his efforts into trying to be the team's best player, he has done everything he can to make the team better. As Ethan has shown us, lifting up those around us is also of great worth. When we help others shine, their light will shine on us in return. Yes, sometimes there is something better than being the best.

① discouraging ② helping ③ verifying
④ abusing ⑤ supporting

정답 ②, ⑤

lifting up은 주위 사람들의 '기운을 북돋아 주는 것'을 의미하므로, helping(도와주는 것)이나 supporting(지지하는 것)으로 바꿔 쓸 수 있다.
① 낙담시키는 것
③ 확인하는 것
④ 학대하는 것

문장5

문장 출제 확률: 1.8%

help+목적어+to-v/동사원형 / 보상[보답]으로

When we help others shine, their light will shine on us in return.

시간의 부사절 현재 시제 / 미래 시제

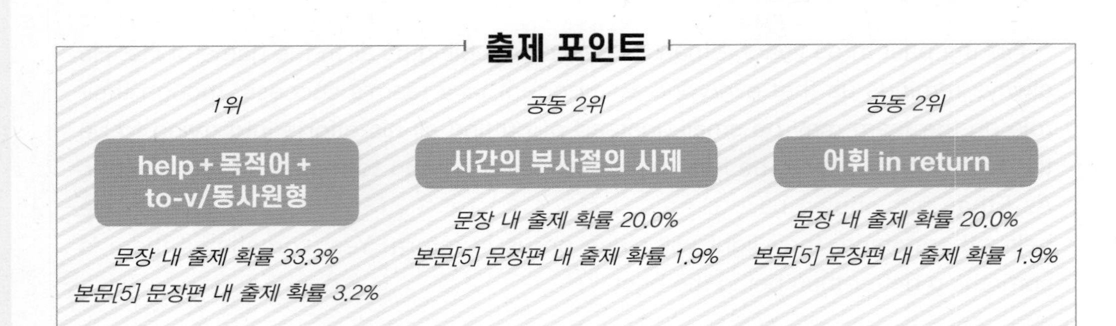

● help+목적어+to-v/동사원형

문장5에서 출제될 가능성은 1.8%이다. 이 문장에서 출제가 된다면 33.3%의 확률로 준사역동사 help의 목적격 보어 형태를 묻는 문제가 나올 수 있다. 〈help+목적어+목적격 보어〉의 5형식 구조로 쓰이며, 목적격 보어로 to부정사와 동사원형이 둘 다 올 수 있다는 점을 기억하자.

Q. 다음 괄호 안에서 알맞은 것을 고르시오.

When we help others (shine / shining), their light will shine on us in return.

정답 shine

help는 목적격 보어로 동사원형이나 to부정사를 쓴다. 따라서, 동사원형 shine이 오는 것이 적절하다.

● 시간의 부사절의 시제

이 문장에서는 20.0%의 확률로 시간의 부사절의 동사 help의 시제를 묻는 문제가 출제될 수 있다. 시간 · 조건의 부사절에서는 미래의 일이더라도 현재 시제를 사용한다. 따라서, 주절의 동사가 will shine으로 미래 시제라도, 부사절의 동사는 미래 시제 will help가 아닌 현재 시제 help로 써야 한다는 것을 잊지 말자. 현재 시제를 써야 하는 곳이 주절이 아닌 부사절이라는 것도 혼동하지 않도록 하자.

Q. 다음 괄호 안에서 알맞은 것을 고르시오.

When we (help / will help) others shine, their light will shine on us in return.
(우리가 다른 사람이 빛나도록 도와줄 때, 그 빛은 보답으로 우리를 비출 것이다.)

정답 help

시간의 부사절에서는 미래 시제를 의미하더라도 현재 시제를 사용한다. 따라서, 빈칸에는 help가 오는 것이 적절하다.

● 어휘 in return

이 문장에서는 20.0%의 확률로 어휘 in return을 묻는 문제가 출제될 수 있다. 다른 사람들이 빛나도록 도와줄 때 '(그에 대한) 보상으로' 자신도 빛날 것이라는 의미로, in return(보상[보답]으로)이 쓰였음을 기억하자.

Q. 다음 글의 밑줄 친 문장에서 어색한 부분을 찾아 바르게 고쳐 쓰시오.

For the past three years, Ethan has been schooling us all in the game of life. He always reminds us that everyone is important to a team's success, though their role on the team may be small. Instead of putting all his efforts into trying to be the team's best player, he has done everything he can to make the team better. As Ethan has shown us, lifting up those around us is also of great worth. <u>When we help others shining, their light will shine on us of return.</u> Yes, sometimes there is something better than being the best.

(1) ______________ → ______________

(2) ______________ → ______________

정답
(1) shining → (to) shine
(2) of → in

help는 목적격 보어로 to부정사나 동사원형을 쓸 수 있다. 따라서, shining을 shine이나 to shine으로 고쳐야 한다. 또한, 의미상 '(~에 대한) 보상[보답]으로'의 의미가 자연스러우므로, of return이 아닌 in return이 되어야 한다.

● 함축 의미

이 문장에서는 13.3%의 확률로 해당 문장의 함축 의미를 묻는 문제가 출제될 수 있다. Ethan의 이야기로 미루어 보았을 때, When we help others shine, their light will shine on us in return이 의미하는 바는, '다른 사람이 빛나도록 도우면, 자신도 빛날 수 있다'는 것이다. 이어지는 there is something better than being the best(최고가 되는 것보다 더 나은 것이 있다)와도 비슷한 맥락이라고 볼 수 있다.

Q. 다음 글의 밑줄 친 부분이 의미하는 바로 가장 적절한 것은?

For the past three years, Ethan has been schooling us all in the game of life. He always reminds us that everyone is important to a team's success, though their role on the team may be small. Instead of putting all his efforts into trying to be the team's best player, he has done everything he can to make the team better. As Ethan has shown us, lifting up those around us is also of great worth. <u>When we help others shine, their light will shine on us in return.</u> Yes, sometimes there is something better than being the best.

① Assisting others can lead to achieving success.
② Only those who become the best player can help others.
③ Helping others is not important for individual's success.
④ Success can only be achieved by putting efforts into being the best.
⑤ Helping others to succeed will hinder one's own success.

정답 ①

Ethan의 이야기로 미루어 보았을 때, 밑줄 친 부분이 말하는 바는, 자기 자신이 최고의 선수가 되려고 노력하는 것보다 남들의 기운을 북돋으며 돕는 것이 더 낫다는 의미이다. 따라서, 밑줄 친 문장의 함축 의미로 가장 적절한 것은 ① '다른 사람을 돕는 것은 성공으로 이어질 수 있다'이다.
② 최고의 선수가 되는 사람만이 다른 사람들을 도울 수 있다.
③ 다른 사람들을 돕는 것은 개인의 성공에 중요하지 않다.
④ 최고가 되기 위해 노력을 기울여야만 성공할 수 있다.
⑤ 다른 사람들이 성공하도록 돕는 것은 자신의 성공을 방해할 것이다.

출제 포인트 95.6% 정복!

문장6

문장 출제 확률: 2.6%

Yes, sometimes there is <u>something better than being the best</u>.

(something better than being the best: 최고가 되는 것보다 더 나은 것 / 후치 수식; being: 동명사 명사 역할 – 전치사의 목적어)

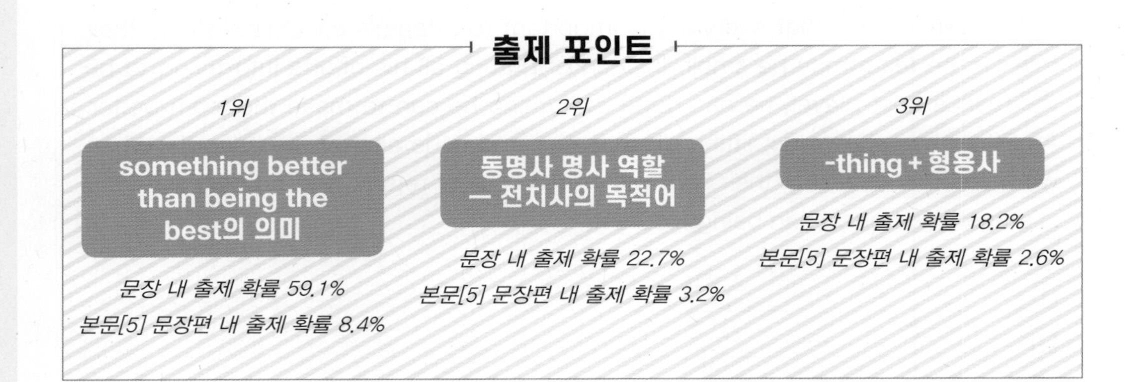

● something better than being the best의 의미

문장6에서 출제될 가능성은 2.6%이다. 이 문장에서 출제된다면 59.1%의 확률로 핵심 어구 something better than being the best를 활용한 문제가 나올 수 있다. 본문[5]는 남들의 기운을 북돋으며 돕는 것이 가치 있으며 자신이 최고의 선수가 되려고 노력하는 것보다 더 낫다는 것을 주제로 한다. 이를 집약한 부분이 something better than being the best이다. 같은 의미를 담는 다른 표현으로 변형되어 출제될 수 있으니, 핵심 의미를 잘 파악해두자. 또한, better, best는 출제 빈도가 높은 어휘이니 꼭 알아두도록 하자.

Q. 다음 글의 밑줄 친 부분이 의미하는 것을 본문에서 찾아 그대로 쓰시오. (5단어)

For the past three years, Ethan has been schooling us all in the game of life. He always reminds us that everyone is important to a team's success, though their role on the team may be small. Instead of putting all his efforts into trying to be the team's best player, he has done everything he can to make the team better. As Ethan has shown us, lifting up those around us is also of great worth. When we help others shine, their light will shine on us in return. Yes, sometimes there is <u>something better</u> than being the best.

____

정답

lifting up those around us 또는 to make the team better

팀에서의 역할이 작더라도 팀을 위해 최선을 다한 풋볼 선수 Ethan의 사례를 통해, 최고보다 더 나은 무언가(something better)는 팀원들을 돕는 것 또는 팀을 더 좋게 만드는 것이라는 점을 유추할 수 있다. 이를 5단어로 나타낸 부분은 lifting up those around us(우리 주변 사람들의 기운을 북돋아 주는 것) 또는 to make the team better(팀을 더 좋게 만드는 것)이다.

● 동명사 명사 역할 – 전치사의 목적어

이 문장에서는 22.7%의 확률로 전치사 than 뒤의 동사 형태를 묻는 문제가 출제될 수 있다. 전치사의 목적어로는 명사가 와야 하므로, 동사원형이 아닌 동명사 being이 와야 한다는 사실을 기억하자.

Q. 다음 글의 밑줄 친 우리말 뜻과 일치하도록 주어진 단어를 활용하여 영작하시오. (4단어)

For the past three years, Ethan has been schooling us all in the game of life. He always reminds us that everyone is important to a team's success, though their role on the team may be small. Instead of putting all his efforts into trying to be the team's best player, he has done everything he can to make the team better. As Ethan has shown us, lifting up those around us is also of great worth. When we help others shine, their light will shine on us in return. Yes, sometimes there is something better 최고가 되는 것보다(be, good).

____

정답
than being the best
'~보다 더 …하다'라는 비교 표현은 비교급 better와 함께 than을 써서 나타낸다. than은 전치사이므로 뒤에 동명사를 쓴다. '최고'라는 의미는 good의 최상급 best를 활용하여 the best로 나타낸다.

● -thing + 형용사

이 문장에서는 18.2%의 확률로 something better에서 형용사의 후치 수식을 묻는 문제가 출제될 수 있다. -thing으로 끝나는 명사는 일반적인 명사와 달리 형용사가 뒤에서 수식(후치 수식)한다. better something이 틀린 표현임에 유의하자.

Q. 다음 글의 (A), (B), (C)의 각 네모 안에서 어법에 맞는 표현으로 가장 적절한 것은?

For the past three years, Ethan has been schooling us all in the game of life. He always reminds us that everyone (A) [is / to be] important to a team's success, though their role on the team may be small. Instead of putting all his efforts into trying to be the team's best player, he (B) [was done / has done] everything he can to make the team better. As Ethan has shown us, lifting up those around us is also of great worth. When we help others shine, their light will shine on us in return. Yes, sometimes there is (C) [something better / better something] than being the best.

	(A)		(B)		(C)
①	is	–	was done	–	something better
②	to be	–	was done	–	something better
③	is	–	has done	–	better something
④	to be	–	has done	–	better something
⑤	is	–	has done	–	something better

정답 ⑤
(A) 접속사 that이 이끄는 명사절의 주어 everyone의 동사가 필요하다. 따라서, to부정사가 아닌 본동사 is가 알맞다.
(B) 그(Ethan)가 모든 것을 '한' 주체이고 뒤에 목적어 everything이 쓰인 것으로 보아, 능동태가 적절하다.
(C) something은 형용사가 뒤에서 수식하므로, something better가 알맞다.

최중요 연습 문제

01

다음 글의 (A), (B), (C)의 각 네모 안에서 어법에 맞는 표현으로 가장 적절한 것은?

For the past three years, Ethan (A) [has been schooling / has been schooled] us all in the game of life. He always reminds us (B) [that / which] everyone is important to a team's success, though their role on the team may be small. Instead of putting all his efforts into trying to be the team's best player, he has done everything he can to make the team better. As Ethan has shown us, lifting up those around us (C) [is / are] also of great worth. When we help others shine, their light will shine on us in return. Yes, sometimes there is something better than being the best.

	(A)	(B)	(C)
①	has been schooling	– that	– is
②	has been schooling	– that	– are
③	has been schooled	– that	– is
④	has been schooled	– which	– is
⑤	has been schooling	– which	– are

02

다음 빈칸에 들어갈 말로 가장 적절한 것은?

For the past three years, Ethan has been schooling us all in the game of life. He always reminds us that everyone is important to a team's success, though their role on the team may be ____________. Instead of putting all his efforts into trying to be the team's best player, he has done everything he can to make the team better. As Ethan has shown us, lifting up those around us is also of great worth. When we help others shine, their light will shine on us in return. Yes, sometimes there is something better than being the best.

① equal ② invaluable
③ significant ④ important
⑤ minor

03

다음 글의 (A), (B), (C)의 각 네모 안에서 문맥에 맞는 낱말로 가장 적절한 것은?

For the past three years, Ethan has been schooling us all in the game of life. He always reminds us that everyone is (A) [important / valueless] to a team's success, though their role on the team may be small. Instead of putting all his (B) [effects / efforts] into trying to be the team's best player, he has done everything he can to make the team better. As Ethan has shown us, lifting up those around us is also of great (C) [worth / wealth]. When we help others shine, their light will shine on us in return. Yes, sometimes there is something better than being the best.

	(A)	(B)	(C)
①	important	– effects	– worth
②	important	– efforts	– wealth
③	important	– efforts	– worth
④	valueless	– efforts	– wealth
⑤	valueless	– effects	– worth

04

우리말 뜻에 맞게, 다음 글의 밑줄 친 부분에서 어법상 틀린 부분을 바르게 고쳐 문장을 완성하시오.

For the past three years, Ethan has been schooling us all in the game of life. He always reminds us that everyone is important to a team's success, though their role on the team may be small. Instead of putting all his efforts into trying to be the team's best player, he has done everything he can to make the team better. As Ethan has shown us, lifting up those around us is also of great worth. When we help others shine, their light will shine on us in return. Yes, <u>sometimes there is something best than is the better</u>.

• 때로 최고가 되는 것보다 더 나은 것이 있다

→ ____________________

05

다음 글의 (A), (B), (C)의 각 네모 안에서 어법에 맞는 표현으로 가장 적절한 것은?

For the past three years, Ethan has been schooling us all in the game of life. He always reminds us that everyone (A) [is / are] important to a team's success, though their role on the team may be small. (B) [Instead / Instead of] putting all his efforts into trying to be the team's best player, he has done everything he can to make the team better. As Ethan has shown us, lifting up those around us is also of great (C) [worth / worthy]. When we help others shine, their light will shine on us in return. Yes, sometimes there is something better than being the best.

	(A)		(B)		(C)
①	is	–	Instead	–	worth
②	is	–	Instead of	–	worth
③	is	–	Instead	–	worthy
④	are	–	Instead of	–	worth
⑤	are	–	Instead of	–	worthy

06

다음 글의 밑줄 친 부분 중, 문맥상 낱말의 쓰임이 적절한 것은?

For the past three years, Ethan has been schooling us all in the game of life. He always reminds us that everyone is important to a team's ① succession, though their role on the team may be ② huge. Instead of putting all his efforts into trying to be the team's ③ worst player, he has done everything he can to make the team better. As Ethan has shown us, lifting up those around us is also of great ④ significance. When we help others shine, their light will shine on us in return. Yes, sometimes there is something ⑤ worse than being the best.

07

다음 빈칸에 들어갈 말로 적절하지 않은 것은?

For the past three years, Ethan has been schooling us all in the game of life. He always reminds us that everyone is ______________ to a team's success, though their role on the team may be small. Instead of putting all his efforts into trying to be the team's best player, he has done everything he can to make the team better. As Ethan has shown us, lifting up those around us is also of great worth. When we help others shine, their light will shine on us in return. Yes, sometimes there is something better than being the best.

① essential ② important
③ valuable ④ meaningful
⑤ insignificant

08

다음 글의 빈칸 (A), (B)에 공통으로 들어갈 말로 적절한 것을 모두 고르시오. (대소문자 무관)

_____(A)_____ he wasn't the one making the actual plays on the field, Ethan's mind was always right there with his teammates. Everyone could sense his love for football, and the coaches admired his commitment.

For the past three years, Ethan has been schooling us all in the game of life. He always reminds us that everyone is important to a team's success, _____(B)_____ their role on the team may be small. Instead of putting all his efforts into trying to be the team's best player, he has done everything he can to make the team better. As Ethan has shown us, lifting up those around us is also of great worth. When we help others shine, their light will shine on us in return. Yes, sometimes there is something better than being the best.

① unless ② even though
③ as though ④ though
⑤ because

09

다음 중, 밑줄 친 to make와 쓰임이 같은 것은?

For the past three years, Ethan has been schooling us all in the game of life. He always reminds us that everyone is important to a team's success, though their role on the team may be small. Instead of putting all his efforts into trying to be the team's best player, he has done everything he can to make the team better. As Ethan has shown us, lifting up those around us is also of great worth. When we help others shine, their light will shine on us in return. Yes, sometimes there is something better than being the best.

① To travel all across Italy is my goal for next year.
② You must study hard to pass the exam.
③ She was so sad to hear the news.
④ The girl grew up to be a doctor.
⑤ I have a lot of things to do today.

10

다음 글의 빈칸 (A), (B)에 공통으로 들어갈 단어를 쓰시오.

For the past three years, Ethan has been schooling us all in the game of life. He always reminds us ___(A)___ everyone is important to a team's success, though their role on the team may be small. Instead of putting all his efforts into trying to be the team's best player, he has done everything ___(B)___ he can to make the team better. As Ethan has shown us, lifting up those around us is also of great worth. When we help others shine, their light will shine on us in return. Yes, sometimes there is something better than being the best.

____

11

다음 글의 밑줄 친 우리말과 같은 뜻이 되도록 〈조건〉에 맞게 영작하시오.

〈조건〉 1. be, something, good, than, best를 모두 사용할 것 (단, 필요시 단어 변형 및 추가 가능)
2. 총 8단어로 쓸 것

For the past three years, Ethan has been schooling us all in the game of life. He always reminds us that everyone is important to a team's success, though their role on the team may be small. Instead of putting all his efforts into trying to be the team's best player, he has done everything he can to make the team better. As Ethan has shown us, lifting up those around us is also of great worth. When we help others shine, their light will shine on us in return. Yes, sometimes 최고가 되는 것보다 더 나은 것이 있다.

____

____

12

다음 글의 (A), (B), (C)의 각 네모 안에서 어법에 맞는 표현으로 가장 적절한 것은?

For the past three years, Ethan (A) [has schooling / has been schooling] us all in the game of life. He always reminds us that everyone is important to a team's success, though their role on the team may be small. Instead of putting all his efforts into trying (B) [to be / being] the team's best player, he has done everything he can to make the team better. As Ethan has shown us, lifting up those around us (C) [is / are] also of great worth. When we help others shine, their light will shine on us in return. Yes, sometimes there is something better than being the best.

	(A)	(B)	(C)
①	has been schooling	to be	are
②	has schooling	to be	is
③	has been schooling	to be	is
④	has schooling	being	are
⑤	has been schooling	being	are

13

다음 글의 (A), (B), (C)의 각 네모 안에서 문맥에 맞는 낱말로 가장 적절한 것은?

For the past three years, Ethan has been schooling us all in the game of life. He always reminds us that everyone is important to a team's success, (A) [as though / even though] their role on the team may be small. Instead of putting all his efforts into trying to be the team's best player, he has done (B) [everything / nothing] he can to make the team better. As Ethan has shown us, lifting up those around us is also of great (C) [worth / wealth]. When we help others shine, their light will shine on us in return. Yes, sometimes there is something better than being the best.

	(A)		(B)		(C)
①	as though	–	everything	–	worth
②	even though	–	everything	–	worth
③	even though	–	nothing	–	worth
④	even though	–	everything	–	wealth
⑤	as though	–	nothing	–	wealth

14

다음 글의 밑줄 친 부분 중, 어법상 틀린 것은?

For the past three years, Ethan has been schooling us all in the game of life. He always ① reminds us that everyone is important to a team's success, though their role on the team may be small. Instead of ② put all his efforts into trying to be the team's best player, he has done everything he can ③ to make the team better. As Ethan ④ has shown us, lifting up those around us is also of great worth. When we help others shine, their light ⑤ will shine on us in return. Yes, sometimes there is something better than being the best.

15

다음 빈칸에 들어갈 말로 가장 적절한 것은?

For the past three years, Ethan has been schooling us all in the game of life. He always reminds us that everyone is important to a team's success, though their role on the team may be small. Instead of putting all his efforts into trying to be the team's best player, he has done everything he can to make the team better. As Ethan has shown us, lifting up those around us is also of great worth. When we help others shine, their light will shine on us in return. Yes, sometimes there is something better than ____________________.

① becoming popular
② having comfort
③ making plans
④ earning wealth
⑤ being the best

16

다음 글의 (A), (B), (C)의 각 네모 안에서 문맥에 맞는 낱말로 가장 적절한 것은?

For the past three years, Ethan has been schooling us all in the game of life. He always reminds us that everyone is (A) [invaluable / insignificant] to a team's success, though their role on the team may be small. Instead of putting all his efforts into trying to be the team's best player, he has done everything he can to make the team (B) [better / worse]. As Ethan has shown us, lifting up those around us is also greatly (C) [meaningful / meaningless]. When we help others shine, their light will shine on us in return. Yes, sometimes there is something better than being the best.

	(A)		(B)		(C)
①	invaluable	–	better	–	meaningful
②	invaluable	–	worse	–	meaningless
③	insignificant	–	better	–	meaningful
④	insignificant	–	better	–	meaningless
⑤	insignificant	–	worse	–	meaningful

17

다음 빈칸에 들어갈 말로 가장 적절한 것은?

For the past three years, Ethan has been schooling us all in the game of life. He always reminds us that everyone is important to a team's success, though their role on the team may be small. Instead of putting all his efforts into trying to be the team's best player, he has done everything he can to make the team better. As Ethan has shown us, lifting up those around us is also of great worth. When we help others shine, their light will shine on us in return. Yes, sometimes there is something ____________ than being the best.

① more important ② more dangerous
③ less popular ④ worse
⑤ smaller

18

다음 글의 밑줄 친 문장 중, 어법상 옳은 것은?

① For the past three years, Ethan have been schooling us all in the game of life. ② He always reminds us that everyone is importantly to a team's success, though their role on the team may be small. ③ Instead of putting all his efforts into try to be the team's best player, he has done everything he can to make the team better. ④ As Ethan has shown us, lifting up those around us are also of great worth. ⑤ When we help others to shine, their light will shine on us in return. Yes, sometimes there is something better than being the best.

19

다음 글의 밑줄 친 lift up의 영영풀이로 가장 적절한 것을 고르시오.

For the past three years, Ethan has been schooling us all in the game of life. He always reminds us that everyone is important to a team's success, though their role on the team may be small. Instead of putting all his efforts into trying to be the team's best player, he has done everything he can to make the team better. As Ethan has shown us, to lift up those around us is also of great worth. When we help others shine, their light will shine on us in return. Yes, sometimes there is something better than being the best.

① to provide support, encouragement, or assistance to someone who may be struggling or in need of help
② to gain or obtain something through one's own efforts or actions
③ to understand or grasp the meaning of something, either through intuition or analysis
④ to successfully complete a task, goal, or objective, usually through efforts and determination
⑤ to assess or judge the quality, value, or effectiveness of something based on specific criteria or standards

20

다음 글의 (A), (B), (C)의 각 네모 안에서 어법에 맞는 표현으로 가장 적절한 것은?

For the past three years, Ethan has been schooling us all in the game of life. He always reminds us (A) [that / what] everyone is important to a team's success, though their role on the team may be small. Instead of putting all his efforts into trying to be the team's best player, he has done everything he can (B) [make / to make] the team better. As Ethan has shown us, lifting up those around us is also of great worth. When we (C) [help / will help] others shine, their light will shine on us in return. Yes, sometimes there is something better than being the best.

	(A)		(B)		(C)
①	that	–	make	–	help
②	what	–	make	–	will help
③	that	–	make	–	will help
④	what	–	to make	–	help
⑤	that	–	to make	–	help

21

다음 빈칸에 들어갈 말로 가장 적절한 것은?

For the past three years, Ethan has been schooling us all in the game of life. He always reminds us that everyone is important to a team's success, though their role on the team may be small. Instead of putting all his efforts into trying to be the team's best player, he has done everything he can to make the team better. As Ethan has shown us, lifting up those around us is also of great worth. When we help others shine, their light will shine on us in return. Yes, sometimes ______________.

① we have to take credit for our work
② ignoring others' opinions is advantageous
③ people shouldn't overestimate their confidence
④ there is something better than being the best
⑤ helping others can put us in dangerous situations

22

다음 글의 (A), (B), (C)의 각 네모 안에서 문맥에 맞는 낱말로 가장 적절한 것은?

For the past three years, Ethan has been schooling us all in the game of life. He always (A) [remains / reminds] us that everyone is important to a team's success, though their role on the team may be (B) [minor / major]. Instead of putting all his efforts into trying to be the team's best player, he has done everything he can to make the team better. As Ethan has shown us, lifting up those around us is also of great worth. When we help others shine, their light will shine on us (C) [in return / in advance]. Yes, sometimes there is something better than being the best.

	(A)		(B)		(C)
①	remains	–	minor	–	in advance
②	remains	–	major	–	in return
③	reminds	–	minor	–	in return
④	reminds	–	major	–	in return
⑤	reminds	–	minor	–	in advance

23

다음 빈칸에 들어갈 말로 가장 적절한 것은?

For the past three years, Ethan has been schooling us all in the game of life. He always reminds us that everyone is important to a team's success, though their role on the team may be small. Instead of putting all his efforts into trying to be the team's best player, he has done everything he can to make the team better. As Ethan has shown us, ______________ those around us is also of great worth. When we help others shine, their light will shine on us in return. Yes, sometimes there is something better than being the best.

① mocking ② criticizing
③ encouraging ④ bringing down
⑤ competing with

24

다음 글의 (A), (B), (C)의 각 네모 안에서 어법에 맞는 표현으로 가장 적절한 것은?

For the past three years, Ethan has been schooling us all in the game of life. He always reminds us that everyone is important to a team's success, though their role on the team may (A) [be / being] small. Instead of putting all his efforts into trying to be the team's best player, he has done everything he can to make the team better. As Ethan has shown us, (B) [lift / lifting] up those around us is also of great worth. When we help others (C) [shine / shining], their light will shine on us in return. Yes, sometimes there is something better than being the best.

	(A)	(B)	(C)
①	be	lift	shine
②	being	lift	shining
③	be	lifting	shine
④	being	lifting	shine
⑤	be	lifting	shining

25

다음 글의 밑줄 친 문장 중, 어법상 틀린 부분이 있는 것을 모두 고르시오.

① For the past three years, Ethan has been schooling us all in the game of life. ② He always reminds us that everyone is important to a team's success, though their role on the team may small. Instead of putting all his efforts into trying to be the team's best player, he has done everything he can to make the team better. ③ As Ethan has shown us, lifting up those around us is also of great worth. ④ When we help others shine, their light will shine on us in return. ⑤ Yes, sometimes there is better something than being the best.

26

다음 글의 밑줄 친 부분 중, 어법상 틀린 것을 모두 고르시오.

For the past three years, Ethan ① has been schooling us all in the game of life. He always reminds us that everyone is important to a team's success, though their role on the team may be small. ② Instead of putting all his efforts into trying to be the team's best player, he has done everything ③ what he can to make the team better. As Ethan has shown us, lifting up those around us is also ④ of great worth. When we help others shine, their light will shine on us in return. Yes, sometimes there is something better than ⑤ to be the best.

27

다음 글의 (A), (B), (C)의 각 네모 안에서 문맥에 맞는 낱말로 가장 적절한 것은?

For the past three years, Ethan has been schooling us all in the game of life. He always reminds us that everyone is important to a team's success, though their role on the team may be small. Instead of (A) [celebrating / concentrating] on being the team's best player, he has done everything he can to make the team better. As Ethan has shown us, lifting up those around us is also of great worth. When we (B) [help / hinder] others shine, their light will shine on us in return. Yes, sometimes there is (C) [something / nothing] better than being the best.

	(A)	(B)	(C)
①	celebrating	help	something
②	celebrating	hinder	nothing
③	concentrating	hinder	something
④	concentrating	help	something
⑤	concentrating	hinder	nothing

28

다음 글의 밑줄 친 부분이 의미하는 바로 가장 적절한 것은?

For the past three years, Ethan has been schooling us all in the game of life. He always reminds us that everyone is important to a team's success, though their role on the team may be small. Instead of putting all his efforts into trying to be the team's best player, he has done everything he can to make the team better. As Ethan has shown us, lifting up those around us is also of great worth. When we help others shine, their light will shine on us in return. Yes, sometimes there is something better than being the best.

① Each individual is not important to team's success.
② Success is only achieved by fortune.
③ Helping others will hinder one's own success.
④ Lifting up those around us is also of great worth.
⑤ A skilled coach can make a team successful.

29

다음 글의 밑줄 친 우리말을 〈조건〉에 맞게 영작하시오.

〈조건〉 1. lift, of, worth, great, up, be, those, also를 모두 사용할 것 (단, 필요시 단어 변형 및 추가 가능)
2. 총 10단어로 쓸 것

For the past three years, Ethan has been schooling us all in the game of life. He always reminds us that everyone is important to a team's success, though their role on the team may be small. Instead of putting all his efforts into trying to be the team's best player, he has done everything he can to make the team better. As Ethan has shown us, 우리 주변 사람들의 기운을 북돋워 주는 것 역시 큰 가치가 있다. When we help others shine, their light will shine on us in return. Yes, sometimes there is something better than being the best.

____

____

30

다음 밑줄 친 우리말을 〈조건〉에 맞게 영작하시오.

〈조건〉 1. 부사적 용법의 to부정사를 사용할 것
2. 총 12단어로 완성할 것
3. make, do, that, can, the team, everything을 사용할 것 (단, 필요시 단어 변형 및 추가 가능)

For the past three years, Ethan has been schooling us all in the game of life. He always reminds us that everyone is important to a team's success, though their role on the team may be small. Instead of putting all his efforts into trying to be the team's best player, 그는 팀을 더 좋게 만들기 위해 할 수 있는 모든 것을 해왔다. As Ethan has shown us, lifting up those around us is also of great worth. When we help others shine, their light will shine on us in return. Yes, sometimes there is something better than being the best.

____

____

본문[5]

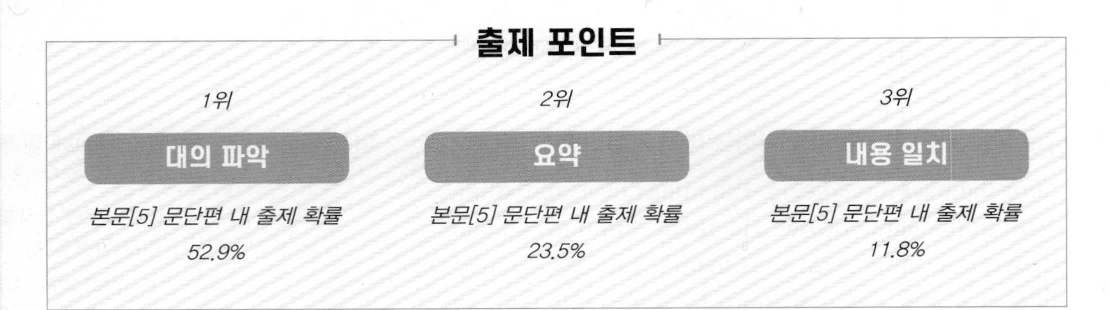

● 대의 파악

본문[5]에서는 대의 파악 문제가 52.9%로 가장 많이 출제되었다. Ethan이 모든 팀원이 중요함을 상기시키고 팀원들의 기운을 북돋아 줌으로써, 자신이 최고가 되기보다는 더 나은 팀을 만들기 위해 노력했다는 내용이다. '팀을 위해서는 역할에 상관없이 모두가 중요하다', '다른 사람을 빛나도록 돕는 사람은 자신도 빛날 것이다'와 같이 Ethan을 통해 얻을 수 있는 교훈이 선지로 나오는 경우가 많으니 기억하자.

Q. 다음 글의 주제로 가장 적절한 것은?

For the past three years, Ethan has been schooling us all in the game of life. He always reminds us that everyone is important to a team's success, though their role on the team may be small. Instead of putting all his efforts into trying to be the team's best player, he has done everything he can to make the team better. As Ethan has shown us, lifting up those around us is also of great worth. When we help others shine, their light will shine on us in return. Yes, sometimes there is something better than being the best.

① necessity of keeping time
② value of praising oneself
③ importance of cheering up others
④ significance of being a top player
⑤ limitation of working hard without talent

정답 ③

Ethan의 사례에서 알 수 있듯이, 팀원들의 기운을 북돋아 줌으로써 팀을 더 좋게 만드는 것이 자신이 최고가 되는 것보다 더 낫다는 내용의 글이다. 따라서, 주제로 가장 적절한 것은 ③ '다른 사람들을 응원하는 것의 중요성'이다.
① 시간을 지키는 것의 필요성
② 자신을 칭찬하는 것의 가치
④ 최고의 선수가 되는 것의 중요성
⑤ 재능 없이 노력하는 것의 한계

● 요약

두 번째로 출제될 가능성이 높은 것은 23.5%의 확률로, 요약 유형이다. 'Ethan이 팀원들에게 팀을 위해 모두가 중요하다고 상기시킨다'는 내용과, 'Ethan이 최고가 되려고 하기보다는 더 나은 팀을 만들기 위해 노력했다'는 내용이 요약문으로 자주 출제된다. 다시 말해, 글의 주제와 직결되는 경우가 많으므로, 주제를 파악하는 것이 중요하다. 본문[5]에서는 '중요한', '최고의', '격려하다'와 같은 키워드가 선지로 출제되는 경우가 많으므로 기억하자.

Q. 다음 글의 내용을 한 문장으로 요약하고자 할 때, 빈칸 (A), (B)에 알맞은 말은?

For the past three years, Ethan has been schooling us all in the game of life. He always reminds us that everyone is important to a team's success, though their role on the team may be small. Instead of putting all his efforts into trying to be the team's best player, he has done everything he can to make the team better. As Ethan has shown us, lifting up those around us is also of great worth. When

정답 ④

팀에서의 역할이 작더라도 모두가 팀에 중요하다는 내용으로, Ethan의 역할은 동료에게 '동기를 부여하고 도와주는' 것이었으므로, (A)에는 motivating, assisting, helping이 가능하다. (B)에는 '중요한'과 비슷한 의미로 쓰이는 '필수적인'을 의미하는 essential이 빈칸에 적절하다.

we help others shine, their light will shine on us in return. Yes, sometimes there is something better than being the best.

Whether it be being the team's best player or ______(A)______ others, every role is ______(B)______ for team's success.

(A) (B)
① motivating – insufficient
② winning – harmful
③ interrupting – trivial
④ assisting – essential
⑤ helping – replaceable

팀 최고의 선수가 되는 것이든 다른 사람들을 돕든, 모든 역할은 팀의 성공에 필수적이다.

① 동기를 부여하는 것 – 불충분한
② 이기는 것 – 해로운
③ 방해하는 것 – 사소한
⑤ 돕는 것 – 대체 가능한

● 내용 일치

이 문단에서는 내용 일치 문제가 11.8%의 확률로 출제될 가능성이 있다. 이 유형 문제를 놓치지 않으려면 글의 세부적인 내용에 유의해야 한다. 특히, 얼핏 보면 일반적으로 맞는 진술로 생각할 수 있는 'Ethan은 최고의 선수가 되기 위해 노력했다' 등의 선지가 글의 내용과 일치하지 않는 것을 고르는 문제의 답으로 자주 출제되었으니 유의하자. 이외에도, 팀을 위해 모든 선수가 중요하다는 Ethan의 가르침도 선지로 출제될 수 있다. 'Ethan은 3년 동안 팀에 있었음', '작은 역할이라도 팀의 성공을 위해 중요함', '주변 사람들의 기운을 북돋워 준 Ethan', '다른 사람이 빛나도록 돕는 것이 자신을 빛나게 하는 것'이라는 세부 내용을 기억해야 한다.

1	For the past three years, Ethan has been schooling us all in the game of life.	7.1%
2	He always reminds us that everyone is important to a team's success, though their role on the team may be small.	21.4%
3	Instead of putting all his efforts into trying to be the team's best player, he has done everything he can to make the team better.	21.4%
4	As Ethan has shown us, lifting up those around us is also of great worth.	7.1%
5	When we help others shine, their light will shine on us in return.	21.4%
6	Yes, sometimes there is something better than being the best.	21.4%

Q. 글의 내용과 일치하면 T, 일치하지 않으면 F에 표시하시오.

(1) 팀의 성공을 위해 모든 사람이 중요하다. (T / F)
(2) Ethan은 최고의 선수가 되기 위해 항상 노력했다. (T / F)
(3) 우리 자신이 빛나도록 노력하는 것이 중요하다. (T / F)
(4) 다른 사람을 가치 있게 만든 만큼 자신도 가치 있게 될 것이다. (T / F)
(5) 최고가 되는 것보다 더 훌륭한 것이 있다. (T / F)
(6) Ethan은 4년 동안 풋볼팀에 있었다. (T / F)
(7) All players have different values depending on their roles. (T / F)
(8) Ethan tried everything to make his team more successful. (T / F)
(9) Being the best is always the best. (T / F)
(10) Ethan has been in the football team for three years. (T / F)
(11) Cheering up others can be as worthy as being the best player. (T / F)
(12) Ethan has shown the value of motivating those around us. (T / F)

정답

1	T	2	F	3	F
4	T	5	T	6	F
7	F	8	T	9	F
10	T	11	T	12	T

(7) 모든 선수들은 역할에 따라 다른 가치를 지닌다.
(8) Ethan은 팀을 더 성공적으로 만들기 위해 모든 것을 시도했다.
(9) 최고가 되는 것은 항상 제일 좋다.
(10) Ethan은 3년 동안 풋볼팀에 있었다.
(11) 다른 사람들을 격려하는 것은 최고의 선수가 되는 것만큼이나 가치가 있을 수 있다.
(12) Ethan은 우리 주변의 사람들에게 동기를 부여하는 것의 가치를 보여주었다.

최중요 연습 문제

01

다음 글의 내용을 요약할 때, 빈칸 (A), (B)에 알맞은 말은?

For the past three years, Ethan has been schooling us all in the game of life. He always reminds us that everyone is important to a team's success, though their role on the team may be small. Instead of putting all his efforts into trying to be the team's best player, he has done everything he can to make the team better. As Ethan has shown us, lifting up those around us is also of great worth. When we help others shine, their light will shine on us in return. Yes, sometimes there is something better than being the best.

> In Ethan's story, we get to know those who ____(A)____ other people will be ____(B)____ for their behavior.

	(A)		(B)
①	betray	–	regretful
②	cheer up	–	repaid
③	offend	–	paying
④	sacrifice	–	neglected
⑤	imitate	–	rewarded

02

다음 글에서 얻을 수 있는 교훈으로 가장 알맞은 것은?

For the past three years, Ethan has been schooling us all in the game of life. He always reminds us that everyone is important to a team's success, though their role on the team may be small. Instead of putting all his efforts into trying to be the team's best player, he has done everything he can to make the team better. As Ethan has shown us, lifting up those around us is also of great worth. When we help others shine, their light will shine on us in return. Yes, sometimes there is something better than being the best.

① 최고가 되기 위해 끊임없이 노력해야 한다.
② 지도자는 때로는 강하게 일을 추진해야 한다.
③ 스포츠에 있어서 공정한 선수 선발이 중요하다.
④ 달성하고자 하는 목표를 계속 상기하는 것이 중요하다.
⑤ 팀을 위하는 것이 최고의 선수가 되는 것보다 중요할 수 있다.

03

다음 글의 주제로 가장 적절한 것은?

For the past three years, Ethan has been schooling us all in the game of life. He always reminds us that everyone is important to a team's success, though their role on the team may be small. Instead of putting all his efforts into trying to be the team's best player, he has done everything he can to make the team better. As Ethan has shown us, lifting up those around us is also of great worth. When we help others shine, their light will shine on us in return. Yes, sometimes there is something better than being the best.

① the need of living one's life alone
② the unexpected benefit from failure
③ the value of encouraging other people
④ the importance of sunlight to one's health
⑤ the irrelevance of teamwork to team's performance

[04~05]

다음 글을 읽고, 물음에 답하시오.

For the past three years, Ethan has been schooling us all in the game of life. He always reminds us that everyone is important to a team's success, though their role on the team may be small. Instead of putting all his efforts into trying to be the team's best player, he has done everything he can to make the team better. As Ethan has shown us, lifting up those around us is also of great worth. When we help others shine, their light will shine on us in return. Yes, sometimes there is something better than being the best.

04

윗글의 제목으로 가장 적절한 것은?

① Everyone Needs a Reminder of Their Value!
② Spend Your Money Wisely Helping Others
③ Be the Loudest Supporter of Yourself
④ Making Others Shine Makes You Shine
⑤ The Way to Make Lifelong Friends

05

윗글의 Ethan에 관한 설명으로 옳지 않은 것은?

① 3년 동안 팀에 있었다.
② 팀의 성공을 위해 모두가 중요함을 일깨워 주었다.
③ 스스로 최고의 선수가 되기 위해 노력했다.
④ 주변 사람들의 기운을 북돋아 주었다.
⑤ 다른 사람을 빛나게 해 주는 사람이었다.

06

다음 글의 내용을 요약할 때, 빈칸 (A), (B)에 알맞은 말은?

For the past three years, Ethan has been schooling us all in the game of life. He always reminds us that everyone is important to a team's success, though their role on the team may be small. Instead of putting all his efforts into trying to be the team's best player, he has done everything he can to make the team better. As Ethan has shown us, lifting up those around us is also of great worth. When we help others shine, their light will shine on us in return. Yes, sometimes there is something better than being the best.

From Ethan who always ____(A)____ them, Ethan's teammates could learn that no one is ____(B)____ for a team's victory.

	(A)		(B)
①	discouraged	–	invaluable
②	inspired	–	invaluable
③	encouraged	–	worthless
④	intimidated	–	worthless
⑤	disturbed	–	trivial

07

다음 글의 제목으로 가장 적절한 것은?

For the past three years, Ethan has been schooling us all in the game of life. He always reminds us that everyone is important to a team's success, though their role on the team may be small. Instead of putting all his efforts into trying to be the team's best player, he has done everything he can to make the team better. As Ethan has shown us, lifting up those around us is also of great worth. When we help others shine, their light will shine on us in return. Yes, sometimes there is something better than being the best.

① Ethan's Shining Face
② Devotion of Ethan to the Team
③ The Reason Ethan Learned Cheerleading
④ How Small Ethan's Role Was in His Team
⑤ Ethan Who Became the Best Player

08

다음 글의 Ethan에 관한 설명으로 옳은 것은?

For the past three years, Ethan has been schooling us all in the game of life. He always reminds us that everyone is important to a team's success, though their role on the team may be small. Instead of putting all his efforts into trying to be the team's best player, he has done everything he can to make the team better. As Ethan has shown us, lifting up those around us is also of great worth. When we help others shine, their light will shine on us in return. Yes, sometimes there is something better than being the best.

① He has been in the team for four years.
② He thinks some of players are unnecessary for the team.
③ He has been eager to make himself more successful.
④ He has always cheered up his teammates.
⑤ He has shown the value of loving oneself.

100점 맞고 싶다면!

기타 연습 문제

1회 등장 포인트

● 동사 remind

He always reminds us that everyone is important to a team's success, though their role on the team may be small.

01

다음 주어진 우리말 뜻과 일치하도록 〈조건〉에 맞게 완성하시오.

그는 팀에서의 역할이 작을지라도, 모두가 팀의 성공을 위해 중요하다는 것을 우리에게 항상 일깨워준다.

1) 〈조건 1〉 4형식 문장

He always reminds __________ __________ everyone is important to a team's __________, though their role on the team may be small.

2) 〈조건 2〉 3형식 문장

He always reminds __________ __________ the importance of every individual to the __________ of a team, though their role on the team may be small.

● instead of

Instead of putting all his efforts into trying to be the team's best player, he has done everything he can to make the team better.

● 부사절을 이끄는 접속사 when - 시간

When we help others shine, their light will shine on us in return.

02

다음 글의 빈칸 (A), (B)에 들어갈 말로 가장 적절한 것은?

For the past three years, Ethan has been schooling us all in the game of life. He always reminds us that everyone is important to a team's success, though their role on the team may be small. ____(A)____ putting all his efforts into trying to be the team's best player, he has done everything he can to make the team better. As Ethan has shown us, lifting up those around us is also of great worth. ____(B)____ we help others shine, their light will shine on us in return. Yes, sometimes there is something better than being the best.

	(A)		(B)
①	Along with	–	When
②	Because of	–	Although
③	In spite of	–	When
④	Due to	–	As
⑤	Instead of	–	As

● 현재완료

As Ethan has shown us, lifting up those around us is also of great worth.

03

다음 글의 (A), (B), (C)의 각 네모 안에서 어법에 맞는 표현으로 가장 적절한 것은?

Over time, however, Ethan became valuable to the team in different ways. His passion for the game was an inspiration to all his teammates. Because Ethan (A) [motivated / was motivated] and encouraged them, they became his most passionate fans. Day in and day out, seeing Ethan's smile, positive attitude, and hard work lifted everyone's spirits. Right before every game, Ethan would always be in the middle of the group offering motivational words. He had a special talent for calming people down and bringing out the best in them. Ethan was also Winston High's loudest supporter. He always observed each play carefully from the sidelines. Although he wasn't the one making the actual plays on the field, Ethan's mind was always right there with his teammates. Everyone could sense his love for football, and the coaches admired his commitment.

For the past three years, Ethan has been schooling us all in the game of life. He (B) [always reminds /

[reminds always] us that everyone is important to a team's success, though their role on the team may be small. Instead of putting all his efforts into trying to be the team's best player, he has done everything he can to make the team better. As Ethan (C) [was shown / has shown] us, lifting up those around us is also of great worth. When we help others shine, their light will shine on us in return. Yes, sometimes there is something better than being the best.

	(A)	(B)	(C)
①	motivated	– always reminds	– was shown
②	was motivated	– always reminds	– was shown
③	motivated	– always reminds	– has shown
④	was motivated	– reminds always	– has shown
⑤	motivated	– reminds always	– has shown

● 표현 put one's efforts into

Instead of putting all his efforts into trying to be the team's best player, he has done everything he can to make the team better.

● 어휘 success

He always reminds us that everyone is important to a team's success, though their role on the team may be small.

04

다음 글의 (A), (B), (C)의 각 네모 안에서 문맥에 맞는 낱말로 가장 적절한 것은?

Although he wasn't the one making the actual plays on the field, Ethan's mind was always right there with his teammates. Everyone could sense his love for football, and the coaches (A) [admired / neglected] his commitment.

For the past three years, Ethan has been schooling us all in the game of life. He always reminds us that everyone is important to a team's (B) [success / succession], though their role on the team may be small. Instead of putting all his (C) [efforts / effects] into trying to be the team's best player, he has done everything he can to make the team better. As Ethan has shown us, lifting up those around us is also of great worth. When we help others shine, their light will shine on us in return. Yes, sometimes there is something better than being the best.

	(A)	(B)	(C)
①	admired	– success	– efforts
②	admired	– success	– effects
③	admired	– succession	– efforts
④	neglected	– succession	– effects
⑤	neglected	– success	– effects

● 무관한 문장

05

글의 흐름과 무관한 문장을 고르시오.

For the past three years, Ethan has been schooling us all in the game of life. ① He always reminds us that everyone is important to a team's success, though their role on the team may be small. ② Instead of putting all his efforts into trying to be the team's best player, he has done everything he can to make the team better. ③ He tried to get along only with promising teammates. ④ As Ethan has shown us, lifting up those around us is also of great worth. ⑤ When we help others shine, their light will shine on us in return. Yes, sometimes there is something better than being the best.

● 글의 순서

● 문장 변형

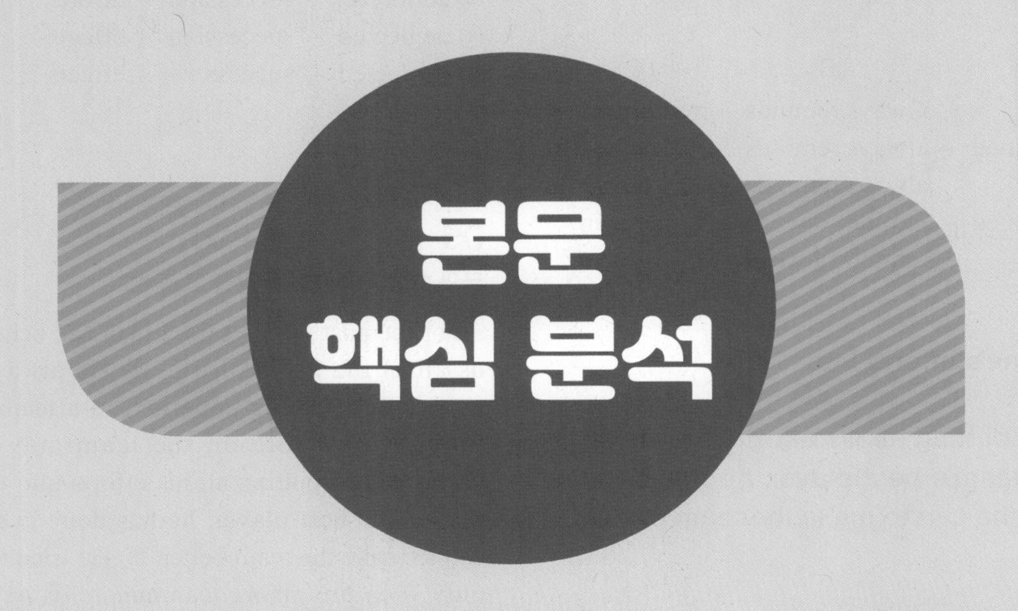
본문
핵심 분석

본문 핵심 분석 1과 - The Part You Play

본문1 윈스턴 고등학교 4학년생들의 마지막 경기에서, Ethan은 처음으로 경기를 뛰었고 동료에게 공을 패스받음

1 The Final Touchdown

to-v 형용사적 용법 S V 과거진행
2 With only two minutes (to play), both teams were fighting for the football.

S1 V1 ≠ the latest (최신의) SC
3 It was the last home game for the seniors of Winston High, and
S2 V2 SC to-v 부사적 용법 〈형용사 수식〉
they were determined to win.
= the seniors

= As[Because] S′ V′ 과거완료 SC′
4 Since it had been a close game the whole evening, the best
S V 과거완료 O
players of each team hadn't left the field.
teams (X)

S′ V′ O′ 접속사 that
5 Once Winston High's coach finally knew [that victory was
S V 수동태
theirs], all the seniors on the sidelines were allowed to play for
= their victory playing (X) during (X)
the last few seconds.

S V SC
6 One of the seniors, Ethan, was especially happy.
senior (X)

S V 과거완료 〈경험〉
7 He had never played in any of the games before.

S V 과거진행 O to-v 형용사적 용법
8 Now, Ethan was finally getting the chance (to step onto the grass).

S
9 When the rival team dropped the ball, one of our players
V1 O V2 player (X)
recovered it and quickly ran down the field with it.
= the ball = the ball

S V to-v 부사적 용법 〈목적〉
10 Ethan ran right after him to catch up.

S′ V′ SC′ S V O
11 As our player got closer to the end zone, he saw Ethan behind
= When
him on his left.

Instead (X) 동명사 S V
12 Instead of running straight ahead, the player kindly passed the
O S′ V′ O′
ball to Ethan so that he could score a touchdown.
= in order that = Ethan

1 마지막 터치다운
2 경기 시간 단 2분을 남기고, 양 팀은 공을 차지하기 위해 싸우고 있었다.
3 이 경기는 윈스턴 고등학교 4학년 학생들의 마지막 홈 경기였고, 그들은 이기려는 의지가 확고했다.
4 저녁 내내 박빙의 경기였었기 때문에, 각 팀의 핵심 선수들은 필드를 떠나지 않았다.
5 윈스턴 고등학교의 감독이 마침내 승리가 자신들의 것임을 알았을 때, 사이드라인에 있던 모든 4학년생 선수들은 마지막 몇 초간 뛸 수 있도록 허락받았다.
6 그 4학년생 선수 중 하나인 Ethan은 특히 기뻤다.
7 그는 이전에 어떤 경기에서도 뛰어본 적이 없었다.
8 이제, Ethan은 마침내 잔디를 밟을 기회를 얻게 된 것이었다.
9 상대 팀이 공을 놓쳤을 때, 우리 선수 중 한 명이 공을 집어 빠르게 뛰었다.
10 Ethan은 그를 따라잡기 위해 그의 바로 뒤에서 뛰었다.
11 우리 선수가 엔드존에 좀 더 가까워졌을 때, 그는 왼쪽 뒤에 Ethan이 있는 것을 보았다.
12 곧장 앞으로 달리는 것 대신에, 그 선수는 Ethan이 터치다운 득점을 할 수 있도록 친절하게 Ethan에게 공을 패스했다.

Words and Phrases

- final a. 마지막의
- fight for ~을 위해 싸우다
- senior n. 마지막 학년
- determined a. 확고한, 단호한
- close game 접전, 치열한 경기
- whole a. 전체의
- field n. 경기장
- victory n. 승리
- be allowed to-v ~하는 것이 허용되다
- especially ad. 특히
- chance n. 기회
- step onto ~에 들어서다, ~를 밟다
- grass n. 잔디
- drop v. 떨어뜨리다
- recover v. 되찾다
- run down 내리 달리다
- right ad. 바로
- catch up v. 따라잡다
- get closer to ~에 가까워지다
- behind prep. 뒤에서
- instead of ~ 대신에
- straight ad. 똑바로
- ahead ad. 앞으로
- pass A to B A를 B에게 패스[전달]하다
- score v. 득점하다

본문2 Ethan은 경기 종료 직전 터치다운에 성공했고, 그 득점은 팀 승리의 결정적인 요인이 아니었음에도 기억할 만한 가치가 있음

all eyes are on: 모두의 시선이 ~에 쏠리다

1 All eyes were on Ethan. (S: eyes, V: were)

with + 명사 + 수식어구(전치사구): ~가 …한 채로[…하면서] / seem to-v: ~인 것 같다

2 With the ball in his hands, everything seemed to be moving in slow motion, like in a Hollywood movie. (S: everything, V: seemed; in: 전치사; it seemed that everything was moving (O))

3 People kept their eyes on him as he made his way to the end zone. (S: People, V: kept, O: their eyes; him = Ethan; as = when; S′: he, V′: made, O′: his way)

지각동사 + 목적어 + 목적격 보어(동사원형/v-ing)

4 They saw him cross the goal line right before the clock ran out. (S: They, V: saw, O: him, OC: cross; crossing (O); S′: the clock, V′: ran out)

5 Unexpectedly, everyone in the crowd leapt to their feet with their hands in the air. (S: everyone, V: leapt; with + 명사 + 수식어구(전치사구): ~가 …한 채로[…하면서])

6 They were bursting with excited shouts and unending cheers for Ethan. (S: They, V: were bursting 과거진행; excited 과거분사, exciting (X); unending 현재분사, unended (X))

7 In this moment, all of Ethan's hard work and dedication was being rewarded with glory. (S: all of Ethan's hard work and dedication, V: was being rewarded 과거진행 수동태; dedication = commitment, devotion)

★ 주제문

8 Ethan's touchdown didn't win the game, but it will be worth remembering. (S1: Ethan's touchdown, V1: didn't win, O: the game; S2: it = Ethan's touchdown, V2: will be, SC: worth remembering; to remember (X))

9 By now you're probably wondering why. (S: you, V: 're wondering 현재진행, O: why; why Ethan's touchdown will be worth remembering (O))

1 모든 시선이 Ethan을 향했다.

2 그의 손에 들린 공과 함께, 모든 것이 할리우드 영화의 한 장면처럼 천천히 움직이는 듯 했다.

3 사람들은 그가 엔드존을 향해갈 때 그에게 시선을 고정했다.

4 그들은 Ethan이 경기 종료 직전 골 라인을 넘어선 것을 보았다.

5 뜻밖에 모든 관중들이 손을 흔들며 벌떡 일어섰다.

6 그들은 Ethan을 향한 들뜬 외침과 끝없는 환호성을 터뜨렸다.

7 이 순간, Ethan의 그 모든 노고와 헌신이 영광으로 보상 받고 있었다.

8 Ethan의 터치다운으로 경기에서 이긴 것은 아니었지만, 그것은 기억할 만한 가치가 있을 것이다.

9 이쯤 되면 여러분은 아마 이유를 궁금해할 것이다.

Words and Phrases

- keep one's eyes on ~에서 눈을 떼지 않다
- make one's way to ~로 나아가다
- cross v. 가로지르다
- run out 다 떨어지다
- unexpectedly ad. 예기치 못하게
- crowd n. 관중
- leap to one's feet 벌떡 일어서다
- burst v. 터뜨리다
- excited a. 신이 난, 흥분한
- shout n. 외침
- unending a. 끝없는
- cheer n. 환호
- hard work 노력
- dedication n. 헌신
- reward v. 보상하다
- glory n. 영광
- be worth v-ing ~할 가치가 있다
- probably ad. 아마도
- wonder v. 궁금해하다

본문 핵심 분석 1과 - The Part You Play

본문3 Ethan은 신체적인 어려움에도 불구하고 윈스턴 고등학교로 전학 온 후 1년 뒤인 2학년 때 풋볼팀에 가입하고 열심히 연습함

1 Well, Ethan is only five feet tall, and his legs unnaturally bend away from each other.
(S1 Ethan / V1 is / SC five feet tall / S2 his legs / V2 bend; feet: foot (X))

2 It is difficult for him to walk, run, or move around.
(가S It / V is / 의미상의 주어 for him / 진S1 to walk / 진S2 run / 진S3 move; for: of (X); (to) run, (to) move)

3 Because of his condition, he decided to leave his crowded high school in the big city.
(S he / V decided / O to leave: to-v 명사적 용법; Because of: Because (X); to leave: leaving (X))

4 He moved to our school in the middle of his first year in high school.
(S He / V moved)

5 That following summer, he asked the coach [if he could join the football team as a sophomore].
(following: 현재분사 / S he / V asked / IO the coach / DO [if ...]; if = whether(~인지 아닌지))

6 The coach wasn't sure at first, but in the end he allowed Ethan to come to practice.
(S1 The coach / V1 wasn't / SC sure / S2 he / V2 allowed / O Ethan / OC to come; to come: coming (X))

★ 주제문

7 Regardless of his physical difficulties, Ethan worked just **as** hard **as** every other player on the team.
(S Ethan / V worked; as+형/부 원급+as: ~만큼 …한; player: players (X))

8 Although he knew [he would never be a valuable player in any of the team's games], he poured his heart and soul into practice every day.
(Although: (Even) Though, Even if (O) / Despite/In spite of (X); S′ he / V′ knew / (that) / S″ he / V″ be / SC″ a valuable player; would: will(X); S he / V poured / O1 his heart / O2 soul)

1 Ethan은 키가 단지 5피트(152.4cm)이고, 그의 다리는 부자연스럽게 바깥으로 구부러졌다.

2 그는 걷고, 뛰고, 움직이는 게 어렵다.

3 그의 상태 때문에, 그는 큰 도시에 있는 붐비던 고등학교를 떠나기로 결정했다.

4 Ethan은 고등학교 1학년 도중 우리 학교로 전학 왔다.

5 이듬해 여름, Ethan은 감독에게 2학년으로서 풋볼팀에 들어갈 수 있는지 물어보았다.

6 감독은 처음에 망설였지만, 결국에는 Ethan을 연습에 오도록 허락했다.

7 Ethan은 신체적 한계와 상관없이, 그 팀의 다른 모든 선수들만큼이나 열심히 연습했다.

8 비록 팀의 어떤 경기에서도 절대 중요한 선수가 될 수 없다는 것을 알았지만, Ethan은 매일매일 연습에 열과 성을 다했다.

Words and Phrases

- unnaturally ad. 부자연스럽게
- bend v. 구부러지다
- away from ~로부터 멀리 떨어져
- condition n. 상태
- decide v. 결정하다
- crowded a. 붐비는
- in the middle of ~의 중간에
- following a. 다음의
- sophomore n. 2학년생
- be sure ~을 확신하다
- at first 처음에
- in the end 결국, 마침내
- allow A to-v A가 ~하는 것을 허락하다
- regardless of ~에 상관없이
- physical a. 신체적인
- difficulty n. 어려움
- although conj. 비록 ~임에도 불구하고
- valuable a. 귀중한, 가치 있는
- pour A into B A를 B에 쏟아 넣다

본문 핵심 분석 1과 - The Part You Play

본문4 Ethan은 신체적 어려움과 상관없이 열정적으로 노력했고, 팀의 자극제이자 지지자로 팀 내에서 중요한 사람이 됨

★ 주제문

1 Over time, however, Ethan became valuable to the team in different ways.
(S: Ethan / V: became / SC: valuable)

2 His passion for the game was an inspiration to all his teammates.
(S: His passion / V: was / SC: an inspiration)

3 Because Ethan motivated and encouraged them, they became his most passionate fans.
(Because of (X) / S′: Ethan / V′1: motivated / V′2: encouraged / S: they / V: became / SC: his most passionate fans / them = they = all his teammates)

4 Day in and day out, seeing [Ethan's smile, positive attitude, and hard work] lifted everyone's spirits.
(S 동명사: seeing ... / V: lifted / O: everyone's spirits / attitude ≠ altitude(고도) aptitude(적성))

5 Right before every game, Ethan would always be in the middle of the group offering motivational words.
(games (X) / S: Ethan / V: would be / offering: as he would offer (O))

6 He had a special talent for [calming people down and bringing out the best in them].
(S: He / V: had / O: a special talent / 동명사 1: calming / 동명사 2: bringing / them = people)

7 Ethan was also Winston High's loudest supporter.
(S: Ethan / V: was / SC: supporter)

8 He always observed each play carefully from the sidelines.
(S: He / V: observed / O: each play / observed ≠ conserve(보존하다) reserve(예약하다) / plays (X))

9 Although he wasn't the one (making the actual plays on the field), Ethan's mind was always right there with his teammates.
(Despite (X) / In spite of (X) / S′: he / V′: wasn't / SC′: the one / 현재분사: making / made (X) / S: Ethan's mind / V: was)

10 Everyone could sense his love for football, and the coaches admired his commitment.
(S1: Everyone / V1: could sense / O: his love / S2: the coaches / V2: admired / O: his commitment / commitment = dedication, devotion)

1 그러나 시간이 지나면서 Ethan은 다른 방식으로 팀에 중요한 사람이 되었다.

2 경기에 대한 그의 열정은 팀 내 모든 선수에게 자극을 주었다.

3 Ethan이 선수들에게 동기를 부여하고 격려했기 때문에, 선수들은 그의 가장 열정적인 팬이 되었다.

4 매일매일 Ethan의 미소와 긍정적인 태도, 엄청난 노력을 보는 것은 모두의 기운을 북돋웠다.

5 매 경기 직전에, Ethan은 의욕을 높이는 말을 해주며 항상 팀의 중심에 있곤 했다.

6 Ethan은 사람들을 침착하게 하고, 그들의 최고의 능력을 끌어내는 특별한 재능이 있었다.

7 Ethan은 윈스턴 고등학교의 가장 큰 지지자이기도 했다.

8 그는 항상 사이드라인에서 각 플레이를 유심히 관찰했다.

9 경기장에서 실제 경기를 뛰는 선수는 아니었을지라도, Ethan의 마음은 항상 같은 팀 선수들과 함께했다.

10 모두가 풋볼을 향한 Ethan의 사랑을 느낄 수 있었고, 코치들은 그의 헌신을 존경했다.

Words and Phrases

- passion n. 열정
- inspiration n. 자극
- motivate v. 동기 부여하다
- encourage v. 격려하다
- day in and day out 매일
- positive a. 긍정적인
- attitude n. 태도
- lift one's spirits ~의 기운을 북돋우다
- right before ~ 직전에
- offer v. 제공하다
- motivational a. 동기 부여의
- talent n. 재능
- calm down 침착하게 하다
- admire v. 존경하다
- commitment n. 헌신, 전념

본문 핵심 분석 1과 - The Part You Play

본문5 Ethan의 이야기를 통해, 우리는 역할이 작을지라도 팀의 성공에는 모두가 중요하다는 것과 최고가 되는 것보다 팀을 더 좋게 만드는 더 나은 일들이 있다는 것을 배울 수 있음

1 For the past three years, Ethan has been schooling us all in the game of life.
(S: Ethan / V: has been schooling 현재완료 진행 〈계속〉 / O: us; For — During (X))

2 He always reminds us [that everyone is important to a team's success, though their role on the team may be small].
(S: He / V: reminds / IO: us / DO: that ~; that: 접속사 that; is — are (X); though — despite (X), in spite of (X))

3 Instead of putting all his efforts into trying to be the team's best player, he has done everything (he can) to make the team better.
(putting: 동명사; trying: 동명사; to be — being (X); Instead of — Instead (X); S: he / V: has done 현재완료 〈계속〉 / O: everything; (that) 생략; he can — he can do (O); to make: to-v 부사적 용법 〈목적〉; · try to-v: 노력하다 · try v-ing: 시험삼아 해보다)

4 As Ethan has shown us, lifting up those (around us) is also of great worth.
(S′: Ethan / V′: has shown 현재완료 / O′: us; S: lifting 동명사 / V: is — are (X); of+추상명사=형용사)

5 When we help others shine, their light will shine on us in return.
(시간의 부사절; S′: we / V′: help / O′: others / OC′: shine — to shine (O); S: their light / V: will shine)

★ 주제문
6 Yes, sometimes there is something better than being the best.
(V: is / S: something better — better something (X); being: 동명사 — be (X))

1 지난 3년간, Ethan은 삶이라는 경기에서 우리 모두를 가르쳐왔다.

2 그는 우리에게 팀에서의 역할이 작을지라도 모두가 팀의 성공을 위해 중요하다는 것을 항상 일깨워준다.

3 팀의 최고 선수가 되기 위해 모든 노력을 쏟아붓는 대신에, Ethan은 팀을 더 좋게 만들기 위해 할 수 있는 모든 것을 해왔다.

4 Ethan이 우리에게 보여준 것처럼, 우리 주변 사람들의 기운을 북돋워 주는 것 역시 큰 가치가 있는 것이다.

5 우리가 다른 사람이 빛나도록 도와주었을 때, 그 빛은 그에 대한 보답으로 우리를 비출 것이다.

6 그렇다, 때로 최고가 되는 것보다 더 나은 것이 있다.

Words and Phrases

- past (a.) 지난
- school (v.) 가르치다
- remind (v.) 상기시키다
- success (n.) 성공
- though (conj.) ~임에도 불구하고
- role (n.) 역할
- put A into B A를 B에 투입하다
- effort (n.) 노력
- try to-v 하기 위해 노력하다
- lift up (정신적으로) 고양시키다
- worth (n.) 가치
- shine (v.) 빛나다
- in return 보답으로

기타 본문

After You Read 적중 MAPPING

이것만 알아도 맞힌다!

Winston High News

Winston High finished its season with an inspiring victory. It defeated Stark High by a score of 20-6. About 30 seconds before the final whistle, victory was already certain. ★★ However, the best moment of the game began shortly after. The coach sent all the seniors onto the field. Among them was Ethan. He joined the team in his sophomore year. Ethan doesn't look like a typical football player. He is only five feet tall and his legs are too weak to run fast. ★★★ Nevertheless, Ethan is the team's most important player, as his great attitude motivates everyone around him. In the game's final seconds, Ethan scored the last touchdown. A teammate passed the ball to Ethan so that he could score. It was a touching moment and a fantastic way to finish the season!

내용 일치

이 글에서 자주 출제된 것은 윈스턴고가 승리한 경기의 점수에 관한 내용이다. 경기 종료 30초 전의 상황에 대한 내용과, Ethan의 운동능력과 태도도 문제로 자주 나오므로 잘 기억하도록 하자.

문장 삽입

문장 삽입 유형의 경우 연결어, 지시어에 주목해야 한다. 전환의 역할을 하는 however, nevertheless와 같은 연결어들이 포함된 문장이 주어지는 경우, 문장과 문장 사이의 흐름을 파악하는 것이 중요하다. 또한, 대명사를 포함한 문장이 주어지는 경우, 대명사가 지칭하는 대상이 언급된 문장을 찾아야 한다.

제목

이 글은 불리한 신체 조건에도 불구하고 팀을 위해 항상 노력한 Ethan이 마지막 승리에 기여한 내용을 말하고 있다. '팀원들의 기운을 북돋우는 능력', '동료들과의 협력', '감동적인 승리'와 같은 키워드를 포함한 선지에 주목하는 것이 좋으며, Ethan을 통해 얻을 수 있는 교훈도 선지로 출제될 수 있음을 기억하자.

출제 1위 문장 ★★★

Nevertheless, Ethan is the team's most important player, as his great attitude motivates everyone around him.

연결어 Nevertheless

연결어 Nevertheless는 글의 흐름을 전환할 때 사용된다. 따라서 Nevertheless를 전후로 반대의 내용이 나오는 경우가 많으니 기억하도록 하자. Ethan이 불리한 신체 조건을 가지고 있었다는 것과, 그가 팀의 가장 중요한 선수였다는 것을 통해 내용의 전환이 있음을 알 수 있다. 유의어로는 Nonetheless, Yet이 있으며, 접속사 Although, 전치사 Despite과 헷갈리지 않도록 주의하자.

출제 2위 문장 ★★

However, the best moment of the game began shortly after.

연결어 However

연결어 However은 글의 흐름을 전환할 때 사용된다. 따라서 However을 전후로 반대의 내용이 나오는 경우가 많으니 기억하도록 하자. 경기 종료 30초 전에 승리가 확정되었다는 것과, 얼마 남지 않은 시간임에도 잠시 후 게임의 하이라이트가 시작되었다는 것을 통해 내용의 전환이 있음을 알 수 있다.

해석

윈스턴고가 감동적인 승리로 시즌을 마쳤다. 윈스턴고는 20-6의 점수로 스타크고를 이겼다. 종료 휘슬이 울리기 약 30초 전, 승리는 이미 확실했다. 그러나 경기 최고의 순간은 그 직후 시작되었다. 감독은 4학년생 모두를 경기장에 내보냈다. 그들 가운데 Ethan이 있었다. 그는 2학년 때 팀에 합류했다. Ethan은 전형적인 풋볼 선수로는 보이지 않는다. 키는 5피트에 불과하고 그의 다리는 너무 약해서 빨리 달릴 수 없다. 그럼에도 불구하고 Ethan은 팀의 가장 중요한 선수인데, 그의 훌륭한 태도가 주변에 모든 사람들을 독려하기 때문이다. 경기의 마지막 순간에, Ethan은 마치막 터치다운을 득점했다. 팀 동료가 Ethan이 득점할 수 있도록 공을 패스했던 것이다. 그것은 감동적인 순간이었고, 시즌을 마치는 환상적인 방식이었다!

1. Liberos in Volleyball

In volleyball, liberos receive the attack or serve and often have the best reaction times and passing skills on their team. Their sole purpose is to defend. Height is not an issue because liberos may not play at the net. This gives shorter players who excel at passing and defending a chance to show off their skills.

2. Punt Returners in American Football

After a football is punted, a punt returner has to catch it and run toward the end zone. Though it seems like only tall and big athletes play American football, this sport actually offers many ways for athletes of all shapes and sizes to contribute to the game. Smaller players are the better choice for punt returns because being quick is more valuable than height or width for this position.

3. Coxswains in Rowing

From their seat at the front of the boat, coxswains steer, pass on the coach's orders, and shout out commands to the crew. They are the lightest among the other rowing team members, but they pull more than their weight by coming up with good race plans and motivating their team to victory. ★★★ Leadership and effective communication skills are a must for this position.

내용 일치

리베로, 펀트 리터너, 타수의 불리한 신체적 조건과 그들이 팀에 기여하는 방법에 관한 내용 일치 문제가 자주 출제되었다. 세 포지션에서 발견되는 공통적인 신체적 특징과 팀에서 그들의 역할에 주목하도록 하자.

제목

세 포지션은 불리한 신체적 조건에도 불구하고 각자의 능력을 통해 팀의 승리에 기여한다는 공통점이 있다. '헌신'이나 '기여'와 같은 키워드에 주목해야 하며, 눈에 띄지 않더라도 팀에 기여하는 선수가 1과의 주요 소재로 다뤄지고 있음을 함께 기억하도록 하자.

출제 1위 문장 ★★★

Leadership and effective communication skills are a must for this position.

빈칸 leadership

팀의 전략적, 정신적인 부분을 책임지는 타수에게 가장 중요하게 요구되는 자질은 리더십일 것이다. 이와 같은 맥락에서 리베로, 펀트 리터너에게 요구되는 능력에는 어떤 것이 있는지 유심히 보도록 하자.

빈칸 a must

팀의 전략적, 정신적인 부분을 책임지는 타수의 역할을 설명한 뒤, 타수의 자질로 요구되는 리더십과 의사소통 능력을 말하는 문장이다. a must 자리에는 '필수조건'이나 '요구조건'과 같은 의미를 지닌 단어들이 대신할 수 있다. 비슷한 의미를 가진 명사 requirements와 바꿔 쓸 수 있으며, 동사 require, need, demand의 수동태 형태인 are required[needed/demanded] 등으로도 바꿔 쓸 수 있다는 것을 기억하자.

해석

1. 배구의 리베로

배구에서 리베로는 공격이나 서브를 받으며, 보통 팀에서 최고의 반응 속도와 패스 기술을 갖는다. 그들의 단 하나의 목표는 방어하는 것이다. 신장은 문제가 되지 않는데, 이는 리베로가 네트 주변에서 뛰지 않을 수도 있기 때문이다. 이것은 패스나 방어에 뛰어난 키가 더 작은 선수들에게 그들의 능력을 자랑할 기회를 제공한다.

2. 미식축구의 펀트 리터너

공이 차진 후에, 펀트 리터너는 그 공을 잡아 엔드존을 향해 뛰어야 한다. 오직 키와 덩치가 큰 운동선수들만이 미식축구를 하는 것 같아 보이지만, 이 스포츠는 사실 모든 체격과 신체 사이즈의 운동선수들이 시합에 공헌할 수 있도록 많은 방법들을 제공한다. 펀트 리턴에 있어서는 더 작은 선수들이 더 나은 선택인데, 왜냐하면 이 포지션을 위해서는 신장이나 덩치보다 빠른 것이 더 유용하기 때문이다.

3. 조정의 타수

보트 앞 부분에 있는 그들의 자리에서 타수는 조종하고, 감독의 지시사항을 전달하고, 팀에게 명령을 외친다. 그들은 여타 조정 팀원 중에서 가장 가볍지만, 좋은 경주 전략을 떠올리고 그들의 팀이 승리하도록 동기 부여를 함으로써 그들의 몸무게보다 더 많이 끌어당긴다. 리더십과 효과적인 의사소통 능력은 이 포지션에 있어서 필수이다.

01

다음 빈칸에 들어갈 말로 가장 적절한 것은?

Winston High finished its season with an inspiring victory. It defeated Stark High by a score of 20-6. About 30 seconds before the final whistle, victory was already certain. _______________, the best moment of the game began shortly after.

① For example ② Otherwise
③ So ④ However
⑤ Moreover

02

다음 글의 밑줄 친 부분과 바꿔 쓸 수 있는 말로 적절한 것은?

Ethan doesn't look like a typical football player. He is only five feet tall and his legs are too weak to run fast. Nonetheless, Ethan is the team's most important player, as his great attitude motivates everyone around him.

① Moreover ② Nevertheless
③ In contrast ④ Furthermore
⑤ As a result

03

다음 빈칸에 들어갈 말로 가장 적절한 것은?

Winston High finished its season with a(n) _____________ victory. It defeated Stark High by a score of 20-6. About 30 seconds before the final whistle, victory was already certain. However, the best moment of the game began shortly after. The coach sent all the seniors onto the field. Among them was Ethan. He joined the team in his sophomore year. Ethan doesn't look like a typical football player. He is only five feet tall and his legs are too weak to run fast. Nevertheless, Ethan is the team's most important player, as his great attitude motivates everyone around him. In the game's final seconds, Ethan scored the last touchdown. A teammate passed the ball to Ethan so that he could score. It was a touching moment and a fantastic way to finish the season!

① crowded ② uncertain
③ determined ④ discouraging
⑤ inspiring

04

글의 흐름으로 보아, 주어진 문장이 들어가기에 가장 적절한 곳을 고르시오.

Nevertheless, Ethan is the team's most important player, as his great attitude motivates everyone around him.

Winston High finished its season with an inspiring victory. It defeated Stark High by a score of 20-6. About 30 seconds before the final whistle, victory was already certain. However, the best moment of the game began shortly after. The coach sent all the seniors onto the field. Among them was Ethan. He joined the team in his sophomore year. Ethan doesn't look like a typical football player. (①) He is only five feet tall and his legs are too weak to run fast. (②) In the game's final seconds, Ethan scored the last touchdown. (③) A teammate passed the ball to Ethan so that he could score. (④) It was a touching moment and a fantastic way to finish the season! (⑤)

[05~07]

다음 글을 읽고, 물음에 답하시오.

(A) In volleyball, liberos receive the attack or serve and often have the best reaction times and passing skills on their team. Their sole purpose is to defend. Height is not an issue because liberos may not play at the net. This gives shorter players who excel at passing and defending a chance to show off their skills.

(B) After a football is punted, a punt returner has to catch it and run toward the end zone. Though it seems like only tall and big athletes play American football, this sport actually offers many ways for athletes of all shapes and sizes to contribute to the game. Smaller players are the better choice for punt returns because being quick is more valuable than height or width for this position.

(C) From their seat at the front of the boat, coxswains steer, pass on the coach's orders, and shout out commands to the crew. They are the lightest among the other rowing team members, but they pull more than their weight by coming up with good race plans and motivating their team to victory. Leadership and effective communication skills are ____________ for this position.

*coxswain: (조정의) 타수

05

윗글의 공통된 제목으로 알맞은 것은?

① Contributors Getting Over Their Physical Weakness
② The Reason Being Fast Is Required in Volleyball
③ Special Players Playing Outside the Field
④ Loud Voice Necessary for Communication
⑤ Importance of Devoted Defenders

06

윗글의 빈칸에 들어갈 말로 가장 적절한 것은?

① a must ② liberty
③ inquiry ④ inaction
⑤ distribution

07

윗글의 내용과 일치하는 것은?

① 리베로는 훌륭한 공격력이 있는 것이 좋다.
② 리베로는 네트 근처에서 플레이한다.
③ 타수는 보트 중앙에 앉는다.
④ 타수는 팀에서 가장 무겁다.
⑤ 타수는 의사소통 기술을 필요로 한다.

08

다음 밑줄 친 부분의 우리말 뜻과 일치하도록 〈조건〉에 맞게 영작하시오.

In the game's final seconds, Ethan scored the last touchdown. A teammate passed the ball to Ethan <u>그가 득점할 수 있도록</u>.

〈조건〉 1. so that을 사용할 것
2. 총 5단어로 영작할 것

09

다음 글을 읽고 답할 수 <u>없는</u> 질문을 한 사람을 <u>모두</u> 고르시오.

Winston High finished its season with an inspiring victory. It defeated Stark High by a score of 20-6. About 30 seconds before the final whistle, victory was already certain. However, the best moment of the game began shortly after. The coach sent all the seniors onto the field. Among them was Ethan. He joined the team in his sophomore year. Ethan doesn't look like a typical football player. He is only five feet tall and his legs are too weak to run fast. Nevertheless, Ethan is the team's most important player, as his great attitude motivates everyone around him. In the game's final seconds, Ethan scored the last touchdown. A teammate passed the ball to Ethan so that he could score. It was a touching moment and a fantastic way to finish the season!

① Tom: By how many points did Winston High beat Stark High?
② Liz: Since when did the coach join the team?
③ Kate: Why is Ethan unable to run fast?
④ Sam: How did Stark High make the last score of the game?
⑤ Bill: Were seniors allowed to play the game?

10

다음 글의 제목으로 가장 적절한 것은?

Winston High finished its season with an inspiring victory. It defeated Stark High by a score of 20-6. About 30 seconds before the final whistle, victory was already certain. However, the best moment of the game began shortly after. The coach sent all the seniors onto the field. Among them was Ethan. He joined the team in his sophomore year. Ethan doesn't look like a typical football player. He is only five feet tall and his legs are too weak to run fast. Nevertheless, Ethan is the team's most important player, as his great attitude motivates everyone around him. In the game's final seconds, Ethan scored the last touchdown. A teammate passed the ball to Ethan so that he could score. It was a touching moment and a fantastic way to finish the season!

① Great Quarterback Ethan
② Winston High's Disappointing Victory
③ Sacrifice of the Coach for His Football Team
④ The Critical Mistake of Ethan in His Last Game
⑤ Unforgettable Win of the Season's Last Game

Listen & Speak

Listen & Speak 1 적중 MAPPING

이것만 알아도 대화문 맞힌다!

[Listen & Speak 1]

W: Where are you going, David?

B: There's a soccer game today. [1]I'm meeting my friends at the field.

W: Did you [2]forget the whole family is going to clean the house this afternoon?

B: Oh, no! That's today? But my friends are waiting for me!

W: We planned this two weeks ago.

B: I forgot. I'm sorry, Mom.

W: Your dad and sister will be [3]disappointed if you [4]don't help out.

B: Okay. I'm going to call [5]and tell my friends that I can't make it today.

여: David, 어디 가니?
남: 오늘 축구 경기가 있어요. 경기장에서 친구들을 만날 거예요.
여: 오늘 오후에 가족 전체가 집을 청소하기로 한 것 잊었니?
남: 오, 이런! 그게 오늘이에요? 하지만 제 친구들이 저를 기다리고 있어요!
여: 우린 2주 전에 이걸 계획했잖아.
남: 깜박했어요. 죄송해요, 엄마.
여: 네가 돕지 않는다면 아빠와 여동생이 실망할 거야.
남: 알았어요. 친구들에게 전화해서 오늘은 못 간다고 말할게요.

핵심 의사소통기능 – 의도 표현하기

√ "I'm going to+동사원형 ~"은 '나는 ~할 것이다'라는 의미로, 의도를 표현한다.
√ 유사 표현 "I will ~", "I'm thinking of ~", "I'm planning to-v ~"로 말할 수도 있다.

집중!

• to 뒤에는 동사원형을 사용해야 한다.
• go의 진행형(be going)과 헷갈리지 않도록 하자.

출제 포인트 1

√ David는 오늘 오후 친구들과 함께 경기장에 갈 것이다. (불일치)
√ David는 친구들과 2주 전에 만남을 약속했다. (불일치)

출제 포인트 2

1) be v-ing: 가까운 미래를 나타내는 현재진행형
현재진행형은 '~하는 중이다'라는 의미로 현재에 진행 중인 일을 나타내지만, 여기서는 '~할 것이다'라는 뜻으로 가까운 미래의 일을 나타낸다.

2) forget (that): 명사절 접속사 that 생략
forget의 목적어절을 이끄는 접속사 that이 생략된 형태이다.

3) disappointed: 감정동사의 과거분사
주어 Your dad and sister(아빠와 여동생)이 실망스러운 감정을 느끼는 것이므로 과거분사를 쓴다.

4) don't help: 조건 부사절의 현재시제
'만약 ~라면'이라는 조건을 나타내는 접속사 if절에서는 미래의 의미일지라도 현재 시제를 쓴다.

5) and tell: 동사 병렬
등위접속사 and가 동사원형 call과 tell을 병렬 연결하고 있다. call과 tell 모두 I'm going to에 이어진다.

[Use It]

M: Welcome to The Steve Johnson Radio Show! We've got some new songs for you, but first let's check out a letter from one of our listeners. "Hi! I'm Larry, and I'm a high school student. I love hanging out with my friends and spending the whole weekend with them. But it has become a problem. One day, I missed a big family event. I realized that I wasn't being a good son or older brother. I'm always playing games or texting while I'm with my family. And I don't ask about their lives. From now on, I promise to do better. I'm sorry, Mom, Dad, and Amy!"

남: 'The Steve Johnson 라디오 쇼'에 오신 것을 환영합니다! 여러분을 위한 신곡들을 마련해 놓았습니다만, 먼저 청취자 중 한 분의 사연을 살펴보겠습니다. "안녕하세요! 저는 Larry이며, 고등학생입니다. 저는 친구들과 어울리고 주말 전부를 그들과 함께 보내는 걸 무척 좋아해요. 그런데 이것이 문제가 되었습니다. 어느 날, 저는 큰 가족 행사를 놓쳤어요. 제가 좋은 아들, 좋은 오빠가 아니라는 것을 깨달았죠. 가족과 있는 동안 저는 항상 게임을 하거나 문자를 합니다. 그리고 가족의 일상에 관해 묻지 않아요. 이제부터는 더 잘할 것을 약속합니다. 죄송해요, 엄마, 아빠, 그리고 Amy!"

[Listen & Speak 2]

G: Nick, do you have any plans this weekend?

B: Not really. I may go for a hike.

G: [1] How about joining me to help the Heritage Heroes group?

B: Oh, I heard about that. Isn't it a volunteer program?

G: Yes. We'd be kind of like a tour guide. We can [2] help share our heritage with visitors through the program.

B: Great! It sounds like a good way [3] to give back to our community.

G: Yeah. As citizens, we should [4] be more interested in our town.

B: And it also sounds fun. I can't wait!

여: Nick, 주말에 무슨 계획 있니?
남: 딱히. 도보 여행할까 생각 중이야.
여: 나와 같이 Heritage Heroes 모임을 돕는 것을 하면 어때?
남: 아, 그것에 대해 들었어. 자원봉사 프로그램 아니니?
여: 맞아. 우리는 일종의 여행 가이드가 될 거야. 이 프로그램을 통해 우리 유산들을 방문객들과 함께 나누는 걸 도울 수 있어.
남: 좋은데! 우리 사회에 되돌려주는 좋은 방법 같아.
여: 응. 시민으로서 우리는 우리 마을에 더 관심을 가져야 해.
남: 그리고 또 재미있을 것 같아. 어서 하고 싶은데!

핵심 의사소통기능 – 도덕적 의무 표현하기

√ "We should ~"는 '우리는 ~해야 한다'라는 의미로, 도덕적으로 마땅히 해야 할 일을 말할 때 쓴다.
√ "We ought to ~", "We must ~", "It's right/wrong to-v ~", "We have to/have got to ~", "We're supposed to-v ~"로 말할 수도 있다.

집중!

• 조동사 should 뒤에는 동사원형이 와야 한다.

출제 포인트 1

√ Nick은 여자가 말하고 있는 프로그램에 대해 들어본 적이 없다. (불일치)
√ Nick은 이번 주말에 여자와 함께 자원봉사를 하러 갈 것이다. (일치)
√ 여자는 사람들이 마을에 더 관심을 가져야 한다고 생각한다. (일치)

출제 포인트 2

1) How about v-ing ~?: 제안 · 권유의 표현
'~하는 것이 어때?'라고 제안이나 권유하는 표현이다. "What about v-ing ~?"로도 말할 수 있다.

2) help+to-v/동사원형
help는 목적어로 to부정사와 동사원형 모두 쓸 수 있다. 여기서는 share을 to share로 바꿀 수 있다.

3) to give: 형용사적 용법의 to부정사
앞의 명사구 a good way(좋은 방법)를 수식하는 형용사적 용법의 to부정사로 '줄 수 있는', '주는'의 의미이다.

4) be more interested in
⟨be interested in⟩은 '~에 관심이 있다'라는 의미로, 여기서는 more를 써서 비교급을 나타내고 있다.

[Use It]

W: Good evening, everyone. I'm Natalie Brown with The Nightly Report. It's been chilly these days, so here's some news to warm you right up! Earlier today, Angela Reynolds, a senior at Garland High School, received the Good Citizen Award. A few days ago, Angela saw a young child fall off the subway platform at Park Station. She bravely rushed onto the subway tracks to rescue him. Others helped pull her and the little boy back up to safety. Because of her quick thinking, Angela saved a young boy's life. I hope her inspiring story will encourage all of you to help your fellow citizens in their time of need!

여: 여러분, 안녕하십니까. 저는 'The Nightly Report'의 Natalie Brown입니다. 근래 쌀쌀했는데요, 여기 여러분을 바로 따뜻하게 해 드릴 뉴스가 있습니다! 오늘 오전에, Garland 고등학교 졸업반 학생 Angela Reynolds가 훌륭한 시민상을 받았습니다. 며칠 전 Angela는 한 어린이가 Park Station 지하철 승강장에서 떨어지는 것을 보았습니다. 그녀는 그를 구하러 곧장 용감하게 지하철 선로로 뛰어들었습니다. 다른 이들은 그녀와 어린 소년이 다시 안전하게 나오도록 끌어당기는 것을 도왔습니다. 그녀의 빠른 생각 덕에 Angela는 어린 소년의 목숨을 구했습니다. 그녀의 고무적인 이야기가 여러분 모두 다른 시민들이 어려울 때에 그들을 돕도록 격려하기를 바랍니다!

Listen & Speak

최중요 연습 문제

[01~02]

다음 대화문을 읽고, 물음에 답하시오.

W: Where ⓐ are you going, David?

B: There's a soccer game today. I am meeting my friends at the field.

W: Did you forget the whole family ⓑ is going to clean the house this afternoon?

B: Oh, no! That's today? But my friends are waiting for me!

W: We ⓒ planned this two weeks ago.

B: I forgot. I'm sorry, Mom.

W: Your dad and sister will be ⓓ disappointing if you don't help out.

B: Okay. I'm going to call and ⓔ tell my friends that I can't make it today.

01

위 대화의 밑줄 친 부분 중, 어법상 어색한 것은?

① ⓐ ② ⓑ ③ ⓒ ④ ⓓ ⑤ ⓔ

02

위 대화의 내용과 일치하지 않는 것은?

① David was supposed to meet his friends at the stadium.
② David's family is planning to clean their home.
③ David made an appointment with his family two weeks ago.
④ David felt sorry when he heard his mom's words.
⑤ David will go out with his friends this afternoon.

[03~04]

다음 대화문을 읽고, 물음에 답하시오.

G: Nick, do you have any plans this weekend?

B: Not really. I may go for a hike.

G: How about joining me to help the Heritage Heroes group this weekend?

B: Oh, I heard about that. Isn't it a volunteer program?

G: Yes. We'd be kind of like a tour guide. We can help share our heritage with visitors through the program.

B: Great! It sounds like a good way to give back to our community.

G: Yeah. As citizens, ______________________.

B: And it also sounds fun. I can't wait!

03

위 대화의 빈칸에 들어갈 말로 가장 적절한 것은?

① it is essential to protect our heritage
② we do not have to take care of our town
③ it's difficult to care for our community
④ it's unnecessary to share our heritage with others
⑤ we should be more interested in our town

04

위 대화의 내용과 일치하지 않는 것은?

① Nick은 여자가 말하고 있는 프로그램에 대해 들어본 적이 있다.
② Nick은 이번 주말에 여자와 함께 자원봉사를 하러 갈 것이다.
③ 여자는 지역 사회의 여행 가이드로 일하는 것에 관심이 있었다.
④ Nick과 여자는 방문객들이 마을의 유산을 보는 것을 도울 것이다.
⑤ 여자는 사람들이 마을에 더 관심을 가져야 한다고 생각한다.

[05~07]

다음 담화문을 읽고, 물음에 답하시오.

W: Good morning, everyone. I'm Natalie Brown with The Nightly Report. It's been chilly these days, so here's some news ⓐ to warm you right up! Earlier today, Angela Reynolds, a senior at Garland High School, ⓑ received the Good Citizen Award. A Few days ago, Angela saw a young child fell off the subway platform at Park Station. Angela rushed onto the subway tracks to rescue him without thinking about the risks. Others helped ⓒ pull her and the little boy back up to safety. ⓓ Because her quick judgement, Angela saved a young boy's life. I hope her inspiring story will encourage all of you ⓔ to help your fellow citizens in their time of need!

05

위 담화의 밑줄 친 부분 중, 어법상 어색한 것은?

① ⓐ ② ⓑ ③ ⓒ ④ ⓓ ⑤ ⓔ

06

위 담화의 목적으로 가장 적절한 것은?

① 지하철 플랫폼 승하차 시 주의사항을 알리려고
② 훌륭한 시민상의 기준을 안내하려고
③ 지하철 근처에서 실종된 소년을 찾으려고
④ 소녀의 이야기를 통해 선행 실천을 독려하려고
⑤ 도움을 쉽게 얻는 방법에 대해 알리려고

07

위 담화의 Angela에 관한 내용과 일치하지 않는 것은?

① She is a senior in High School.
② She won the Good Citizen Award.
③ She saw a boy falling off the subway platform.
④ She fell off the subway platform by mistake.
⑤ She rescued a young child.

[08~10]

다음 담화문을 읽고, 물음에 답하시오.

M: Welcome to The Steve Johnson Radio Show! We ⓐ have got some new songs for you, but first let's check out a letter from one of our listeners. "Hi! I'm Larry, and I'm a high school student. (①) I love hanging out with my friends and ⓑ spending the whole weekend with them. (②) One day, I missed a big family event. (③) I realized ⓒ that I wasn't being a good son or older brother. (④) I'm always playing games or ⓓ text while I'm with my family. (⑤) And I don't ask about their lives. From now on, I promise ⓔ to do better. I'm sorry, Mom, Dad, and Amy!"

08

위 담화의 밑줄 친 부분 중, 어법상 어색한 것은?

① ⓐ ② ⓑ ③ ⓒ ④ ⓓ ⑤ ⓔ

09

위 담화의 흐름으로 보아, 주어진 문장이 들어가기에 가장 적절한 곳은?

But it has become a problem.

① ② ③ ④ ⑤

10

위 담화의 내용과 일치하는 것은?

① Larry shared a story because he couldn't get along with his friends.
② Larry often talks about his daily life with his mom, dad, and Amy.
③ The speaker is Larry, a listener of The Steve Johnson Radio Show.
④ Larry has come to the realization after missing an important family event.
⑤ Larry usually plays games or sends messages when he is with his friends.

Grammar & Vocabulary

이 단원의 핵심 문법

√ 전치사의 목적어로서의 동명사

√ 진주어 to부정사와 의미상의 주어

Grammar & Vocabulary

최중요 연습 문제

01

다음 우리말과 같은 뜻이 되도록 〈조건〉에 맞게 주어진 말을 알맞게 배열하시오.

우리가 지역 사회에 관심을 갖는 것은 중요하다.

〈보기〉 important / it / to care for / be / us / our community / .

〈조건〉 1. 필요시 〈보기〉에 주어진 말을 변형하거나 추가할 것
2. 의미상의 주어를 사용할 것

02

다음 문장 중, 어법상 옳은 것은?

① All the furniture design by the famous artist was stolen yesterday.
② He walked away without say goodbye and never came back.
③ As he has taught students for a long time, he is used to dealing with them.
④ Many people in the room that is wearing dresses are my guests.
⑤ The purpose of this meeting is of team members to learn how to share materials.

03

다음 중, 밑줄 친 부분의 쓰임이 나머지 넷과 다른 것은?

① I avoid eating junk foods as much as possible.
② Do you mind me opening the window for fresh air?
③ We hopelessly saw the train leaving the platform.
④ You can relieve your stress by keeping a diary.
⑤ I get accustomed to drinking a lot of water.

04

다음 우리말과 같은 뜻이 되도록 〈조건〉에 맞게 주어진 말을 바르게 배열하시오.

당신이 저에게 연필을 빌려주는 것이 가능한가요?

〈보기〉 possible / to / it / for / would / a pencil / you / me / be / lend / ?

〈조건〉 1. 〈보기〉에 주어진 말을 한 번씩만 사용할 것
2. 단어를 변형하거나 추가하지 않을 것

05

다음 빈칸에 공통으로 들어갈 말로 가장 적절한 것은?

- I ______________ writing in English every day.
- He didn't do his best in ______________.

① score
② recover
③ wonder
④ release
⑤ practice

06

다음 중, 단어의 영영풀이가 적절하지 않은 것은?

① effort: a powerful or major influence
② physical: relating to the body of a person
③ passion: a strong feeling of excitement for something
④ attitude: the way you think and feel about something
⑤ bend: to curve out of a straight line

07

다음 문장 중, 어법상 틀린 것은?

① It is hard for him to adapt to high school life.
② Is it easy for you to walk for an hour?
③ She is interested in joining the club.
④ I am looking forward to working with him.
⑤ He was afraid of make mistakes during the presentation.

08

다음 중, 단어의 영영풀이가 적절하지 않은 것은?

① necessity: something that you must have or do
② realize: to understand or become aware of something
③ dedication: a feeling of very strong support for or loyalty to someone or something
④ heritage: the groups that people can be divided into based on certain physical qualities
⑤ rescue: to save someone or something from danger or harm

시험 문제 미리보기

1회

01

다음 중, 어법상 틀린 문장의 개수는?

ⓐ You should be sorry for be late.
ⓑ It was kind of her to help the old lady.
ⓒ We are really looking forward to work with you.
ⓓ I'm accustomed to express my feelings to others.
ⓔ It is necessary of me to get up early in the morning.
ⓕ I want to improve my writing skills by practicing every day.

① 1개 ② 2개 ③ 3개 ④ 4개 ⑤ 5개

02

다음 담화문을 읽고, Angela에 관한 설명으로 틀린 것을 고르시오.

W: Good evening, everyone. I'm Natalie Brown with The Nightly Report. It's been chilly these days, so here's some news to warm you right up! Earlier today, Angela Reynolds, a senior at Garland High School, received the Good Citizen Award. A few days ago, Angela saw a young child fall off the subway platform at Park Station. She bravely rushed onto the subway tracks to rescue him. Others helped pull her and the little boy back up to safety. Because of her quick thinking, Angela saved a young boy's life. I hope her inspiring story will encourage all of you to help your fellow citizens in their time of need!

① Garland 고등학교의 졸업반 학생이다.
② 오늘 '훌륭한 시민 상'을 받았다.
③ Park역에서 아이가 철로로 떨어지는 것을 보았다.
④ 빠른 판단으로 역무원에게 도움을 요청했다.
⑤ 안전하게 철로에서 빠져나올 수 있었다.

03

다음 대화문의 (A), (B), (C)의 각 네모 안에서 어법상 알맞은 말로 바르게 연결된 것은?

G: Nick, do you have any plans this weekend?
B: Not really. I may go for a hike.
G: How about joining me to help the Heritage Heroes group?
B: Oh, I heard about that. Isn't it a volunteer program?
G: Yes. We'd be kind of like a tour guide. We can help (A) [to share / sharing] our heritage with visitors through the program.
B: Great! It (B) [sounds / sounds like] a good way to give back to our community.
G: Yeah. As citizens, we should be more (C) [interesting / interested] in our town.
B: And it also sounds fun. I can't wait!

	(A)		(B)		(C)
①	to share	–	sounds	–	interesting
②	sharing	–	sounds	–	interested
③	to share	–	sounds like	–	interested
④	sharing	–	sounds like	–	interested
⑤	to share	–	sounds like	–	interesting

04

다음 중, 단어의 영영풀이가 바르지 않은 것은?

① attitude: a feeling, opinion or position about something or someone
② score: to win or get a goal in a competition, sport, or game
③ determined: strongly wanting to do something and not letting anyone stop you
④ reward: to give a person advantages because they have been successful
⑤ sophomore: a student in their final year of high school

[05~07]

다음 글을 읽고, 물음에 답하시오.

With only two minutes ⓐ to play, both teams were fighting for the football. (①) It was the last home game for the seniors of Winston High, and they were determined to win. Since it ⓑ has been a close game the whole evening, the best players of each team hadn't left the field. (②) Once Winston High's coach finally knew that victory was ⓒ theirs, all the seniors on the sidelines were allowed to play for the last few seconds. (③) One of the seniors, Ethan, was especially happy. He had never played in any of the games before. (④)

When the rival team dropped the ball, one of our players recovered it and quickly ran down the field with it. Ethan ran right after him ⓓ to catch up. (⑤) As our player got closer to the end zone, he saw Ethan behind him on his left. Instead of ⓔ run straight ahead, the player kindly passed the ball to Ethan so that he could score a touchdown.

05

윗글의 흐름으로 보아, 주어진 문장이 들어가기에 가장 적절한 곳을 고르시오.

Now, Ethan was finally getting the chance to step onto the grass.

① ② ③ ④ ⑤

06

윗글의 밑줄 친 ⓐ~ⓔ 중, 어법상 어색한 것을 모두 고르시오.

① ⓐ ② ⓑ ③ ⓒ ④ ⓓ ⑤ ⓔ

07

윗글의 내용과 일치하는 것은?

① Winston High was confident of their victory throughout the game.
② It was the first time ever that Ethan was allowed to play in the game.
③ Winston High's players were no longer willing to fight two minutes before the end of the game.
④ Unlike their opponents, Winston High's key players left the field near the end of the game.
⑤ Ethan was not one of the senior players on the sidelines.

[08~10]

다음 글을 읽고, 물음에 답하시오.

All eyes were on Ethan. With the ball in his hands, (가) everything seemed to be moving in slow motion, like in a Hollywood movie. People kept their eyes on him as he made his way to the end zone. They saw him (A) [cross / crossed] the goal line right before the clock ran out.

Unexpectedly, (나) everyone in the crowd leapt to their feet with their hands in the air. They were bursting with (B) [exciting / excited] shouts and unending cheers for Ethan. In this moment, all of Ethan's hard work and dedication was being rewarded with glory. Ethan's touchdown didn't win the game, but it will be worth (C) [remembering / to remember]. By now you're probably wondering why.

08

윗글의 (A), (B), (C)의 각 네모 안에서 어법에 맞는 낱말로 가장 적절한 것은?

	(A)	(B)	(C)
①	crossed	excited	to remember
②	cross	excited	remembering
③	cross	excited	to remember
④	crossed	exciting	remembering
⑤	cross	exciting	remembering

09

윗글의 밑줄 친 (가)를 의미 변화 없이 어법에 맞게 다시 쓰시오. (단, 7단어로 쓸 것)

it seemed ______________________________

____

10

윗글의 밑줄 친 (나) everyone in the crowd leapt to their feet with their hands in the air가 의미하는 바로 가장 적절한 것은?

① they were already expecting Ethan's touchdown
② they were very surprised and happy with Ethan's touchdown
③ they wanted to give cheers to one another as their team won the game
④ they felt uncomfortable because they kept standing up during the game
⑤ they thought that Ethan's touchdown was of no use for the game

[11~12]

다음 글을 읽고, 물음에 답하시오.

Well, Ethan is only five feet tall, and ⓐ his legs unnaturally bend away from each other. (A) [It / That] is difficult for him to walk, run, or move around. Because of ⓑ his condition, he decided to leave his crowded high school in the big city. He moved to our school in the middle of his first year in high school. That following summer, he asked the coach if he could join the football team as a sophomore. The coach wasn't sure at first, but in the end ⓒ he allowed Ethan to come to practice. (B) [Regardless of / Though] his physical difficulties, Ethan worked just as hard as every other player on the team. (C) [Despite / Although] ⓓ he knew he would never be a valuable player in any of the team's games, ⓔ he poured his heart and soul into practice every day.

11

윗글의 (A), (B), (C)의 각 네모 안에서 어법에 맞는 표현으로 가장 적절한 것은?

	(A)	(B)	(C)
①	It	Regardless of	Despite
②	It	Regardless of	Although
③	It	Though	Despite
④	That	Regardless of	Although
⑤	That	Though	Although

12

윗글의 밑줄 친 ⓐ~ⓔ 중, 가리키는 대상이 나머지 넷과 다른 것은?

① ⓐ ② ⓑ ③ ⓒ ④ ⓓ ⑤ ⓔ

[13~15]

다음 글을 읽고, 물음에 답하시오.

Over time, however, Ethan became ① valuable to the team in different ways. His passion for the game was an inspiration to all his teammates. Because Ethan motivated and encouraged them, they became his most passionate fans. Day in and day out, ② seeing Ethan's smile, positive attitude, and hard work ______(A)______(lift) everyone's spirits. Right before every game, Ethan would always be in the middle of the group ③ offered motivational words. He had a special talent for ______(B)______(calm) people down and bringing out the best in them. Ethan was also Winston High's loudest supporter. He always observed each ④ play carefully from the sidelines. Although he wasn't the one ⑤ making the actual plays on the field, Ethan's mind was always right there with his teammates. Everyone could sense his love for football, and the coaches admired his commitment.

13

윗글의 밑줄 친 부분 중, 어법상 틀린 것을 고르시오.

① ② ③ ④ ⑤

14

Ethan에 관한 윗글의 내용과 일치하지 않는 것은?

① 긍정적인 태도로 늘 노력하여 동료들에게 귀감이 되었다.
② 동료들이 경기에 들어가기 전에 응원의 말을 해 주었다.
③ 상대 팀이 연습하는 모습을 유심히 관찰하여 전략을 세웠다.
④ 풋볼에 대한 사랑과 열정이 매우 컸다.
⑤ 윈스턴 고등학교 감독에게도 헌신을 인정받았다.

15

윗글의 주어진 괄호 속 동사를 알맞은 형태로 바꿔 빈칸 (A), (B)를 채우시오.

(A) ____________ (B) ____________

[16~18]

다음 글을 읽고, 물음에 답하시오.

For the past three years, Ethan has been schooling us all in the game of life. He (A) [reminds always / always reminds] us that everyone is important to a team's success, though their role on the team may be small. Instead of putting all his efforts into trying (B) [to be / being] the team's best player, he has done everything he can to make the team better. As Ethan has shown us, lifting up those around us (C) [is / are] also of great worth. When we help others shine, their light will shine on us in return. Yes, sometimes there is something better than ____________________.

16

윗글의 (A), (B), (C)의 각 네모 안에서 어법에 맞는 표현으로 가장 적절한 것은?

	(A)	(B)	(C)
①	always reminds	to be	are
②	reminds always	to be	is
③	always reminds	to be	is
④	reminds always	being	are
⑤	always reminds	being	are

17

윗글의 빈칸에 들어갈 말로 가장 적절한 것은?

① becoming popular
② having comfort
③ making plans
④ earning wealth
⑤ being the best

18

윗글의 내용을 한 문장으로 요약하고자 할 때, 빈칸 (A), (B)에 알맞은 말을 고르시오.

> Rather than being the ______(A)______ player, Ethan contributed to making his team better by ______(B)______ his teammates.

	(A)		(B)
①	top	–	encouraging
②	top	–	ignoring
③	ordinary	–	motivating
④	ordinary	–	discouraging
⑤	outstanding	–	neglecting

[19~20]

다음 글을 읽고, 물음에 답하시오.

With only two minutes to play, both teams were fighting for the football. It was the last home game for the seniors of Winston High, and they were (A) [determined / ashamed] to win. Since it had been a close game the whole evening, the best players of each team hadn't left the field. Once Winston High's coach finally knew that victory was theirs, all the seniors on the sidelines were (B) [banned / allowed] to play for the last few seconds. One of the seniors, Ethan, was especially happy. He had never played in any of the games before. Now, Ethan was finally getting the chance to step onto the grass.

When the rival team dropped the ball, one of our players recovered it and quickly ran down the field with it. Ethan ran right after him to catch up. As our player got closer to the end zone, he saw Ethan behind him on his left. Instead of running straight ahead, the player kindly passed the ball to Ethan (C) [so that / in that] he could score a touchdown.

19

윗글의 (A), (B), (C)의 각 네모 안에서 문맥상 맞는 표현으로 가장 적절한 것은?

	(A)		(B)		(C)
①	determined	–	allowed	–	in that
②	ashamed	–	allowed	–	in that
③	determined	–	allowed	–	so that
④	ashamed	–	banned	–	so that
⑤	determined	–	banned	–	in that

20

윗글의 상황에 나타난 분위기로 가장 적절한 것은?

① calm and peaceful
② urgent and scary
③ dynamic and frightening
④ dull and boring
⑤ tense and exciting

[21~22]

다음 글을 읽고, 물음에 답하시오.

All eyes were on Ethan. ① With the ball in his hands, everything seemed to be moving in slow motion, like in a Hollywood movie. ② People kept their eyes on him as he made his way to the end zone. They saw him cross the goal line right before the clock ran out.

③ Unexpectedly, everyone in the crowd led to their feet with their hands in the air. ④ They were bursting with excited shouts and unending cheers for Ethan. ⑤ In this moment, all of Ethan's hard work and dedication was being rewarded with glory. Ethan's touchdown didn't win the game, but it will be worth remembering. By now you're probably wondering why.

21

윗글의 밑줄 친 문장 중, 문맥상 어색한 낱말을 포함하고 있는 것은?

① ② ③ ④ ⑤

22

윗글의 내용과 일치하는 것은?

① Ethan이 공을 가지고 느리게 움직였기 때문에 시선이 집중되었다.
② Ethan은 경기가 종료된 후 득점을 했기 때문에 결과에 영향을 미치지 못했다.
③ Ethan이 득점을 하기 전부터 모든 관중이 환호하기 시작했다.
④ Ethan은 성실한 선수라기보다는 재능을 타고난 선수였다.
⑤ Ethan의 터치다운이 경기에서의 승리에 있어 결정적인 요인은 아니었다.

23

다음 글의 밑줄 친 부분 중, 문맥상 적절하지 않은 것은?

Well, Ethan is only five feet tall, and his legs unnaturally bend away from each other. It is difficult for him to walk, run, or move around. Because of his ① condition, he decided to ② leave his crowded high school in the big city. He moved to our school in the middle of his first year in high school. That following summer, he asked the coach if he could join the football team as a sophomore. The coach wasn't sure at first, but in the end he ③ allowed Ethan to come to practice. Regardless of his ④ physical difficulties, Ethan worked just as hard as every other player on the team. Although he knew he would never be a ⑤ worthless player in any of the team's games, he poured his heart and soul into practice every day.

[24~27]

다음 글을 읽고, 물음에 답하시오.

Over time, however, Ethan became __________ to the team in different ways. His passion for the game ① was an inspiration to all his teammates. ② Because Ethan motivated and encouraged them, they became his most passionate fans. Day in and day out, ③ to see Ethan's smile, positive attitude, and hard work lifted everyone's spirits. Right before every game, Ethan would always be in the middle of the group (A) 의욕을 높이는 말을 해주며. He had a special talent for calming people down and ④ bring out the best in them. Ethan was also Winston High's loudest supporter. He always observed each play carefully from the sidelines. ⑤ Although he wasn't the one making the actual plays on the field, Ethan's mind was always right there with his teammates. Everyone could sense his love for football, and the coaches admired his commitment.

24

윗글의 밑줄 친 부분 중, 어법상 어색한 것은?

① ② ③ ④ ⑤

25

윗글의 빈칸에 들어갈 말로 가장 적절한 것은?

① indifferent
② worthless
③ replaceable
④ priceless
⑤ unacceptable

26

윗글의 밑줄 친 (A)의 우리말 뜻에 맞게 분사구문과 〈보기〉의 단어를 사용하여 문장을 완성하시오.

〈보기〉 motivational, offer, words

____

27

Ethan에 관한 윗글의 내용과 일치하는 것은?

① 실전 경기에서 두각을 나타내 중요한 선수가 되었다.
② 팀원들을 고무시킬 만큼 대단한 열정을 갖고 있었다.
③ 작은 체구의 소극적인 성격의 학생이었다.
④ 팀원들에게서 최고를 이끌어내는 감독을 존경했다.
⑤ 친구들로부터 많은 조언과 격려의 말을 받곤 했다.

[28~30]

다음 글을 읽고, 물음에 답하시오.

Day in and day out, seeing Ethan's smile, positive attitude, and hard work lifted everyone's spirits. Right before every game, Ethan would always be in the middle of the group offering motivational words. He had a special talent for ① calming people down and bringing out the best in them. Ethan was also Winston High's loudest supporter. He always observed each play carefully from the sidelines. Although he wasn't the one ② making the actual plays on the field, Ethan's mind was always right there with his teammates. Everyone could sense his love for football, and the coaches admired his commitment.

For the past three years, (가) Ethan은 삶이라는 경기에서 우리 모두를 가르쳐왔다. He always reminds us that everyone is important to a team's success, though their role on the team may be small. Instead of ③ putting all his efforts into ④ trying to be the team's best player, he has done everything he can to make the team better. When we help others shine, their light will shine on us in return. Yes, sometimes there is something better than ⑤ being the best.

28

윗글의 밑줄 친 부분 중, 쓰임이 나머지 넷과 다른 것은?

① ② ③ ④ ⑤

29

윗글의 밑줄 친 우리말 (가)를 〈조건〉에 맞게 영작하시오.

〈조건〉
- 현재완료 진행형을 사용할 것
- 총 11단어로 문장을 완성할 것
- school, of, all, the game, in, life를 모두 사용할 것 (단, 필요시 단어 변형 및 추가 가능)

____

____

30

윗글을 읽고, 다음 빈칸 (a), (b)에 들어갈 말로 알맞게 짝지어진 것을 고르시오.

Q: According to the passage, what lesson has Ethan shown us?
A: He has shown that ____(a)____ others around us is also ____(b)____.

	(a)		(b)
①	observing	–	of importance
②	respecting	–	of no significance
③	supporting	–	of no use
④	lifting up	–	of great value
⑤	imitating	–	of great worth

2회

[01~02]

다음 대화문을 읽고, 물음에 답하시오.

W: Where are you going, David?
B: There's a soccer game today. I'm meeting my friends at the field.
W: Did you forget the whole family is going to clean the house this afternoon?
B: Oh, no! That's today? But my friends are waiting for me!
W: We planned this two weeks ago.
B: I forgot. I'm sorry, Mom.
W: Your dad and sister will be disappointed if you don't help out.
B: Okay. I'm going to call and tell my friends that ________________.

01

위 대화의 내용과 일치하는 것은?

① David는 오늘 친구들과 야구 경기를 보러 갈 것이다.
② David의 가족은 3주 전에 대청소를 하기로 계획했다.
③ David는 아빠 덕분에 대청소하는 날임을 알게 되었다.
④ David가 경기를 보러 간다면 여동생은 실망할 것이다.
⑤ David의 아빠는 출장으로 인해 청소에 참여할 수 없다.

02

위 대화의 빈칸에 들어갈 말로 알맞은 것은?

① I can't make it today
② I can't help clean the house
③ I will bring my sister with me
④ I can't wait to watch the game
⑤ I cannot help attending the game

03

다음 중, 어법상 틀린 문장을 모두 고른 것은?

ⓐ It was foolish of me to believe his words.
ⓑ The dog is accustomed to walking along the river.
ⓒ She is good at taking care of others and to help them.
ⓓ It was so sweet of you to coming to my birthday party.
ⓔ Is it possible for you to keep silent while I'm reading?
ⓕ My sister is scared of to stay at home alone.

① ⓐ, ⓑ, ⓓ
② ⓑ, ⓒ, ⓔ
③ ⓑ, ⓓ, ⓔ
④ ⓒ, ⓓ, ⓕ
⑤ ⓓ, ⓔ, ⓕ

04

다음 중, 단어의 영영풀이가 바르지 않은 것은?

① make one's way: to move forward usually by following a path
② observe: to watch something or someone carefully
③ run out: to come to an end
④ admire: to provide or supply something
⑤ catch up: to reach someone who is in front of you by moving faster

[05~08]

다음 글을 읽고, 물음에 답하시오.

With only two minutes (a) to play, both teams were fighting for the football. It was the last home game for the seniors of Winston High, and they were ① unwilling to win. Since it had been a ② close game the whole evening, the best players of each team (b) hadn't left the field. Once Winston High's coach finally knew that victory was theirs, the coach (c) was allowed all the seniors on the sidelines to play for the last few seconds. One of the (d) seniors, Ethan, was especially ③ happy. He had never played in any of the games before. Now, Ethan was finally getting the chance (e) to step onto the grass.

When the rival team dropped the ball, one of our players ④ recovered it and quickly ran down the field with it. Ethan ran right after him to catch up. As our player got closer to the end zone, he saw Ethan behind him on his left. ⑤ Instead of running straight ahead, the player kindly passed the ball to Ethan (A) so that he could score a touchdown.

05

윗글의 밑줄 친 (a)~(e) 중, 어법상 어색한 것은?

① (a) ② (b) ③ (c) ④ (d) ⑤ (e)

06

윗글의 밑줄 친 ①~⑤ 중, 문맥상 낱말의 쓰임이 적절하지 않은 것은?

① ② ③ ④ ⑤

07

윗글의 밑줄 친 (A)와 의미가 일치하도록 〈조건〉에 맞게 영작하시오.

〈조건〉 - to부정사를 사용할 것
- 의미상의 주어를 사용할 것
- 총 6단어로 쓸 것

____

____

08

윗글의 내용과 일치하지 않는 것은?

① Winston High's players had a strong will to win even when only two minutes were left in the game.
② Ethan had played in a few games before.
③ When the rival team's player dropped the ball, one of Winston High's players picked it up and ran fast.
④ Ethan's teammate, who was running to the end zone with the ball, passed it to Ethan.
⑤ Winston High played a close game with its opponent.

[09~11]

다음 글을 읽고, 물음에 답하시오.

All eyes ① were on Ethan. With the ball in his hands, everything seemed ② to be moving in slow motion, like in a Hollywood movie. People kept their eyes on him ③ as he made his way to the end zone. They saw him ④ to cross the goal line right before the clock ran out.

Unexpectedly, everyone in the crowd leapt to their feet with their hands in the air. They were ⑤ bursting with excited shouts and unending cheers for Ethan. In this moment, all of Ethan's hard work and dedication (A) 영광으로 보상받고 있었다. Ethan's touchdown didn't win the game, but it will be worth remembering. By now you're probably wondering why.

09

윗글의 밑줄 친 부분 중, 어법상 어색한 것은?

① ② ③ ④ ⑤

10

윗글의 주어진 우리말 (A)를 〈보기〉의 단어를 모두 활용하여 어법에 맞게 영작하시오. (단, 5단어로 쓸 것)

〈보기〉 glory, reward, with

____

11

윗글의 내용과 일치하지 않는 것은?

① Everyone was watching Ethan reaching the end zone.
② Ethan passed the goal line before the game ended.
③ It was expected that everyone would stand up cheering Ethan.
④ Ethan was a hard-working, dedicated player.
⑤ Ethan's touchdown did not lead the team to win the game.

[12~14]

다음 글을 읽고, 물음에 답하시오.

Well, Ethan is only five feet tall, and his legs unnaturally bend away from each other. It is difficult ① for him to walk, run, or move around. Because of his condition, he decided ② to leave his crowded high school in the big city. He moved to our school in the middle of his first year in high school. That following summer, he asked the coach ③ if he could join the football team as a sophomore. The coach wasn't sure at first, but in the end he allowed Ethan ④ to come to practice. Regardless of his physical difficulties, Ethan worked just ⑤ as hardly as every other player on the team. Although he knew ______________________________, he poured his heart and soul into practice every day.

12

윗글의 밑줄 친 부분 중, 어법상 적절하지 않은 것은?

① ② ③ ④ ⑤

13

윗글의 빈칸에 들어갈 말로 가장 적절한 것은?

① the coach wouldn't accept him as a football team player
② one day he would be appreciated as an invaluable player
③ he would never be a valuable player in any of the team's games
④ his teammates would help him win his first game
⑤ he didn't want to play football unless his condition was treated

14

윗글의 내용과 일치하지 않는 것은?

① Ethan used to go to a crowded high school in the big city.
② Ethan was in his first year when he moved to Winston High.
③ Ethan has no trouble running fast despite his physical limitations.
④ The coach let Ethan join the football team as a sophomore.
⑤ Ethan participated in the team's practice just like other players.

[15~16]

다음 글을 읽고, 물음에 답하시오.

Over time, however, Ethan became ① valuably to the team in different ways. His passion for the game was an inspiration to all his teammates. ② Because of Ethan motivated and encouraged them, they became his most passionate fans. Day in and day out, seeing Ethan's smile, positive attitude, and hard work ③ was lifted everyone's spirits. Right before every game, Ethan would always be in the middle of the group offering motivational words. He had a special talent for calming people down and ④ being brought out the best in them. Ethan was also Winston High's loudest supporter. He always observed each play carefully from the sidelines. Although he wasn't the one ⑤ made the actual plays on the field, Ethan's mind was always right there with his teammates. Everyone could sense his love for football, and the coaches admired his commitment.

15

윗글의 밑줄 친 부분을 어법상 바르게 고치지 못한 것은?

① → valuable ② → Because
③ → lifting ④ → bringing
⑤ → making

16

윗글의 내용과 일치하는 것은?

① Ethan was so loud that he distracted the players in the field.
② Ethan was jealous of his teammates for making the actual plays.
③ Ethan recorded each play from the sidelines to spot the team's weaknesses.
④ Ethan gave inspiring words to his teammates before every game.
⑤ Some teammates were uncomfortable about Ethan's presence.

[17~18]

다음 글을 읽고, 물음에 답하시오.

Ethan was also Winston High's ① loudest supporter. He always observed each play carefully from the sidelines. Although he wasn't the one ② making the actual plays on the field, Ethan's mind was always right there with his teammates. Everyone could sense his love for football, and the coaches admired his commitment.

For the past three years, Ethan ③ has been schooled us all in the game of life. He always reminds us that everyone is important to a team's success, though their role on the team may be small. Instead of ④ putting all his efforts into trying to be the team's best player, he has done everything he can to make the team better. As Ethan has shown us, lifting up those around us is also ______________. When we help others shine, their light will shine on us in return. Yes, sometimes there is ⑤ something better than being the best.

17

윗글의 밑줄 친 부분 중, 어법상 적절하지 않은 것은?

① ② ③ ④ ⑤

18

윗글의 빈칸에 들어갈 말로 가장 적절한 것은?

① worthless ② optional
③ pointless ④ irrelevant
⑤ valuable

[19~20]

다음 글을 읽고, 물음에 답하시오.

Over time, however, Ethan became valuable to the team in different ways. His passion for the game was an inspiration to all his teammates. Because Ethan motivated and encouraged them, they became his most passionate fans. Day in and day out, seeing Ethan's smile, positive attitude, and hard work lifted everyone's spirits. Right before every game, Ethan would always be in the middle of the group offering motivational words. He had a special talent (A) 사람들을 침착하게 하고, 그들에게서 최선을 이끌어내는.

19

윗글의 Ethan의 태도가 주는 교훈으로 옳은 것은?

① Nothing is better than being the best.
② The role of the coach in sports is critical.
③ You should pay back for what you were granted.
④ Only the team's star players determine the outcome of the game.
⑤ The one who cheers up other people will be rewarded.

20

윗글의 밑줄 친 (A)를 〈조건〉에 맞게 영작하시오.

〈조건〉 - 등위접속사 and와 전치사 for를 사용할 것
- calm down, bring out을 변형하여 사용할 것
- 총 11단어로 쓸 것

[21~23]

다음 글을 읽고, 물음에 답하시오.

With only two minutes to play, both teams were fighting for the football.

(A) All eyes were on Ethan. With the ball in his hands, everything seemed to be moving in slow motion, like in a Hollywood movie. People kept their eyes on (a) him as he made his way to the end zone. They saw him ① cross the goal line right before the clock ran out. Unexpectedly, everyone in the crowd leapt to their feet with their hands in the air. They were bursting with excited shouts and unending ② cheers for Ethan. In this moment, all of Ethan's hard work and dedication was being rewarded with glory. Ethan's touchdown didn't win the game, but it will be worth remembering. By now you're probably wondering why.

(B) Now, Ethan was finally getting the chance to step onto the grass. When the rival team dropped the ball, (b) one of our players recovered it and quickly ran down the field with it. Ethan ran right after him to catch up. As (c) our player got closer to the end zone, he saw Ethan behind (d) him on his left. Instead of running straight ahead, (e) the player kindly ③ passed the ball to Ethan so that he could score a touchdown.

(C) It was the last home game for the seniors of Winston High, and they were determined to win. Since it had been a close game the whole evening, the ④ best players of each team hadn't left the field. Once Winston High's coach finally knew that victory was theirs, all the seniors on the sidelines were ⑤ forbidden to play for the last few seconds. One of the seniors, Ethan, was especially happy. He had never played in any of the games before.

21

주어진 글 다음에 이어질 순서로 가장 적절한 것은?

① (A) – (B) – (C) ② (B) – (A) – (C)
③ (B) – (C) – (A) ④ (C) – (A) – (B)
⑤ (C) – (B) – (A)

22

윗글의 밑줄 친 (a)~(e) 중, 가리키는 대상이 나머지 넷과 다른 것은?

① (a) ② (b) ③ (c) ④ (d) ⑤ (e)

23

윗글의 밑줄 친 ①~⑤ 중, 문맥상 낱말의 쓰임이 적절하지 않은 것은?

① ② ③ ④ ⑤

[24~25]

다음 글을 읽고, 물음에 답하시오.

Over time, however, Ethan became ① invaluable to the team in different ways. His passion for the game was an inspiration to all his teammates. Because Ethan motivated and (A) [encourage / encouraged] them, they became his most ② passionate fans. Day in and day out, (B) [see / seeing] Ethan's smile, ③ negative attitude, and hard work lifted everyone's spirits. Right before every game, Ethan would always be in the ④ middle of the group (C) [offer / offering] motivational words. He had a special talent for calming people down and bringing out the best in them. Ethan was also Winston High's loudest supporter. He always observed each play ⑤ carefully from the sidelines.

24

윗글의 밑줄 친 부분 중, 문맥상 낱말의 쓰임이 적절하지 않은 것은?

① ② ③ ④ ⑤

25

윗글의 (A), (B), (C)의 각 네모 안에서 어법에 맞는 표현으로 가장 적절한 것은?

	(A)	(B)	(C)
①	encourage	see	offer
②	encouraged	seeing	offer
③	encourage	seeing	offering
④	encouraged	seeing	offering
⑤	encourage	see	offering

[26~27]

다음 글을 읽고, 물음에 답하시오.

Regardless of his physical difficulties, Ethan worked just ⓐ as hard as every other player on the team. Although he knew ⓑ that he would never be a valuable player in any of the team's games, he poured his heart and soul into practice every day. Over time, however, Ethan became valuable to the team in different ways. His passion for the game was an inspiration to all his teammates. ⓒ Because Ethan motivated and encouraged them, they became his most passionate fans. Day in and day out, ⓓ seeing Ethan's smile, positive attitude, and hard work lifted everyone's spirits. Right before every game, Ethan would always be in the middle of the group ⓔ offering motivational words.

26

윗글의 밑줄 친 ⓐ~ⓔ의 어법 설명으로 적절하지 않은 것은?

① ⓐ: '~만큼 열심히'의 의미인 원급 비교
② ⓑ: 동사 know의 목적어절을 이끄는 접속사
③ ⓒ: 이유를 나타내는 접속사
④ ⓓ: 주어 역할을 하는 동명사
⑤ ⓔ: 목적어 역할을 하는 동명사

27

Ethan에 관한 윗글의 내용과 일치하는 것은?

① 신체적 한계로 인해 풋볼 연습을 관찰하기만 했다.
② 언젠가는 팀에서 중요한 선수가 될 거라 믿고 열심히 연습했다.
③ 동료들로부터 자극을 받아 더 열정적으로 풋볼 연습에 참여했다.
④ 동료들에게 동기를 부여하는 말을 해주며 늘 팀의 중심에 있었다.
⑤ 마지막 홈 경기에서 그의 최고의 능력을 끌어냈다.

[28~30]

다음 글을 읽고, 물음에 답하시오.

Ethan was also Winston High's loudest supporter. He always observed each play carefully from the sidelines. Although he wasn't the one (a) <u>that</u> was making the actual plays on the field, Ethan's mind was always right there with his teammates. Everyone could sense (b) <u>that</u> he did love football, and the coaches admired (c) <u>that</u> commitment.

For the past three years, Ethan has been schooling us all in the game of life. He always reminds us (d) <u>that</u> everyone is important to a team's success, though their role on the team may be small. Instead of putting all his efforts into trying to be the team's best player, he has done everything (e) <u>that</u> he can to make the team better. As Ethan has shown us, (A) <u>우리 주변 사람들의 기운을 북돋워 주는 것 역시 큰 가치가 있다</u>. When we help others shine, their light will shine on us in return. Yes, sometimes ____________________.

28

윗글의 빈칸에 들어갈 말로 가장 적절한 것은?

① we have to take credit for our work
② ignoring others' contributions is advantageous
③ people shouldn't overestimate their confidence
④ there is something better than being the best
⑤ helping others can put us in dangerous situations

29

윗글의 밑줄 친 (a)~(e) 중, 〈보기〉의 밑줄 친 <u>that</u>과 쓰임이 같은 것을 <u>모두</u> 고르시오.

〈보기〉 The doctor recommended <u>that</u> he get more exercise.

① (a)　② (b)　③ (c)　④ (d)　ⓔ (e)

30

윗글의 밑줄 친 (A)의 우리말을 〈조건〉에 맞게 영작하시오.

〈조건〉 - lift, of, worth, great, up, be, those, also를 모두 사용할 것 (단, 필요시 단어 변형 및 추가 가능)
- 총 10단어로 쓸 것

____

정답표

자세한 해설

리딩 본문[1]

문장편 최중요 연습 문제

01 were allowed to play

02 ③

03 ③

04 ③

05 ①

06 ④

07 ④

08 so that he could score a touchdown

09 ①, ③, ⑤

10 ④

11 ⑤

12 for him to score a touchdown

13 ⑤

14 ④

15 ④

16 ②

17 ②

18 allowed all the seniors on the sidelines to play

19 all the seniors on the sidelines were allowed to play for the last few seconds by the coach / all the seniors on the sidelines were allowed to play by the coach for the last few seconds

20 ⑤

21 ③

22 ⑤

23 ⑤

24 ③

25 ②

26 ⑤

27 ④

28 Instead of running straight ahead, the player passed the ball to Ethan so that he could score a touchdown.

29 ③

30 ④

문단편 최중요 연습 문제

01 ⑤

02 ④

03 ⑤

04 ⑤

05 ③

06 ④

07 ②

08 ⑤

09 ③

10 ⑤

11 ③

12 ④

기타 연습 문제

01 (A) – ②, (B) – ④, (C) – ①, (D) – ③

02 ③

03 losing → getting

04 (A) dropped (B) score

05 ④

06 ④

07 ④

08 ①

09 ①, ②

10 one of our players recovered it

11 ③

12 ②

리딩 본문[2]

문장편 최중요 연습 문제

01 ①

02 ④

03 were bursting with excited shouts and unending cheers

04 ②

05 ②

06 ④

07 ④ were being rewarded → was being rewarded

08 it will be worth remembering

09 ②

10 ①

11 ④

12 ④

13 ④

14 ①

15 ④

16 ④

17 ①

18 ⑤

19 ⑤

20 ②

문단편 최중요 연습 문제

01 ②

02 ⑤

03 ③

04 ③

05 ②

06 ④

07 ①

08 ②

09 ②

10 (C) – (A) – (B) – (D)

11 ⑤

12 ②

13 ③

14 ④

15 ①

16 ⑤

기타 연습 문제

01 ⑤

02 ④

03 ②

04 ③

05 ⑤

리딩 본문[3]

문장편 최중요 연습 문제

01 ②

02 ⑤

03 ③, ⑤

04 ③

05 ⑤

06 ②

07 ③

08 ①, ②, ③

09 ②, ③

10 (1) 키가 단지 5피트이다.
(2) 다리가 부자연스럽게 바깥으로 구부러졌다.

11 ⓔ → Although he knew he would never be a valuable player in any of the team's games

12 ③, ⑤

13 It is difficult for him to walk, run, or move around.

14 Although he knew he would never be a valuable player

15 ②

문단편 최중요 연습 문제

01 ③

02 ④

03 ⑤

04 ①

05 ③

06 ③

07 ⑤

08 ③

09 ②, ⑤

10 ③

11 ④

12 ②

기타 연습 문제

01 ④

02 ②

03 ③

04 ⑤

05 ①

리딩 본문[4]

문장편 최중요 연습 문제

01 ⑤

02 ④

03 ②, ④, ⑤

04 ④

05 ⑤

06 seeing Ethan's smile, positive attitude, and hard work lifted everyone's spirits

07 ③

08 ③

09 ④

10 ⑤

11 ①, ③

12 ①

13 ①, ⑤

14 ②

15 ④

16 ③

17 Though he was not the one making the actual plays on the field

18 ④

19 ③

20 ①, ②

21 ⑤

22 ②

23 ③

24 ④

25 ⑤

26 (b) games → game
(d) brings → bringing

27 ③

28 ③

29 offering motivational words

30 Ethan's mind was always right there with his teammates

문단편 최중요 연습 문제

01 ③

02 ①

03 ⑤

04 ③

05 ③

06 ③

07 ④

08 ③

09 ④

10 ④

11 ④

12 ③

기타 연습 문제

01 ⑤

02 He always observed each play carefully from the sidelines.

03 ②

04 field

05 ③

리딩 본문[5]

문장편 최중요 연습 문제

01 ①

02 ⑤

03 ③

04 sometimes there is something better than being the best

05 ②

06 ④

07 ⑤

08 ②, ④

09 ②

10 that

11 there is something better than being the best

12 ③

13 ②

14 ②

15 ⑤

16 ①

17 ①

18 ⑤

19 ①

20 ⑤

21 ④

22 ③

23 ③

24 ③

25 ②, ⑤

26 ③, ⑤

27 ④

28 ④

29 lifting up those around us is also of great worth

30 he has done everything that he can to make the team better

문단편 최중요 연습 문제

01 ②

02 ⑤

03 ③

04 ④

05 ③

06 ③

07 ②

08 ④

기타 연습 문제

01 1) us that, success
2) us of, success

02 ⑤

03 ③

04 ①

05 ③

기타 본문, Listen & Speak, Grammar & Vocabulary

기타 본문 최중요 연습 문제

01 ④

02 ②

03 ⑤

04 ②

05 ①

06 ①

07 ⑤

08 so that he could score

09 ②, ④

10 ⑤

Listen & Speak 최중요 연습 문제

01 ④

02 ⑤

03 ⑤

04 ③

05 ④

06 ④

07 ④

08 ④

09 ②

10 ④

Grammar & Vocabulary 최중요 연습 문제

01 It is important for us to care for our community.

02 ③

03 ③

04 Would it be possible for you to lend me a pencil?

05 ⑤

06 ①

07 ⑤

08 ④

시험 문제 미리보기

1회

01 ④

02 ④

03 ③

04 ⑤

05 ④

06 ②, ⑤

07 ②

08 ②

09 that everything was moving in slow motion

10 ②

11 ②

12 ③

13 ③

14 ③

15 (A) lifted (B) calming

16 ③

17 ⑤

18 ①

19 ③

20 ⑤

21 ③

22 ⑤

23 ⑤

24 ④

25 ④

26 offering motivational words

27 ②

28 ②

29 Ethan has been schooling us all in the game of life

30 ④

2회

01 ④

02 ①

03 ④

04 ④

05 ③

06 ①

07 for him to score a touchdown

08 ②

09 ④

10 was being rewarded with glory

11 ③

12 ⑤

13 ③

14 ③

15 ③

16 ④

17 ③

18 ⑤

19 ⑤

20 for calming people down and bringing out the best in them

21 ⑤

22 ①

23 ⑤

24 ③

25 ④

26 ⑤

27 ④

28 ④

29 ②, ④

30 lifting up those around us is also of great worth

밀당PT 영어 2023 합격 후기

서울대 의예과 등 4개 의대 합격

수강생 최OO 학생

합격 대학 학과 서울대 의예과 / 연세대 의예과 / 부산대 의예과 / 경상대 의예과

밀당PT 수강 후 성적 변화 모의고사 영어 2등급 > **1등급**

• 밀당PT를 선택한 이유

우선 이동시간이 없으니까 그 시간을 아껴 공부에 투자할 수 있다는 점이 가장 유익했습니다. 그래서 계속 자습을 하다가도 흐름이 끊기지 않고 바로 공부를 이어갈 수 있어 효율적이었습니다. 그리고 인강 같은 경우에 QnA 게시판이 있기는 해도 답변을 받으려면 적어도 하루는 기다려야 했습니다. 하지만 밀당의 경우 선생님과 실시간으로 질의응답을 할 수 있어 궁금한 점을 그때그때 해결할 수 있었습니다. 특히, 선생님들께서 단순히 정답을 알려주시는 게 아니라 제가 오답을 선택한 근거를 먼저 물어보시고 그 부분을 수정한 다음, 정답의 근거를 말씀해주셔서 더욱 기억에 남고 학습태도를 교정할 수 있었습니다. 또한, 제 풀이 과정을 하나하나 살펴보시고 잘못된 부분을 짚어내주셔서 학원이나 인강에서는 얻을 수 없었던 걸 많이 배웠습니다.

• 밀당PT의 장점

선생님과 실시간 질의응답이 가장 도움이 되었습니다. 궁금한 건 그때그때 해결해야 기억에 남고 다음 공부로 넘어갈 수 있는데 밀당은 바로바로 질문할 수 있어 학습하는데 찝찝함이 안남아서 좋았습니다. 또, 밀당 안에서 제공하는 강의도 텍스트로 설명을 듣는 것만으로는 이해가 안 되었던 것을 이해할 수 있게 해줘서 좋았습니다. 저는 보통 오답을 할 때 '왜 내가 고른 게 답이 아니지?' 라는 의문을 자주 품는데, 선생님께서 제 답이 오답인 이유를 근거를 들어 설명해주십니다. 그런 후 정답의 근거를 설명해주셔서 이해가 정말 잘 되었습니다 :) 항상 제가 자신감이 떨어지지 않도록 잘 하고 있다고 격려와 칭찬을 마구마구 해주셔서 수업이 끝날 때 쯤이면 항상 기분이 좋았던 것 같습니다 ㅎㅎ

영어 본문 암기 프로그램이 정말 유용했습니다. 내신 영어는 아무래도 암기가 가장 큰 비중을 차지하는데 밀당영어의 본문 암기 프로그램을 통해서 지문 암기가 쉽게 되어서 실제 시험 때 큰 도움을 받았습니다. 또, 제가 원하는 변형 문제를 선생님께 말씀드리면 바로 문제들을 넣어주셔서 정말 유익했습니다.

• 나만의 필승 공부법

어떤 문제집을 풀기 시작하거나, 강의를 듣기 시작해서 중간에 포기하지 않고 끝까지 완주하는 게 중요합니다. 특히, 계획을 처음부터 무리하게 세우고 중간에 포기하면 자신감도 떨어지고 학습에 있어서 결코 도움이 되지 않습니다. 흔히 말하는 여러 권 찍먹 대신 한 권을 풀더라도 제대

1 등급, 최상위권 합격 비결을 알고싶다면?